Beginning Java® SE 6 Game Programming, Third Edition

Jonathan S. Harbour

Course Technology PTR

A part of Cengage Learning

COURSE TECHNOLOGY
CENGAGE Learning™

Australia • Brazil • Japan • Korea • Mexico • Singapore • Spain • United Kingdom • United States

COURSE TECHNOLOGY
CENGAGE Learning™

Beginning Java® SE 6
Game Programming, Third Edition
Jonathan S. Harbour

Publisher and General Manager,
Course Technology PTR: Stacy L. Hiquet

Associate Director of Marketing:
Sarah Panella

Manager of Editorial Services:
Heather Talbot

Marketing Manager: Jordan Castellani

Senior Acquisitions Editor: Emi Smith

Project Editor: Jenny Davidson

Technical Reviewer: Dustin Clingman

Interior Layout Tech: MPS Limited, a Macmillan
Company

Cover Designer: Mike Tanamachi

Indexer: Larry Sweazy

Proofreader: Michael Beady

For product information and technology assistance, contact us at
Cengage Learning Customer & Sales Support, 1-800-354-9706

For permission to use material from this text or product,
submit all requests online at **www.cengage.com/permissions**
Further permissions questions can be emailed to
permissionrequest@cengage.com

Oracle and Java are registered trademarks of Oracle and/or its affiliates. All other trademarks are the property of their respective owners.

All images © Cengage Learning unless otherwise noted.

Library of Congress Control Number: 2010942436

ISBN-13: 978-1-4354-5808-6

ISBN-10: 1-4354-5808-7

Course Technology, a part of Cengage Learning
20 Channel Center Street
Boston, MA 02210
USA

Cengage Learning is a leading provider of customized learning solutions with office locations around the globe, including Singapore, the United Kingdom, Australia, Mexico, Brazil, and Japan. Locate your local office at: **international.cengage.com/region**

Cengage Learning products are represented in Canada by Nelson Education, Ltd.

For your lifelong learning solutions, visit **courseptr.com**

Visit our corporate website at **cengage.com**

Printed in the United States of America
1 2 3 4 5 6 7 14 13 12 11 10

For Kaitlyn Faye

Acknowledgments

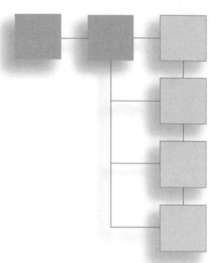

Thank you to my wife, Jennifer, and kids—Jeremiah, Kayleigh, Kaitlyn, and Kourtney—for keeping me on my toes and getting me out of the office from time to time for a needed break! Special thanks to artists Ari Feldman (www.flyingyogi.com) and Reiner Prokein (www.reinerstileset.de) for the 2D sprite artwork used in the examples and final game (without their free collections of sprites, Galactic War would have featured programmer art—yikes!). A big thank you to Emi Smith, Jenny Davidson, and Dustin Clingman.

About the Author

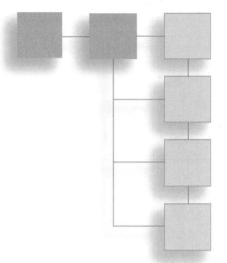

Jonathan S. Harbour has been programming video games since the 1980s. His first video game system was an Atari 2600 that he disassembled on the floor of his room at age 9. He has written on languages and subjects that include C++, C#, Basic, Java, DirectX, Allegro, Lua, DarkBasic, XNA Game Studio, Pocket PC, Nintendo GBA, and game console hacking. He is the author of *Visual Basic Game Programming for Teens, Third Edition*; *Visual C# Game Programming for Teens*; *Beginning Game Programming, Third Edition*; *Multi-Threaded Game Engine Design*; and *XNA Game Studio 4.0 for Xbox 360 Developers*. Visit his blog and forum at www.jharbour.com.

CONTENTS

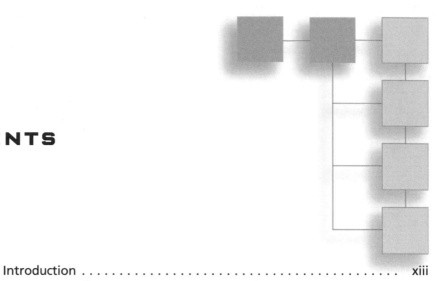

INTRODUCTION

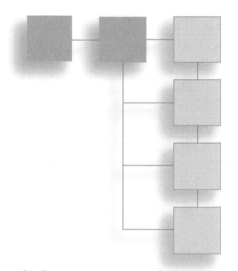

This book will teach you how to create games with the awesome Java language. Previous editions emphasized the casual game market with chapter projects designed to run in AppletViewer or in a web browser. While still relevant, the code in this new edition is a bit simpler, using a JFrame more often instead of an applet, so that examples can be run as a Java application. Some chapters still feature applet projects, while many others are now JFrame-based applications. The final Galactic War project in Part III is still an applet, since a focus of the book is an emphasis on the casual game market. Game programming is a challenging subject, and it can be difficult to figure out how to get started. This book takes away some of the mystery of game programming by explaining how to create a game in Java. I assume that you have a *little* Java programming experience, but if you have never used Java before you should be able to keep up. Chapter 2 provides a quick summary of the language.

This book takes the approach that we can have fun while learning how to program games. Typing in long source code listings out of a book is not fun, so I don't ask you to do that very much. Instead, you will learn to write short programs that demonstrate the major topics, and over time you will get the hang of it. There is no memorization required here, as I'm a firm believer that repetition and practice is the best way to learn, not theory and memorization.

Definition

Java is a programming language, invented by Sun Microsystems, now owned by Oracle, and largely maintained as a loosely constrained community project. The primary design goal of Java was to build runtime binary files that will run on any computer system in the world without being recompiled. This "compile one, run many" philosophy works! The Java compiler creates a *bytecode* binary file containing virtual machine instructions that the JRE (Java Runtime Environment) can execute on any computer system on which it is installed.

You will learn how to write a simple Java program in the first chapter. From there, you will learn the details of how to write games that will run in a web browser or as an application. We cover source code at a pace that will not leave you behind. By the end of this book, you will have learned to create a complete game called Galactic War, and will be able to deploy it to your website in a Java Archive (JAR) file. I'm not talking about some half-baked *simulation* posing as a game. I'm talking about a high-quality game, suitable for publishing in the casual game market. There are thousands of casual gamers who are paying to download games of this type from the many casual game sites on the web today—such as Real Arcade (now www.GameHouse.com). By learning how to create a casual game, you may even be preparing for a career in the game industry, developing games for Microsoft Xbox Live Arcade and other commercial endeavors.

Definition

Web-based games are video games that are installed on a website and run in a web browser, so that the end-users do not need to install the game. Some games are able to store high-score lists and player data on the web server. The most popular type of web game is a "Casual Game" such as Farmville on Facebook.

While we're on the subject of casual games, you can even program your own Xbox 360 games, distributed on Xbox Live Arcade, using Microsoft's free XNA Game Studio Express software. Although this subject is beyond the scope of this book, I bring it up because Microsoft's C# language is unabashedly similar to Java. I have another book on this subject titled *XNA Game Studio 4.0 for Xbox 360 Developers* that you might want to check out.

It all begins here! Are you serious about this subject and willing to learn? As a course developer and instructor of game development, I am scrutinized daily by students who eat, drink, and breathe video games. I cannot create something that stinks or I'll never hear the end of it! So I am as motivated to teach you cutting-edge game development techniques here as I am in a real classroom setting, by students who are paying a lot more than the retail cost of this book to learn these concepts. I have used this book in several Java courses already, so you are guaranteed high-quality material in these pages that will not be a waste of your time. In other words, this book has already been through the flames of scrutiny twice before, so you are guaranteed a solid read and good, working code.

What Will You Learn in This Book?

This book will teach you the difference between Java applications and applets (which run in a web browser). You will then learn about Java's graphics classes and begin writing graphics code. You will learn how to get input from the user, and how to play sound effects and music—all within the context of an online game. From there, the sky's the limit! Figure 1 shows the game you will learn to create in this book. Starting with the basics (and I'm talking about *extreme* basics here!), you will write a simple 2D game using vector graphics (using lines and filled polygons).

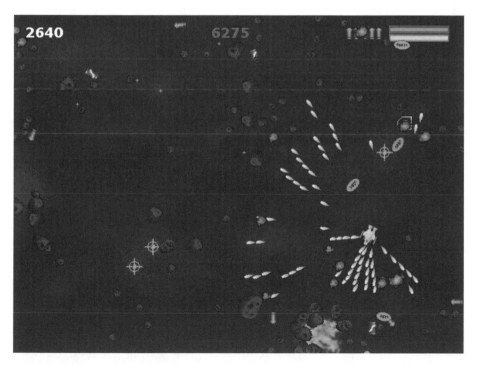

Figure 1
You will learn how to create this game from scratch!

You will then learn new techniques in each chapter, such as how to load a bitmap file and render it on the 2D applet window using Java 2D classes like Graphics2D. You will eventually put the handful of game-related classes together in an event-driven game engine. As you can see from this screenshot, the final game uses some attractive artwork and is chock full of small details! You will learn about simple bitmaps and then sprites before getting into animation. Along the way, you will learn how to use Java's advanced 2D library to rotate and scale sprites, and I'll show you some interesting code that moves bullets, power-ups, asteroids, and other game objects on the screen smoothly and realistically. The end result is a professional sprite-based game engine that packs a serious punch! By learning how to create this retail-quality *casual game*, you will have learned enough to create your own games, suitable for sale in the casual game market (where games are played over the web).

Definition

An *applet* is a limited type of Java program designed to run in a web browser. Due to security restrictions, an applet is not able to access the file system on a user's PC like a Java application, which is installed like any other application software.

Since this book is dedicated to teaching the basics of game programming, it will cover a lot of subjects very quickly, so you'll need to read the chapters of this book sequentially for best results. I use a casual writing style to make the subjects easy to understand and use repetition rather than memorization to nail the points home. You will learn by practice and will not need to struggle with any one subject, because you will use them several times throughout the book. Each chapter builds on the one before. The Galactic War game developed in Part III refers back to previous chapters, so I recommend reading one chapter at a time, in order, to fully understand everything that is going on. I tend to just *use* code after explaining how it works the first time, and often do not explain something over and over again because the book moves along at a brisk pace. We have a lot to cover in a limited amount of space, so I recommend reading the book from start to finish.

WHAT ABOUT THE PROGRAMMING LANGUAGE?

This book is about game programming, and it assumes that you already know at least *some* Java. I recommend that you acquire a Java primer to read before delving into this book, or to keep handy for those parts that may confuse you. For starters, you can pick up *Java Programming for the Absolute Beginner*, by Joseph P. Russell (Cengage Learning). We do not utilize any advanced features of Java SE 6, even though this is the latest version of Java, so if you are new to the language you should be able to make the best of it by following along.

While covering some of the basics over the first three chapters, you'll have created a complete casual game in Java that runs in a web browser, which will be a milestone as well as a measure of your own skill level at that point. As I mentioned, this book is not a primer on the Java language, but rather, makes use of this very capable, high-level language to create games. You will find the code in this book much easier to understand if you have at least read a primer on the subject. We discuss game programming, not basic Java programming.

All of the projects in this book will compile with the Java SE 6 development kit. While later versions (such as Java SE 7) will compile the code, older versions of Java may complain about classes or methods that are not recognized.

What IDE Should You Use?

You will be able to compile the programs in this book using the javac.exe program, and will run the programs using appletviewer.exe. We use an awesome little editor called TextPad that can tie in to these command-line tools to compile and run your Java code. We also explore and use NetBeans as an alternative development environment (if you're looking for a more professional experience).

The first version of this book focused on a professional IDE (Integrated Development Environment) called JBuilder to help organize Java game projects. However, much has changed in the five years since the first edition came out. Borland JBuilder Foundation was a free trial version of JBuilder, and we were able to support the 2005 and 2006 versions at the time. But Borland sold its development tools division to Embarcadero, and it is a proprietary tool now for enterprise development. We simply do not need to use commercial software to build Java code—there are some great options in open source software today!

If a revision is meant to update a book, then it may seem odd to step away from using a professional IDE. But that is exactly what many professional Java programmers are doing—utilizing a simple text editor and the Java SE 6 development kit directly. There are many reasons why this is preferable, and the best explanation may be a desire to avoid the adoption of any single IDE since there are no standard project files in the industry, and each one is dramatically different. I recommend using NetBeans or TextPad. NetBeans is absolutely free and fully featured, but it's kind of large and complex. TextPad is not free, but it is very inexpensive (under $30) and has the great advantage of being lightweight and simple. The main advantage to NetBeans is the programmer pop-up help built into the editor that shows function parameters and class member lists. For those who prefer Eclipse, we do spend some time with that IDE as well.

Avoiding any single IDE allows us to focus more on the Java code and this helps with cross-platform development. The code in this book will compile and run on the following systems:

- Windows (x86, x64, Itanium)

- Linux (x86, x64, Itanium)

- Solaris (SPARC, x86, x64)

Definition

Cross-platform development is the ability to compile and run the same code on many different computer systems. Java code *and* executable files are supported on many platforms. You do not need to recompile your Java code for every system, as the same .class file will run on all of them!

Due to this extensive list of supported operating systems, it is obvious why we would not want to limit ourselves to a single IDE, but would prefer to support all of these systems. As a consequence, none of the source code in the book resource files include any project files, but merely source code files and assets (image and sound files).

Tip

You will be using Java SE 6 (i.e. "Java Standard Edition 6"), which is the lightweight version of Java best suited for creating standalone and web-based games. Our text editor of choice is TextPad 5.0, which can compile your Java source code files with a macro key.

TextPad is a small, easy-to-use source code editor that *recognizes* the Java Development Kit and is able to compile your Java code with a simple macro (Ctrl+1). By using TextPad as our "IDE", you'll be working directly with the file system on your hard drive rather than a virtual project manager (such as the one in NetBeans). In TextPad, you'll see the actual files on your drive, and there is no concept of "adding" files to a "project" because you are working with your source files directly. I recommend purchasing a license of TextPad from www.textpad. com. Sure, there are free editors available, but none that I have found with the feature set and stability of TextPad. For example, two freeware products, Programmer's Notepad and Notepad++, both seem to have stability problems in Windows 7.

CONVENTIONS USED IN THIS BOOK

The following styles are used in this book to highlight portions of text that are important. You will find these highlighted boxes here and there throughout the book.

Note

This is what a note looks like. Notes are additional information related to the text.

Tip

This is what a tip looks like. Tips give you pointers in the current tutorial being covered.

Caution

This is what a caution looks like. Cautions provide you with guidance and what to do or not do in a given situation.

Definition

This is what a definition looks like. Definitions will explain the meaning behind a technical concept or word.

COMPANION WEB SITE DOWNLOADS

You may download the companion website files from www.courseptr.com/ downloads. Please note that you will be redirected to our Cengage Learning site.

PART I

JAVA FOR BEGINNERS

The first part of the book will get you started programming in Java. You will learn how to install and configure the Java Development Kit from Java SE 6 and test your Java installation on your PC by writing your first game—a version of *Asteroids* that runs either standalone or in a web browser. The first chapter covers all the groundwork with programming environments, showing how to compile a Java program with NetBeans, Eclipse, or just a command prompt. The choice will be yours which environment you choose to use!

- Chapter 1: Getting Started with Java
- Chapter 2: Java Programming Essentials
- Chapter 3: Creating Your First Java Game

CHAPTER 1

GETTING STARTED WITH JAVA

Java can be a complex programming language and a challenge to learn in its entirety, but it is easy to get up and running very quickly using freely available development tools and basic code. Java is one of the most rewarding programming languages I have used, and I'm sure you will agree as you gain experience with the language that it's worth your investment of time. This chapter will help you get started with Java and will be especially helpful if you have had no prior experience with this language. This chapter explains what you need, where to get it, and how to configure your system to prepare it for building Java-based games. Several Java-enabled development tools will be presented so you can choose the one that will best meet your needs, including TextPad, NetBeans, Eclipse, and command line.

Here are some of the topics that will be addressed in this chapter:

- Java and the web
- The casual games market
- Installing and configuring Java
- Your first Java program

JAVA AND THE WEB

Let's take a look at game design for a moment and see how Java fits in, because this is the core subject of the book. What truly has changed in the world of gaming since the "good old days"? By that term, I am referring to the infancy of the game industry that entertains the world today, back in the 1980s when arcade game machines were at the top of their game. Many readers were probably *born* in the 1980s and have no recollection of the games of that era, except perhaps those that were ported to the second-generation consoles of the early 1990s (Nintendo SNES, Sega Genesis, Atari Jaguar). You have seen the various anthology collections from Namco, Atari, Midway, and Taito, featuring classics such as *Joust*, *Dig Dug*, *Pac-Man*, *Space Invaders*, *Defender*, and others (some of which date back to even the 1970s).

Note

Nintendo has given some of its classic games an overhaul and released them on the extraordinary Nintendo DS handheld system. Good move! Not only are some classics, such as the original *Super Mario Bros.*, outselling most other handheld games, but re-releases, such as *The Legend of Zelda: A Link to the Past* (for the Game Boy Advance), have outsold most console and PC games.

Studying the Market

The game industry is pushed forward by gamers, not by marketing and business executives, which makes this industry somewhat unique in the world of entertainment. Isn't it obvious that professional sports (NFL, NBA, NHL, and MLB here in the States) are not advanced or directed by the fans? On the contrary, the fans are often derided and ignored by not only the team franchises, but by the organizations themselves. This is an example of how centralized management can lead to problems. Unfortunately for sports fans, they are more than willing to put up with the derision given to them because they love the sport. This is a level of loyalty that simply doesn't exist in any other industry. If you love sports, you ignore all the problems and just enjoy the game, but that doesn't change the fact that it's a seller's market (although digital entertainment is drawing fans away from professional sports in droves).

How is the game industry a buyer's market (meaning, gamers have a lot of influence over the types of games that are created)? Most games are created specifically for a consumer segment, not for the general public. The decision makers at game publishing companies choose projects that will reach as many core constituents as possible, while also trying to reach casual gamers and hardcore fans of other game genres. For instance, Blizzard Entertainment (a subsidiary of

Vivendi Universal Games, which also owns Sierra Entertainment) targets mainly two genres: real-time strategy games (*WarCraft* series, *StarCraft*), and role-playing games (*Diablo* series, *World of WarCraft*).

Can you think of a game that Blizzard has published that does not fit into these two genres? Blizzard has consistently hit the mark dead on with their games in terms of target audience, quality, polish, and subsequent mass appeal. *World of WarCraft* has sold millions of copies with millions of simultaneous players supported on its multitude of servers. *WarCraft III* has sold more than five million units (including the add-ons), while the entire *WarCraft* series has sold twelve million units since its debut in 1994. *StarCraft* has sold nine million copies since 1998 (including add-ons), while *StarCraft II*, released this year, increases the series total.

Why do you suppose Blizzard has been so successful? Certainly not through aggressive advertising campaigns! Gamers have traditionally been immune to marketing, relying primarily on word-of-mouth recommendations from friends, online review sites, and bloggers for their game purchase decisions. If any of Blizzard's games had not been up to par with the gamers, they would not have continued to play the game. But the sales figures shown here reveal products that have had a very long shelf life due to continued sales.

Design Rules

I could go into other companies with equally impressive success stories, as well as those that have been dismal failures. But my goal is to demonstrate to you that the game industry is indeed a buyer's (gamer's) market. It's not dictated and ruled by the board of directors of one company or another or by marketing people, who have been stymied by the reluctance of gamers to go along with traditional promotional theories. In other words, gamers are a tough audience! It's an empowering position to be in, knowing that your personal preferences and tastes are shared by millions of others who demand excellence and innovative gameplay, and that these demands are met, more or less. Companies that produce excellent games are rewarded by gamers, while those that fall short quickly close up shop and move on.

Would you like another real-world example? A few years ago, a new publisher emerged in the game industry by the name of Eidos. This company's bank account was padded by millions of PlayStation owners who had all fallen in love with Lara Croft. Eidos seems to have misinterpreted the market, believing that gamers loved the *image* and *motif* of this Bond-esque heroine. Eidos created a new hotshot team in Texas made up of some industry veterans in an endeavor called *Ion Storm*. The belief was that marketing the "rock-n-roll" hype of these developers would lead to millions of preorder sales for their games (coming from the successes of the two *Tomb Raider* sequels).

Eidos failed to recognize that gamers bought into Lara Croft because the games were fun, not because of the image. When *Ion Storm* was launched, Eidos printed two-page spreads in major game magazines showing the team rather than the upcoming games in development. The developers of *Daikatana* were not able to keep up with the marketing explosion and were derided for producing an average game that would have been well received were it not blacklisted by gamers after *years of hype*. The impression was very strong that it was all about sales, not a gaming experience, and gamers rejected that notion. Eidos has moved on from the experience too, having published some fantastic games such as *LEGO: Star Wars*, *Deus Ex*, and *Anachronox*.

In my experience, the fun factor of video games has risen exponentially in the last two decades, along with the complexity of modern games. Let's face it; you can only play *Pac-Man* for an hour or so until it becomes tedious. The same applies to most of the classic arcade games. At one time, you could fit every video game in existence in a single room, and those quarter-fueled machines were housed in stand-up cabinets. Since that time, there have been about a half million games created, though we might narrow down that figure to a few thousand good games, out of which we find a few hundred "Hall of Fame" greats.

THE CASUAL GAMES MARKET

In recent years a new game genre called *casual games* arose in the game industry. This genre has been relegated to secondhand status for many years, while the numbers of gamers has risen from the hardcore "geek" fans to include more and more people. The average gamer plays games for a few hours a week, whereas the hardcore gamer spends 20 or more hours playing games every week (like a part-time job). Casual gamers, on the other hand, will only spend a few minutes playing a game now and then—perhaps every day, but not always. The casual gamer does not become addicted to any game the way a hardcore gamer does, with games such as *World of WarCraft, Star Wars: The Old Republic, Lord of the Rings Online,* and so on.

So, what is a casual game anyway? A casual game is any game that can be played in a short timeframe and requires no instructions on how to play. In this context, almost every classic arcade game ever made falls into this category. It is only recently that publisher and game industry pundits have begun to realize that gamers really don't want the long, drawn-out experience of installing a game, downloading a patch, and spending eight hours learning how to play it. Sometimes it is refreshing to just fire up a game and play for 10 or 20 minutes without having to *screw* with it all evening! This was a gripe of mine for a long time. It is why I spend far more time playing console games than PC games, and I'm sure many readers share that sentiment.

No Manual Required

Yes, there are some PC games that are so compelling or innovative that they are worth the effort to get them installed and running. The best example of late is *World of WarCraft*. I have spoken to many gamers who claim that if Blizzard's games were not so darned much fun, they would boycott Blizzard altogether! (How's that for a contradiction?) The impression I get is that these gamers have a love/hate relationship with Blizzard and many other game publishers as well. (Lest you suspect that I suffer from memory lapse over Blizzard, let me clear up one important point—I love their games, but dislike their terrible installers!)

Case in point, I could not install *World of WarCraft* on my decently equipped laptop. First, the installer locked up and a subsequent install attempt reported an error on disc two. I got around these issues by copying all four discs to the hard drive and installed it from there with no more problems. However, as soon as I fired up the game and logged in to my account, it dropped out to download a 260MB update to the game. When that was done, three more small updates were installed just to bring the game up to the latest version. Are these problems tolerable? Yes and no. On the one hand, this is the most advanced and complex MMORPG (*massively multiplayer online role-playing game*) ever created, and Blizzard has a full-time team continually creating new content and improving the game, which I applaud. But on the other hand, that sure was a lot of work just to get the game installed, and it took three hours of my time (which is why hardcore gamers tend to have more than one PC).

Would a casual gamer be willing to devote that much time just to install a game that will end up requiring hundreds of hours of gameplay in order to rise through the ranks within the game world? Most casual gamers do not have the time or patience to jump through so many hoops for Blizzard, unless a friend helps them get started. Such is the target audience for casual games! Have you ever given serious thought to this issue? If you are an IT (*information technology*) professional or a hardcore gamer, you are used to dealing with computer problems and coping with them without incident. But do you ever wonder, if you—a smart, experienced, knowledgeable computer expert—are having problems with a game, how on earth will an average user figure out these problems? Well, the short answer is, *they don't*, which accounts for most game returns.

Casual Games

Casual gamers include professionals such as doctors and lawyers, business executives, software developers, and, well, *everyone else*. Casual games attract people from all cultures, classes, genders, religions, ethnicities, and political orientations. Given that most *potential* game players are not willing or able to cope with the issues involved in PC games, is it any wonder that this burgeoning market has been inevitable for several years now? While casual games are currently played mainly in a web browser using technology such as Java and Flash, the console systems are featuring online gameplay as well, and this trend will continue to gain popularity.

The casual game market was limited a few years ago. Only recently has this subject started to show up on the radar of publishers, schools, and retail stores, even though gamers have been playing casual games for two decades. (I predicted casual games would take off a few years ago, but my dog ate that article.) Casual games are a win-win situation because they are just as easy to create as they are to play, so the developer is able to create a casual game in a short timeframe, and the gamer has an enjoyable experience with a lot of choices. Casual games have a very simple distribution model (most are put up on a website for online play), a respectable compensation model (developers receive a percentage of net sales or a single lump sum), an often meager development cycle measured in weeks or a few months, and almost no testing required. As a casual game developer, you can come up with an innovative game idea, develop the game, and get it onto store shelves (that is, a website) all within the timeframe of just the concept-art stage of a full-blown retail game.

Jay Moore was an evangelist for Garage Games who promoted the Torque game engine around the country at conferences and trade shows. He spoke at the 2005 Technology Forum at the University of Advancing Technology, where he addressed the possibility of earning a living as a casual game developer. Garage Games' Torque engine has been ported to Xbox 360, and they have published two games on Xbox Live Arcade that you can download and play if you are a Live user. *Marble Blast* is one such game, and Garage has many more games planned for release on Live and through retail channels. In fact, when you purchase the entire Torque game engine for $100, you have the option of publishing through Garage Games, which does the contractual work and provides you with a contract (subject to quality considerations, of course).

Microsoft has really embraced casual games by making it possible for independent developers to publish games directly on Xbox Live Arcade without going through retail channels. Xbox 360 is the first console video game system in history to provide downloadable games right out of the box without first purchasing retail software. If you are interested in casual games, you can enjoy playing on Xbox Live Arcade without buying a retail game at all, because many games are available for free trial and purchase on Xbox Live Arcade (with a membership account, that is). Indie developers can use XNA Game Studio to develop games for Windows, Xbox 360, Zune, and Windows Phone 7 for a small annual membership fee.

I attended the Austin Game Conference in 2005, and the focus of the show was about casual games. Microsoft's booth was titled "Microsoft Casual Games," and they were giving away USB flash drives with the MSN Messenger SDK and showcasing some of their Xbox Live Arcade games, as just one example. These early efforts to promote casual game development on Microsoft's platforms has paid off in a huge way today with Xbox Live seeing huge earnings for both Microsoft and all of their publishers and indie developers alike, thanks to a very reasonable 70/30 royalty rate.

One of the earliest downloadable games on Xbox Live Arcade was *RoboBlitz*. This game was built using the Unreal Engine 3 (which Epic Games developed for *Unreal Tournament III*). *RoboBlitz* also makes use of the impressive Ageia

PhysX physics engine to produce realistic gameplay. Another innovative game on Xbox Live Arcade from the creators of *Project Gotham Racing* is *Geometry Wars*. This game is unique and compelling, with gameplay that involves gravity and weapons that resemble geometric shapes.

If you feel as if I've been leading you along a train of thought, you would be right to trust your feelings. The focus of this book is about programming games using Java with a strong emphasis on casual games, and we will learn to do just that shortly. Since Java is the pioneer language of casual game development, I will be emphasizing this aspect of gaming while creating web-based projects in the chapters to come. But for those interested in just Java game programming without concern for the web or the casual market, most of the projects will be presented as standalone applications that do not need AppletViewer or a web browser.

Installing and Configuring Java

As you might have guessed, Java applet games run in a web browser—Internet Explorer and Mozilla Firefox work equally well for running Java games. Java programs can also run on a desktop system locally without going to a website. These types of programs are called *Java applications* and require the Java Runtime Environment (JRE) to be installed. The web browser runtime is the same as the desktop application runtime, which is installed with the JDK. Users who do not need the Java development tools will just install the JRE, which is what happens when a user installs "Java"—a reference to the JRE.

When you install Java Standard Edition 6 (Java SE 6), the runtime includes an update for web browsers automatically. So if you write a Java game using features from Java SE 6, the runtime might need to be updated on an end user's PC before it will run the game properly. In some cases, the compiled Java program (which ends up being a file with an extension of .class or .jar) will run on older versions of Java, because some updates to the Java language have no impact on the resulting compiled files. The games we write will run as an applet or as an application with a little bit of tweaking. In the interest of simplifying the code as much as possible, we will create an application in most cases using a JFrame. Why?

A JFrame gives us the Graphics context we need to draw with Java 2D. An Applet project has a Graphics context, but a standard console-style application does not, unless a JFrame is used. What this does is give us a window for drawing. By default, an application will just work with the console for text input and output, but we need a graphical window on which to render, and that is what a JFrame provides. It's actually very easy to use, and we'll begin working with it soon.

Installing Java

The Java SE 6 development kit is available for download from http://www.oracle.com/technetwork/java/javase/downloads. You will want to get the latest version of the JDK, which is "Update 22" at the time of this writing (see Figure 1.1). When you install the JDK, the installer will not automatically modify your system's environment variables, which is something we will need to do so that you can run the Java compiler (javac.exe) using a command prompt or shell window. The current version at the time of this writing is Java SE 6 Update 22, and the install file is called jdk-6u22-windows-i586.exe. If you are using a system other than Windows you will need to visit the Java website to download the appropriate version for your system.

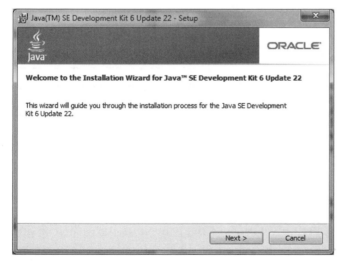

Figure 1.1
Installing Java SE 6.

Configuring the Java Command-Line Compiler

Java will be installed by default in the folder C:\Program Files\Java (on the Windows platform; obviously, this will be different depending on your system). In this folder are two folders called jdk1.6.0_22 and jre6, containing the development kit and runtime environment, respectively. We need to focus our attention on the first folder containing the JDK, in particular. This folder contains a folder called bin, in which you will find all of the Java programs needed to compile and run Java code. The most important programs in this folder are javac.exe (the Java compiler) and appletviewer.exe (the applet viewer utility). We need to add this folder to the system's environment variables so that we can invoke the Java compiler from any location on the hard drive.

I'm going to focus my attention on Windows since it is the most widely used operating system. Depending on the system you're using, the steps will be different but the concept will be similar. You need to add the jdk1.6.0_22/bin folder to your system path—the list of folders searched when you invoke a program at the command line. In Windows, open the Control Panel and run the System utility. Select the Advanced tab, as shown in Figure 1.2. Here you will find a button labeled Environment Variables. Click on it.

Tip

The System Properties dialog in Windows 7 can be found in Control Panel, System, Advanced system settings.

Scroll down the list of system variables until you find the Path variable. Select it, then click the Edit button. Add the following to the end of the path variable (including the semicolon):

```
;C:\Program Files\Java\jdk1.6.0_22\bin
```

If you have installed a different version, you will need to substitute the version shown here with the actual folder name representing the version you installed on your system. Click the OK button three times to back out of the dialogs and

Figure 1.2
The System utility in Windows Control Panel.

save your settings. Now let's verify that the path has been configured properly by testing the Java installation.

To open a command prompt in Windows, open the Start menu, Program Files (or All Programs), and you will find it in Accessories. The command prompt should appear as shown in Figure 1.3.

If you are using a system like Linux, just open a shell if you don't have one open already, and the commands and parameters should be the same. Now that you have a command prompt, type the following command and press Enter:

```
javac -version
```

This will invoke the Java compiler and instruct it to merely print out its version number, as shown in Figure 1.4. The version reported here is just what you would expect: 1.6.0_22 represents Java SE 1.6 Update 22.

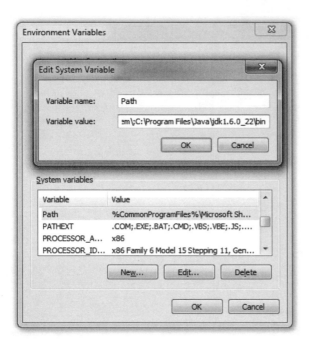

Figure 1.3
Adding the JDK folder to the system path.

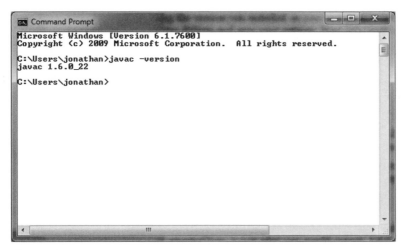

Figure 1.4
The Java compiler reports its version number.

If you were able to see the version number show up on your system, then you will know that Java has been installed correctly, and you're ready to start writing and compiling code! On the other hand, if you received an error such as "Bad command or file name," then your environment variable has not been set correctly, as explained previously. There is an alternative to editing the system's environment variable—you can just modify the path from the command prompt. However, when you do this, the change is not permanent, and you will have to set the path every time you open a command prompt. But just for reference, here is how you would do it:

```
set path=%path%;C:\Program Files\Java\jdk1.6.0_22
```

At this point, you are ready to start writing and compiling Java code. So let's do just that, to further test your Java installation. In a moment, we'll write a Java application that prints something out to the console (or shell). See the section below titled "Your First Java Program."

Java Version Numbers

Java's versioning can be confusing, but it's something you might want to understand. The official latest version of Java at the time of this writing is Java Standard Edition 6 Update 22, or Java SE 6u22. However, the actual version number is 1.6.0. The computer industry is anything but consistent, given the extraordinary changes that have taken place on the Internet and in software development in general. But one thing has been agreed upon in the computer industry regarding versioning. The first release of a software product is version 1.0. Often a revision or build number will be appended, such as 1.0.8392, which helps technical support or call center personnel identify the version or sub-revision of software that a customer is using when a problem arises. The revision number is, in every case, not part of the retail packaging and product name, but rather a tracking tool. Table 1.1 lists the Java version history.

The interesting thing about this table is that it is very consistent in the second column (Version), but there are a lot of inconsistencies in the third column (Marketed Name), which is not a great surprise since marketing campaigns seldom makes sense. If you were to follow the progression from one version to the next and tally them, you might note that there have been seven major versions of Java (while the eighth version is 1.7, and not yet released). Product

Table 1.1 Java Version History

Year	Version	Marketed Name	Code Name
1996	1.0	Java 1.0	
1997	1.1	Java 1.1	
1998	1.2	Java 2	Playground
2000	1.3	J2SE 1.3	Kestrel
2002	1.4	J2SE 1.4	Merlin
2004	1.5	J2SE 5.0	Tiger
2006	1.6	Java SE 6	Mustang
2010	1.7*	Java SE 7	Dolphin

*1.7 is still in a pre-release state at the time of this writing, as it has been for two years.

branding is a very expensive and time-consuming process, which is why businesses defend their brand names carefully.

When Sun released Java 2 as a trademarked name, the name caught on, and the version we are using now, Java SE 6, is still known internally as version 1.6.0. Java fans love these quirks, which are not flaws but endearing traits, and it's not a problem once you understand how it has evolved over the past decade.

Java SE 6 Development Kit

The Java SE 6 Development Kit (the "JDK") is available for these platforms:

- Linux
- Linux Intel Itanium
- Linux x64
- Solaris SPARC
- Solaris x64
- Solaris x86
- Windows
- Windows Intel Itanium
- Windows x64

We are focusing primarily on the Windows platform because that is the most popular platform, but the code and examples will absolutely build and run on all of the supported platforms without any modifications.

There are several components that extend the basic functionality of Java that are of interest to us with regard to game programming.

Java 2D is an API containing classes for advanced 2D graphics rendering and image manipulation, with support for vector (line-based) shapes, font-based text, image formats, and advanced RGBA color manipulation. This API works great for building 2D games with Java, and is what we will be using in this book. Among other things, we can perform transforms (rotation, translation, and scaling) on 2D images.

Java 3D is an API that allows rendering of 3D graphics in a Java application or web-based applet with high-level constructs for building 3D scenes. The websites are java3d.dev.java.net and www.java3d.org. This API works very well for building 3D games with Java.

Java Development Environments

There are a variety of Java development environments we can use for our Java game projects, from the fairly large and complex Eclipse to a text editor with command-line compiler. In most cases, you will want to install the Java Development Kit (JDK) first, because all of the integrated development environments (IDEs) require the JDK.

Caution

The JDK must be installed *first* if you choose to install and use an IDE such as Eclipse or NetBeans. These IDEs support Java, but do not include the JDK, and the JDK is a prerequisite in order for the IDEs to automatically locate and plug in links to the JDK if it's installed. If you install an IDE first, then it won't be automatically set up and you will have to manually link it to the JDK. Optionally, you may install a special version of NetBeans *with* the JDK.

Command Prompt/Shell

The simplest way to create and run a Java program is with a text editor and the Java command-line tools javac.exe, java.exe, and appletviewer.exe. Any text editor will work, including Notepad, although there are better choices out there, some of which offer Java source code syntax highlighting to improve your productivity. The point is, once you have installed the JDK, you can technically get by with nothing more than this. In many ways, just using the simple command-line tools is preferable to the large and complex projects created by the professional IDEs, which is why I often take this route when I just want to write a small program in Java. If you are using Linux or Mac OS, then the shell is likely your preferred choice.

TextPad

One such editor with Java source code highlighting is TextPad, available for download from www.textpad.com. We'll be using TextPad quite a bit in the next section of this chapter so I'll refer you there for screenshots showing what TextPad looks like. There are many other editors like TextPad, but TextPad is unique (and helpful!) with its built-in support for the JDK tools that makes it possible to compile and run Java code right from inside the text editor. The latest version of TextPad (5.4 at the time of this writing) now supports a Workspace feature, which puts TextPad into the realm of a "mini IDE." A project workspace in TextPad can now be saved so that all of the configured tools and source files are retained in the project, saved to a workspace file with an extension of .tws. Since TextPad is so incredibly easy to use, this will be our tool of choice, with NetBeans a close second.

NetBeans

NetBeans IDE (currently at version 6.9.1) is a free development environment with support for Java, C++, PHP, and Ruby projects, and is available for Windows, Mac OS, and Linux. This is the *official* development environment for Java. The complete NetBeans distribution requires a separate installer for the Java Development Kit (JDK), and it can be downloaded from http://netbeans .org. Another distribution of the JDK is available *with* NetBeans 6.9.1 already included! If you are new to Java development, then this is the version I recommend using because it only requires one install to get both the JDK and IDE up and running. If you have already installed the latest JDK, then just use the independent NetBeans installer.

Eclipse

Eclipse is another community-supported development environment with support for multiple languages, including Java. The home page for Eclipse is at www .eclipse.org. There is a package for Java development ready to be downloaded and installed called "Eclipse IDE for Java Developers" at http://www.eclipse.org/

downloads. Eclipse can be rather difficult to use, especially if you're *really* new to programming, but it is jam packed with incredible features right out of the box, so to speak, and is a quite mature development environment. But, with complexity comes difficulty of use. In fairness to the developers and fans of Eclipse, we will at least see a simple example of an Eclipse project later in the chapter but it will not be our tool of choice.

YOUR FIRST JAVA PROGRAM

I want to take you through the steps of creating a new Java program to test the JDK and a Java applet project to test web-browser integration right away so we can begin programming. Let's start at the very beginning so that when you have written a full-featured game down the road, you'll be able to look back and see where you started.

Java Application

The following program, shown in Figure 1.5, is called DrinkJava. Type it into a text file and save the file as DrinkJava.java.

```java
import java.io.*;
public class DrinkJava {
    public static void main(String args[]) {
        System.out.println("Do you like to drink Java?");
    }
}
```

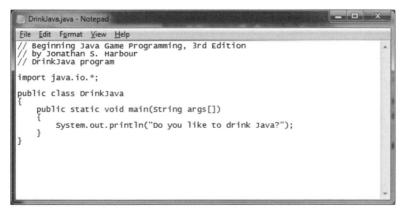

Figure 1.5
The DrinkJava program can be edited using any text editor.

Tip

The perhaps undocumented but *assumed* coding standard for Java has always placed opening brackets for a small block of code at the end of a statement. Large blocks of code typically have the bracket on the next line to improve readability and reduce potential bugs. You may feel free to put opening brackets on the next line if you prefer. I am doing it this way to stay in line with the JDK examples.

Now let's compile the program. You'll need to open a command prompt window again, or you can continue using the one discussed earlier if you still have it open. Use the `cd` command to change the directory to the where you saved the .java file—for instance, `cd \chapter01\DrinkJava`. Once in the correct folder, you can then use the javac.exe program to compile your program, assuming you have added the JDK to the system path as described earlier:

```
javac DrinkJava.java
```

The Java compiler (javac.exe) should spend a few moments compiling your program, and then return the command prompt cursor to you. If no message is displayed, that means everything went okay. You should then find a new file in the folder called DrinkJava.class. You can see the list of files by typing `dir` at the command prompt, or just open Windows Explorer to browse the folder graphically.

To run the newly compiled DrinkJava.class file, you use the java.exe program:

```
java DrinkJava
```

Note that I did not include the .class extension, which would have generated an error. Let Java worry about the extension on its own. By running this program, you should see a line output onto the command prompt like this:

```
Do you like to drink Java?
```

Perhaps without realizing it, what you have done here is created a Java *application*. This is one of the two types of Java programs you can create. The other type is called an *applet*, which describes a program that runs in a web browser and is really the goal of what we want to do in order to create Java games. You can certainly write a Java game as an application and run it on a local system, but the real point of this book is to create Java applets that run in a web browser.

Java Applet

Now let's create a Java applet and note how its code is different from a Java application. This applet that you're about to write will run in a web browser, or you can run it with appletviewer.exe (one of the JDK tools). Open your favorite text editor (Notepad, TextPad, Emacs, or whichever it may be) and create a new file called FirstApplet.java with the following source code. TextPad is shown in Figure 1.6. Before you try to run the program, though, we'll have to create a mini web page container, which we'll create shortly.

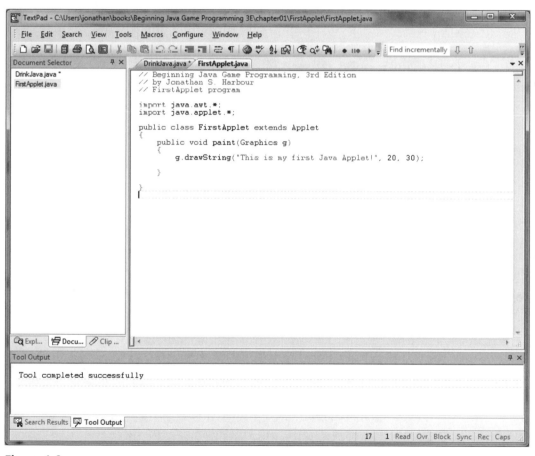

Figure 1.6
The FirstApplet source code in TextPad.

Tip

The trial edition of TextPad has a pop-up that appears every time it is opened. You can register it at www.textpad.com for a small fee to get rid of the pop-up message, which will cause TextPad to start up much faster. I encourage you to support this developer if you find TextPad useful.

```java
import java.awt.*;
import java.applet.*;
public class FirstApplet extends Applet {
    public void paint(Graphics g) {
        g.drawString("This is my first Java Applet!", 20, 30);
    }
}
```

The applet code is a little different from the application-based code in the DrinkJava program. Note the extends Applet code in the class definition and the lack of a static main method. An applet program extends a class called Applet, which means the applet will receive all of the features of the Applet class (which has the ability to run in a web browser). Essentially, all of the complexity of tying in your program with the web browser has been done for you through class inheritance (your program inherits the features of the Applet class). You can compile the program with this command:

```
javac FirstApplet.java
```

TextPad Configuration

Now, if you happen to be using TextPad (refer to Figure 1.6), you can compile the program from within TextPad without having to drop to the command prompt to compile it manually. As Figure 1.7 shows, TextPad has a macro that will launch the Java compiler for you and report the results of the compile. If there are no errors in the Java code, it will report "Tool completed successfully."

If you don't see the Java tools listed in this menu, then there's a way to add them manually. Open the Configure menu and choose Preferences to bring up the Preferences dialog. The last item in the list of preferences is Tools. Select it. Click the Add button and choose "Java SDK Commands" from the list. This will add the Java tools to the list of external tools, as shown in Figure 1.8.

The next change is optional, but I think it's helpful. Select the "Run Java Application" item under Tools, which was just added. There's a check option called "Capture output," as shown in Figure 1.9. Check this option. This will

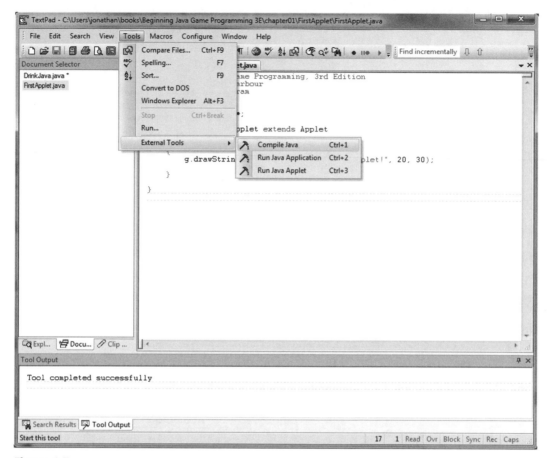

Figure 1.7
Compiling Java code is a cinch in TextPad.

cause the Java output to go to the output window rather than causing a new window to open.

Figure 1.10 shows the change with the "Capture output" option enabled. Now, instead of TextPad bringing up a new window to show the Java program running, it displays the output directly in the Output window at the bottom of the TextPad window!

Applet Web Container

Java Applets can only run in a web browser or in the appletviewer. This is a basic web page containing the code to embed an applet on the page. We'll be creating

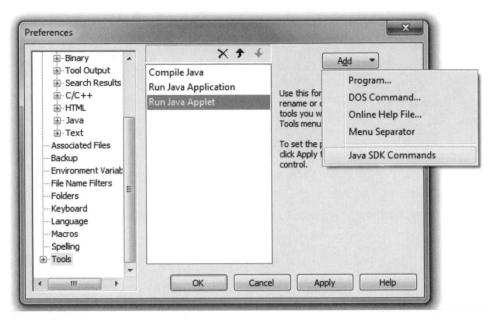

Figure 1.8
Adding the Java tools to the TextPad.

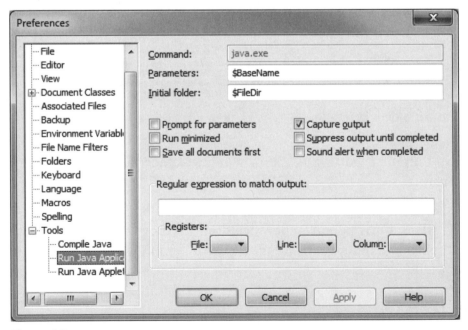

Figure 1.9
Configuring the Run Java Application tool.

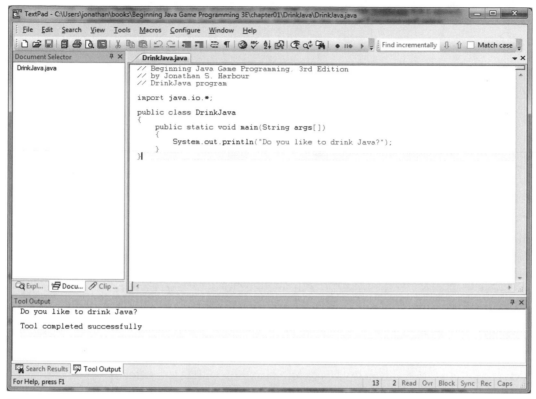

Figure 1.10
Java console output now goes to the Output window in TextPad.

one of these containers for every program in the book. But don't worry, our development tools will generate the web container file for us. Here is what it looks like:

```
<html>
<head><title>FirstApplet</title></head>
<body>
<applet
  codebase = "."
  code = "FirstApplet.class"
  name = "FirstApplet"
  width = "640"
  height = "480"
  hspace = "0"
```

```
  vspace = "0"
  align = "middle"
>
</applet>
</body></html>
```

This container web page code includes an embedded `<applet>` tag with parameters that specify the Java applet class file and the width and height of the applet, among other properties. You can now open this file with Applet Viewer like so:

```
appletviewer FirstApplet.html
```

The Applet Viewer window appears with the FirstApplet program running, as shown in Figure 1.11.

You can also open the FirstApplet.html file in your favorite web browser. Using Windows Explorer, locate the folder containing your project and locate the FirstApplet.html file, then double-click it to open it in the default web browser. Figure 1.12 shows the applet running in Internet Explorer.

TextPad can generate the web container file for us! From the Tools menu, choose External Tools, then Run Java Applet. TextPad will automatically generate a web container file and launch it in AppletViewer, as shown in Figure 1.13.

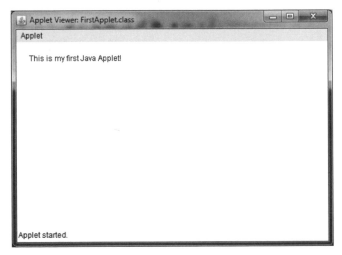

Figure 1.11
The FirstApplet program is running inside the Applet Viewer utility.

Figure 1.12
FirstApplet is running as an embedded applet in Internet Explorer.

Now that we've seen how to compile the program from the command line as well as from within the very simple to use editor, TextPad, we'll look at how to compile a Java program with two major integrated development environments (IDEs): NetBeans and Eclipse.

Creating a NetBeans Project

NetBeans is a pretty good IDE, balancing features with usability without adding too much complexity. Let's see how to create and configure a new Java Application project in NetBeans as a reference for all future projects. First, open the File menu and select New Project (see Figure 1.14).

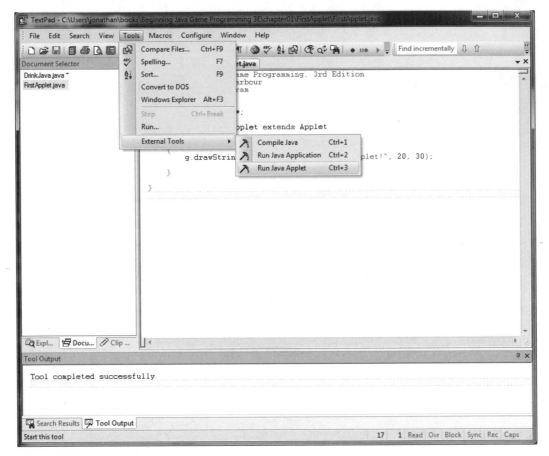

Figure 1.13
Launching an applet from TextPad.

The New Project dialog will appear (Figure 1.15). This dialog has many options and will look a bit different depending on the version of NetBeans that you have installed (this is the complete version with all tools installed). Choose the Java category in the list to the left, and Java Application from the list on the right.

A second project configuration dialog now comes up, titled New Java Application (Figure 1.16). Enter the new project name in the field. Unless you specifically want to change the location of the new project, the other options can be left alone.

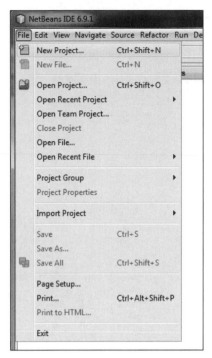

Figure 1.14
Creating a new Java project in NetBeans.

At this point, the new project will be created with a sample source code file (Figure 1.17).

Add the following line of code to the main() function in the Main.java file. You can then run the project by pressing the F6 key or by opening the Run menu and selecting Run Main Project, as shown in Figure 1.18. The output is shown in the Output window at the bottom.

```
System.out.println("NetBeans makes Java programming easier!");
```

Creating an Eclipse Project

Eclipse is *somewhat* similar to NetBeans when it comes to creating a new project and running the Java code. There are a few extra steps that are a bit unusual, though, so a quick walkthrough is needed. This should help anyone who intends to use Eclipse for the projects in the book. First, open the File menu, choose New, Java Project, as shown in Figure 1.19.

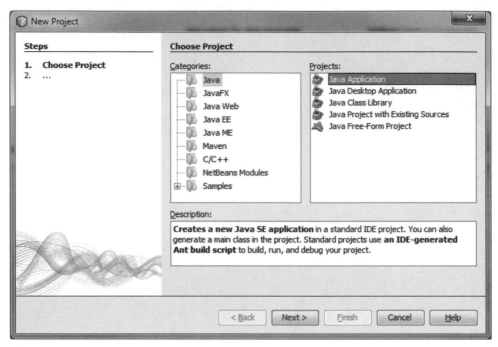

Figure 1.15
The New Project dialog in NetBeans.

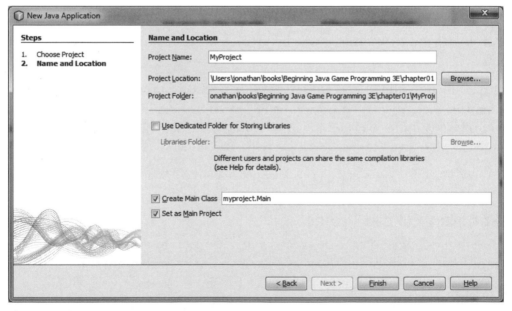

Figure 1.16
The New Java Application project configuration dialog.

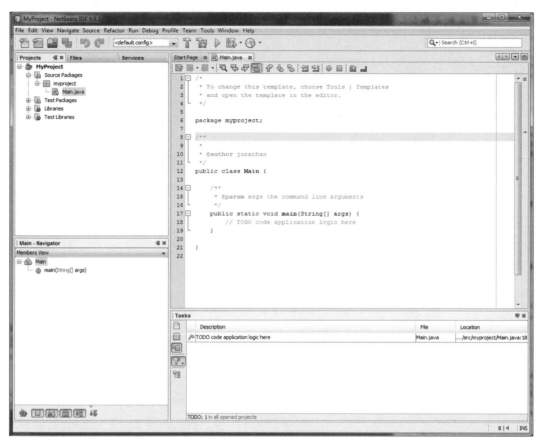

Figure 1.17
The new Java project has been created in NetBeans.

This brings up the New Java Project dialog, shown in Figure 1.20. Enter the project name, choose the Java runtime to use (default shown here is JavaSE-1.6, as expected). One option I recommend setting is "Use project folder as root for sources and class files." The other option will generate too many subfolders, making the project even more difficult to manage.

Eclipse does not use any project files to manage projects, but instead uses a workspace containing one or more project folders with source code files, such that no "file" is even related to the workspace—it's just a bunch of folders containing sources. It's definitely a different approach than the way most development tools work, and it can be difficult to use until you get the hang of working within a

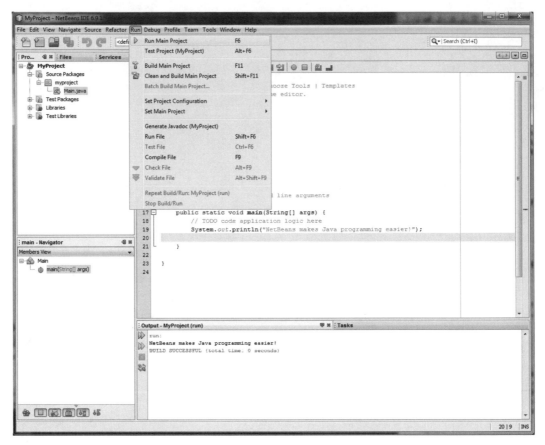

Figure 1.18
Compiling and running the project in NetBeans.

workspace. Note in Figure 1.21 that there are two "projects" listed in the Package Explorer. By default, a new project like the one we just created has no source code files—we have to add the first source file to the project.

Right-click on the project name in the Package Explorer, then choose New, Class, as shown in Figure 1.22.

The New Java Class dialog appears (Figure 1.23). Choose your desired source folder and enter a name such as "Main." Be sure to check the option "public static void main(String[] args)," as this will generate our main function for us. If you don't select the option, you'll just have to type in extra code.

Now that the source file has been created, add this line to the main() function:

```
System.out.println("Doing Java in Eclipse. Yay!");
```

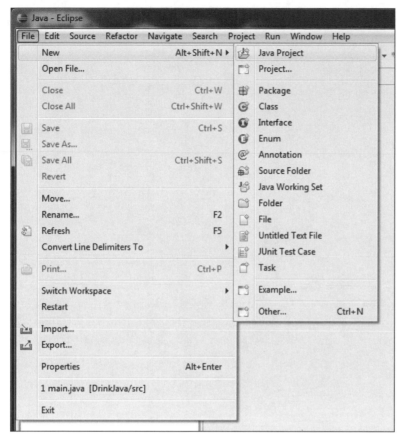

Figure 1.19
Creating a new Java project in Eclipse.

Run the program by clicking the green "Run" icon on the toolbar, as shown in Figure 1.24. The output is down at the bottom in the Console window.

JFrame-Powered Application

As mentioned earlier, JFrame makes it possible to do graphics in a Java application that is normally limited to just console output. JFrame provides a Graphics context, as does the Applet class, which can be used for drawing. The source code for a JFrame-based application is not any *less* code than an Applet project, but it foregoes the need of a web browser (or appletviewer), meaning we can run such a program with java.exe. The JFrameDemo project is shown in Figure 1.25, and the source code listing for the program follows. This is a bit more code than we've seen so far, but this program *does* more than any previous code.

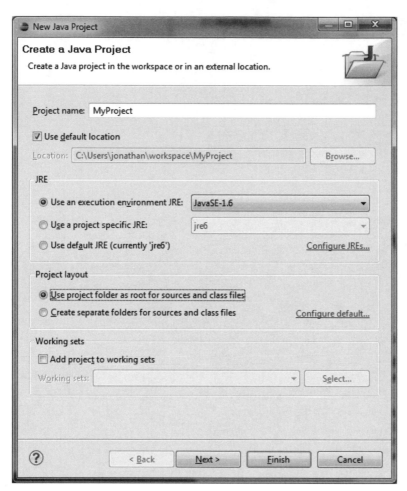

Figure 1.20
Setting the properties for a new Java project in Eclipse.

```java
package jframedemo;
import javax.swing.*;
import java.awt.*;
public class JFrameDemo extends JFrame
{
    public JFrameDemo()
    {
        super("JFrameDemo");
        setSize(400,400);
        setVisible(true);
```

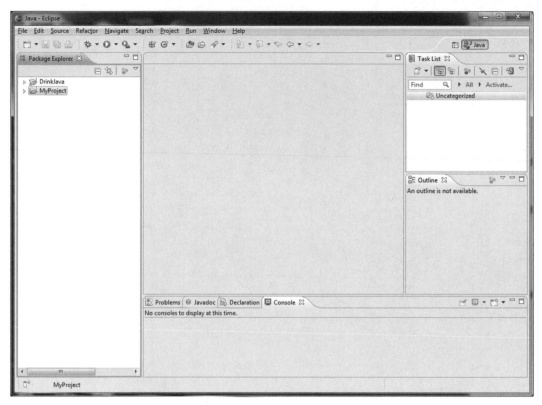

Figure 1.21
Managing projects in an Eclipse workspace.

```
        setDefaultCloseOperation(JFrame.EXIT_ON_CLOSE);
    }
    public void paint(Graphics g)
    {
        super.paint(g);
        g.setColor(Color.WHITE);
        g.fillRect(0, 0, 400, 400);
        g.setColor(Color.orange);
        g.setFont(new Font("Arial", Font.BOLD, 18));
        g.drawString("Doing graphics with a JFrame!", 60, 200);
    }
    public static void main(String[] args)
    {
        new JFrameDemo();
    }
}
```

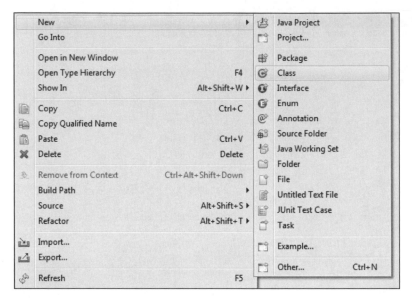

Figure 1.22
Adding a new source file to the project.

Let's go over this code. It's important to understand this basic code because all of our game projects coming up will be based on the code you see here—extending JFrame, with a main() method, a paint() method, and a constructor.

First, we need javax.swing, which owns the JFrame class, while java.awt makes the Graphics class available. The JFrameDemo class is the main class of the program, which extends JFrame, meaning that our class *is* a JFrame. There are some things that come with a JFrame class, such as the paint() method, which renders the window when the program first starts up. We still need our main() function, and it has a single purpose: to launch the JFrame-powered class, JFrameDemo. The JFrameDemo() method is actually the constructor for the class, meaning it runs when the class is first created. Anything you want to happen when the window is first created and comes up, you could put in the constructor. So, we set the window title, the dimensions, and other useful properties. Figure 1.26 shows the output.

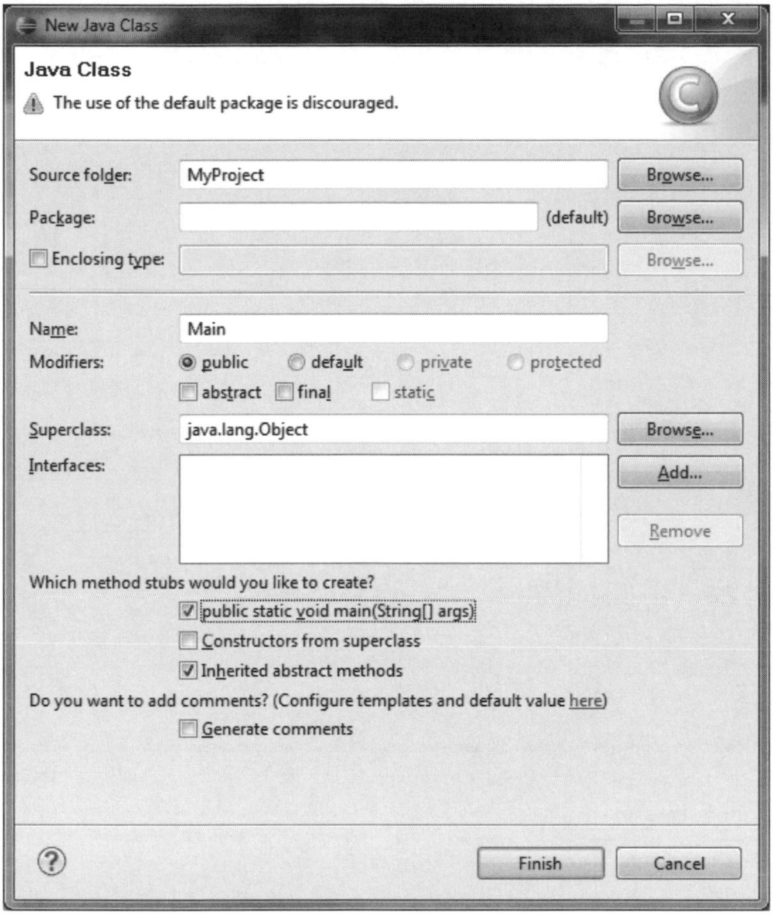

Figure 1.23
Adding a source file with the New Java Class dialog.

WHAT YOU HAVE LEARNED

Well, this has been a pretty heavy chapter that covered a lot of introductory information about working with several Java development tools, but the goal was to get the basics covered so that we can jump right into Java game programming in the next chapter. Consider this a reference chapter on creating

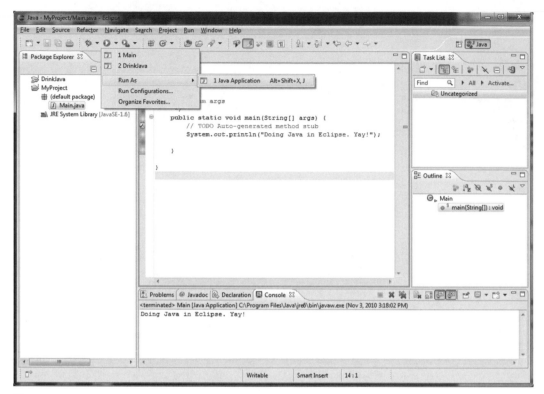

Figure 1.24
Running our first Java program in Eclipse.

Java projects with the various development tools, and come back here any time you need to create a new project but can't quite remember all of the steps. You learned about:

- Casual games, what they are, and their importance
- The Java Development Kit (JDK) and Java versions
- Editing and compiling Java code
- Standalone Java applications and Java applets
- Using Eclipse, NetBeans, and TextPad

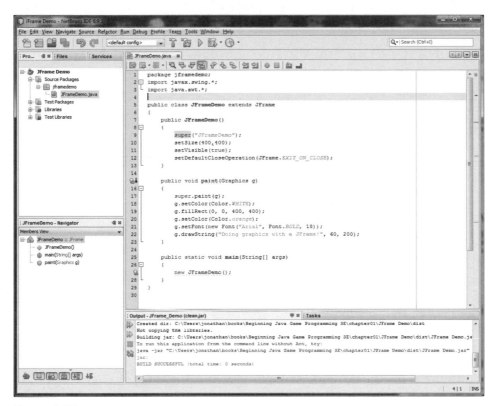

Figure 1.25
The JFrameDemo project.

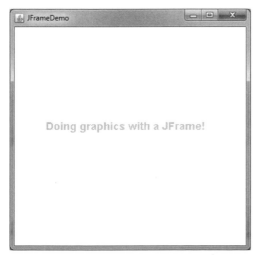

Figure 1.26
A JFrame window with a Graphics context for drawing.

REVIEW QUESTIONS

The following questions will help you to determine how well you have learned the subjects discussed in this chapter. The answers are provided in Appendix A, "Chapter Quiz Answers."

1. What does the acronym "JDK" stand for?

2. What version of the JDK are we focusing on in this book?

3. What is the name of the company that created Java?

4. Where on the web will you find the text editor called TextPad?

5. In what year was Java first released?

6. Where on the web is the primary download site for Java?

7. What type of Java program do you run with the java.exe tool?

8. What type of Java program runs in a web browser?

9. What is the name of the command-line tool used to run a web-based Java program?

10. What is the name of the parameter passed to the paint() event method in an applet?

ON YOUR OWN

Use the following exercises to test your grasp of the material covered in this chapter.

Exercise 1

Modify the FirstApplet program so that it displays your own message on the screen below the current message.

Exercise 2

The JFrame Demo program displayed a message with orange text over a white background. See if you can change the background color to black and the text color to green.

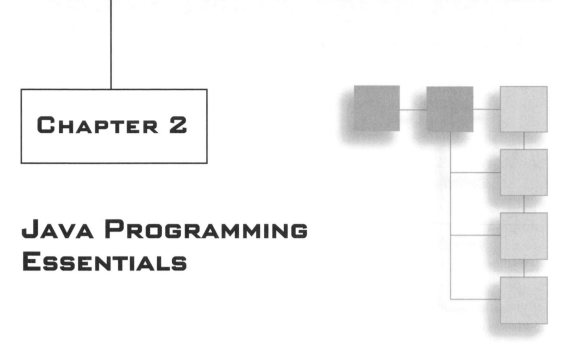

CHAPTER 2

JAVA PROGRAMMING ESSENTIALS

Java is a mature programming language that offers many good features and capabilities that make it popular on many computer systems. Java is quite popular among Linux server programmers and administrators, as well as Windows application programmers. The key aspect of Java that makes it so appealing is its built-in library support. The C++ language cannot even begin to do what Java can do *out of the box*, so to speak. That is, you can't do any graphics programming in C++ without an extra graphics library (such as OpenGL or Direct3D). Java, on the other hand, has everything built in (while still supporting add-on libraries). If you are just getting started as a Java programmer, then this chapter will help you gain some familiarity with the Java language. You will learn most of the basics in this chapter that you will need to write a game. There is a lot more to the Java language than what you will learn about in this sole chapter, obviously—many whole books have been written on Java programming. This chapter will help give you a jumpstart if you are new to Java. If you have experience with Java, you may find the information to be overly simple, but it is more important for a beginner to understand concepts rather than standards.

Here is what you will learn in this chapter:

- Writing Java code using applets
- How to use the Java data types

- The basics of object-oriented programming
- Writing Java classes

JAVA APPLETS AND APPLICATIONS

There are two different types of programs you can compile with Java: applications and applets. A Java *application*—the most common type of Java program—is a program compiled to run on a computer as a standalone application. A Java *applet*, on the other hand, is compiled specifically to run in a web browser. Java applications are usually written to run as server programs or just for one user, whereas applets run as client programs in a networked environment. For example, Java Web Server (JWS) is a Java application that hosts web page files to a web browser (such as Internet Explorer or Mozilla Firefox), and it is comparable to Microsoft's Internet Information Server (IIS) web server and the open-source Apache web server. But, Java applications are not solely devoted to services, as we can use the Swing library and the Abstract Windowing Toolkit (AWT) to bring up a graphical window for an application with all the same features as an applet window. Since applications are much easier to use, requiring fewer steps to compile and run, this is the approach we are taking in this new edition. The final game of Galactic War in the last chapter will support both.

Web Server Technology Explained

The main difference is that Microsoft's web server (IIS) and the Apache web server were written in C++, while JWS was written in Java. JWS can host regular HTML web pages and custom Java Server Pages (JSP), which are custom web server programs written in Java. A Java applet is different: An applet is a "client-side" program that runs entirely in the web browser, not on the web server. A JSP application literally runs on the web server and sends content to the web browser, whereas an applet runs only in the web browser. For this reason, we say that server programs run on the "back end," and applets run on the "front end."

An applet is like an HTML file that a web browser (like Firefox) downloads from the web server and then displays to the user. Microsoft's IIS web server has gained in popularity and market share in recent years, thanks in part to the new .NET

Framework, ASP.NET, and Web Services technologies. Active Server Pages .NET (ASP.NET) pages are similar to JSPs in concept, but ASP sites are written in Basic or C#, while JSP sites are built entirely with Java. If you don't know much about web servers and web applications, don't worry—we will only be writing web *client* programs, not server programs.

Hosting Java Applets

If you really find that you enjoy Java, then you may want to consider creating or enhancing your own website with Java applets. You can build an entire website as one large applet or you can embed many different applets inside a standard HTML page to enhance your website. One of the strong suits of Java is that you don't need any special type of web server in order to use Java on your website. Java has been around since 1995, and web browsers have supported Java since Java 1.1. Microsoft Internet Explorer and Mozilla Firefox support the latest version of Java. To update your browser, simply install Java SE 6, and the installer will add a plug-in to your web browser automatically. This is necessary if you want to run the applet examples in this book.

Compiling Java Code

The easiest way to compile a Java program is by using the command-line compiler. As you may recall from Chapter 1, you use the javac.exe program to compile a .java file into a .class file. You then use the appletviewer.exe program in conjunction with an .html container file with an embedded applet tag to run your Java applet in the Applet Viewer program. You can also open this HTML test file in a web browser to run the applet. One of the main reasons why TextPad is such a useful editor is that it generates the HTML container file automatically when it invokes AppletViewer, which is a real time saver if you're in a hurry.

We looked at NetBeans and Eclipse in the previous chapter. These are relatively large Integrated Development Environments (IDEs) for building software projects. For simple games, I recommend using a text editor like TextPad and the command-line tools. But one really great feature of both NetBeans and Eclipse is syntax lookup, which lists the contents of classes and parameters for functions, effectively eliminating the need for a manual! This is one feature you won't get with a text editor, and so I recommend using one of these IDEs for larger game projects.

The Java Language

There are many built-in classes in Java, but we will only be using a few of them to build games. Now then, I suppose even a word like "class" might be a mystery if you are new to programming. A class is a sort of container that holds both data and functions. Do you have any experience with the C++ language? Java was based on C++ by "borrowing" all of the best features of C++ and dropping the more difficult aspects of the language. The programmers who developed the Java specification created a language that is more of an evolution than something created. C++ is a powerful language used to build everything from cell phone games to operating systems to supercomputer simulations. Linux was built with C++. Microsoft Windows was built with C++. The Java Development Kit was built with C++! The power of C++ makes it difficult for beginners to grasp, and even professionals who have spent many years working with databases and web applications may be stymied when confronted with a mysterious C++ error message. It is a world-class language, and there are dozens of compilers for it on every computer system, but it is very difficult to master. Here is a list of software built with the C++ language:

- Microsoft Windows
- Microsoft Office
- Microsoft Visual Studio
- NVIDIA video card drivers
- Mozilla Firefox
- Linux core
- Mac OS X
- Apple iOS (iPod, etc.)
- OpenOffice

I could go on and on, listing *thousands* of operating systems, productivity applications, video card device drivers, compilers, assemblers, interpreters, and so on, that were built with C++.

Now consider Java. There is just one compiler for it, the Java Development Kit (JDK), which is available for most computer systems. Java is innovative enough to be called a new language, but it was heavily influenced by C++. Java is much easier to program than C++. Java automatically handles memory management for you—all you do is allocate memory for new variables and objects, and then you don't really need to worry about freeing up the memory afterward. Java uses a technology called *garbage collection* to remove unused things from memory that your program no longer needs. To give you an analogy, in the realm of Java, you don't even need to carry the trashcan out to the street for pickup because the garbage collector just picks up all the trash thrown about in your house. The garbage collector is sort of like a little robot that scurries about the house searching for trash to pick up. When you are done with your Chinese takeout, just pitch the container and your napkin, and the little trash robot will find it and clean it up for you.

This *could* lead to sloppy programming habits if you spend many years programming in Java and then switch to a more demanding language like C++, so Java makes it possible for you to write solid code that cleans up after itself if you wish to use it. There is a drawback to garbage collection, though: You can't tell it specifically *when* to pick up the trash (variables and objects that are no longer used), only that there is trash to be picked up (as with the real-world garbage collectors most of the time!).

Java Data Types

Let's now learn about the basic data types available in Java, because you will be using these data types throughout the book (and presumably for the rest of your programming career).

Integer Numbers

Java supports many data types, but probably the most basic data type is the *integer*. Integers represent whole numbers, which are numbers that have no decimal point. There are several types of integer that you may use depending on the size of number you need to store. Table 2.1 shows the types of integers you can use and their attributes.

Since Java programs can run on a wide variety of computer systems (this is called *cross-platform support*), you might be wondering whether these data type values will be the same on every system. After all, a Java program can run on a

Table 2.1 Integer Data Types

Type	Size in Bits	Range
byte	8 bits	−128 to 127
short	16 bits	−32,768 to 32,767
int	32 bits	−2,147,483,648 to 2,147,483,647
long	64 bits	−9,223,372,036,854,775,808 to 9,223,372,036,854,775,807

little cell phone or it can run on a supercomputer, such as a Cray Red Storm system.

Tip

For more information about supercomputers, check out www.top500.org for a list of the top 500 supercomputers in the world. At the time of this writing, the most powerful computer is Oak Ridge National Laboratory's 224,162-core Jaguar, based on a Cray XT5-HE, which achieves a peak of 2,331,000 GFlops. Four years ago, when the second edition of this book was published, the top supercomputer was IBM's BlueGene/L at 280,000 GFlops—a nearly ten-fold increase.

Java gets around the data type inconsistency in C++ by defining that data types will be exactly the same, regardless of the computer system on which the Java program is running. It's the job of the Java Runtime Environment (JRE) to determine at runtime how the current computer system will handle the data types your Java program is trying to use, and it does this seamlessly behind the scenes.

Definition

FLOPS is an acronym that stands for **FL**oating point **OP**erations per **S**econd, used to measure computer performance.

Floating-Point Numbers

There are two data types available in Java for working with floating-point numbers. A floating-point represents a decimal value. The float data type stores a 32-bit single-precision number. The double data type stores a 64-bit double-precision number. Table 2.2 shows the specifics of these two data types.

Table 2.2 Floating-Point Data Types

Type	Size in Bits	Range
float	32 bits	1.4E-45 to 3.4028235E+38
double	64 bits	4.9E-324 to 1.7976931348623157E+308

The easiest way to determine the range for a numeric data type is to use the MIN_VALUE and MAX_VALUE properties of the base data type classes. Although we use lowercase to specify the type of a numeric variable (byte, short, int, long, float, and double), these base numeric types are actually instances of Java classes (Byte, Short, Integer, Long, Float, and Double). Therefore, we can take a peek inside these base classes to find some goodies. The MIN_VALUE and MAX_VALUE properties will give you the range of values for a particular data type.

I have written a program called DataTypes that displays these values in an applet window. The output is shown in Figure 2.1, and the source code listing follows. This program is on the companion website (www.courseptr.com/downloads) in the \sources\chapter02\DataTypes folder.

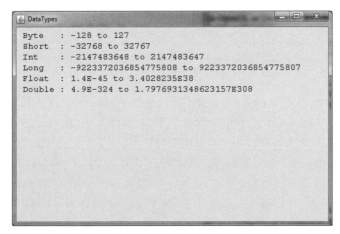

Figure 2.1
The DataTypes program displays the range for each numeric data type.

```java
import java.awt.*;
import javax.swing.*;
public class DataTypes extends JFrame {
    public DataTypes() {
        super("DataTypes");
        setSize(600,400);
        setVisible(true);
        setDefaultCloseOperation(JFrame.EXIT_ON_CLOSE);
    }
    public void paint(Graphics g) {
        g.setFont(new Font("Courier New", Font.PLAIN, 16));
        g.drawString("Byte : " +
            Byte.MIN_VALUE + " to " + Byte.MAX_VALUE, 20, 50);
        g.drawString("Short : " +
            Short.MIN_VALUE + " to " + Short.MAX_VALUE, 20, 70);
        g.drawString("Int : " +
            Integer.MIN_VALUE + " to " + Integer.MAX_VALUE, 20, 90);
        g.drawString("Long : " +
            Long.MIN_VALUE + " to " + Long.MAX_VALUE, 20, 110);
        g.drawString("Float : " +
            Float.MIN_VALUE + " to " + Float.MAX_VALUE, 20, 130);
        g.drawString("Double : " +
            Double.MIN_VALUE + " to " + Double.MAX_VALUE, 20, 150);
    }
    public static void main(String[] args) {
        new DataTypes();
    }
}
```

Characters and Strings

There are two data types in Java for working with character data: char and
String. Note that char is a base data type, while String is automatically
recognizable as a class (due to the uppercase first letter). Java tries to make
programming easy for C++ programmers by using many of the same basic data
types in order to make it easier to convert C and C++ programs to Java. So we
have a base char and a String class; of course, as you now know, every data type
in Java is a class already.

You define a char variable like this:

```
char studentgrade;
char examscore = 'A';
```

The char data type can only handle a single character, not an entire string. Note that a character is identified with single quotes ('A') rather than double quotes, necessary for strings. The String data type (or rather, class) is very easy to use and is used by many of the Java library methods. (Remember, a method is a function.) For instance, you have seen a lot of the Graphics class so far in this chapter because it is the main way to display things (such as text) in an applet window. Here are a couple of different ways to create a string:

```
String favoritegame = "Sid Meier's Civilization V";
String username;
username = "John" + " R. " + "Doe";
```

In addition to supporting the plus operator for combining strings (something that C programmers look upon with envy), the String class also comes equipped with numerous support methods for manipulating strings. I won't go over every property and method in the String class here because that is the role of a Java reference book—to cover every single detail.

Tip

If you are enjoying Java so far and you think you will stick with it, you will definitely need a comprehensive Java language reference book. I recommend Herbert Schildt's *Java: The Complete Reference, 7th Edition* (McGraw-Hill Osborne Media, 2006). A good introductory book for beginners is John Flynt's *Java Programming for the Absolute Beginner, Second Edition* (Cengage, 2006). If you want just a good online reference, the online docs for Java can be found at http://java .sun.com/reference/api/.

One good example of a function we've been using in this chapter is Graphics .drawString(). This function has many overloaded versions available (overloading is explained later in this chapter, in the section entitled "Object-Oriented Programming") that give you a lot of options for printing text to the applet window, but the main version I use is this:

```
drawString(String str, int x, int y)
```

Table 2.3 String Class Methods

Method	Description
contains	Returns true if one string is contained in another string
endsWith	Returns true if the string ends with a certain string
equalsIgnoreCase	Compares strings without considering uppercase or lowercase
length	Returns the length of the string
replace	Replaces all occurrences of a sub-string with another sub-string in a string
trim	Removes blank spaces from the start and end of a string

Note

We have just scratched the surface of Java 2D (with the Graphics and Graphics2D classes). This will be the focus of most of Part II, covering Chapters 4 through 10. You will learn about class inheritance later in this chapter.

Table 2.3 lists just *some* of the useful methods in the String class. This is by no means a complete list.

If you want to see all of the properties and methods in a class (such as String), the easiest way to get a list, aside from using a reference book, is to create an instance of a class (such as String s) and then use the dot operator (.) to cause NetBeans or Eclipse to bring up the contents of the class. This built-in "look" feature works with the Java language classes as well as classes you have written yourself, as shown in Figure 2.2.

Possibly the single-most beneficial advantage to using an IDE is the built-in help system, which is available in tools such as NetBeans. If you aren't using an IDE that provides context-sensitive help and class member lists, then you will need a good reference book or website.

Tip

If you are looking for help on a specific Java language term or class, the easiest way to look up that information is by using Google. Search "java *keyword*" to quickly locate the reference. For example, the first Google result for "java graphics2d" will most likely be a URL to one of Sun's own Java reference pages. Or you can just go straight to the source and search through the class listings at http://java.sun.com/reference/api/. Looking up the reference instead of using the editor's pop-up help may not be as convenient, but it will make you a stronger programmer.

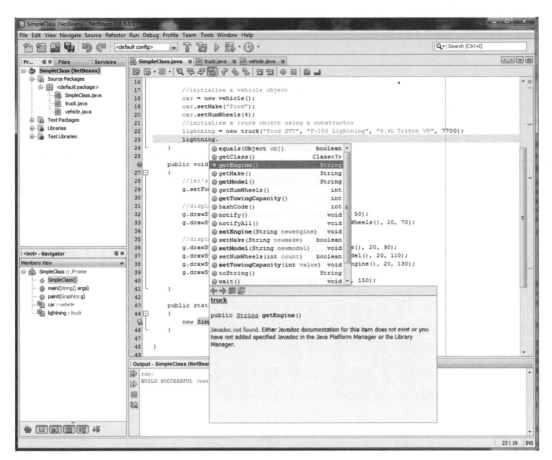

Figure 2.2
NetBeans displays the contents of a class with a pop-up window.

Booleans

The Boolean data type can be set to either *true* or *false*, and it is useful as a return value for methods. For instance, in some of the example programs you've seen so far, there have been methods that returned a Boolean based on whether the code succeeded. You can declare a `boolean` variable like so:

```
boolean gameover = false;
```

Here is a short method that returns a Boolean value based on whether a value is within a boundary of a minimum and maximum value:

```
public boolean checkBounds(long val, long lower, long upper) {
    if (val < lower || val > upper)
```

```
            return false;
        else
            return true;
    }
```

Here is an example of using the checkBounds method to determine whether a sprite's position on the screen (in the horizontal orientation) is within the screen's boundary:

```
spriteX = spriteX + 1;
if (checkBounds(spriteX, 0, 639) == true)
    spriteX = 0;
```

This short example assumes that the spriteX variable has already been declared earlier in the program. The sprite's X position on the screen will wrap around to the left edge anytime the sprite moves off the right edge of the screen. This Boolean method can also be written like this, where the == true is assumed in the if statement:

```
if (checkBounds(spriteX, 0, 639)) ...
```

Note that I have left out the == true in this line of code. This is possible because Java evaluates the return value of the checkBounds method and replaces the method call with the return value when the program is running. Thus, if the checkBounds method returns true, the if statement becomes this:

```
if (true) ...
```

This is why we can leave the == true out of the equation. Conversely, when you want to test for a false return value, you can insert == false in the if statement or you can use the logical negative operator (!) in the statement:

```
if (!checkBounds(spriteX, 0, 639)) ...
```

The result is that if checkBounds returns false, the if statement will execute the code that follows; otherwise, the code is not executed. Speaking of which, you may include a single line of code after an if statement, or you may include a code block enclosed in curly braces as follows. This is especially helpful if you want to do more than one thing after a conditional statement returns true or false:

```
public boolean checkBounds(long val, long lower, long upper) {
    if (val < lower || val > upper) {
        ...
```

```
        return false;
    } else {
        ...
        return true;
    }
}
```

The use of curly braces in this new version of checkBounds might not change anything, but it does allow you to add more lines of code before each of the return statements. (For instance, you may want to display a message on the screen before returning.)

Arrays

An *array* is a collection of variables of a specific data type that are organized in a manageable container. An array is created using one of the base data types, a Java library class, or one of your own classes. To tell Java that you want an array, attach brackets to the data type in your variable declaration:

```
int[] highScoreList;
```

But there are *two* steps to creating an array because an array must first be defined, and *then* memory must be allocated for it. First, you define the data type and array variable name, then you allocate the array by specifying the number of elements in the array with the new operator:

```
int[] studentGrades;
studentGrades = new int[30];
```

Note that I have allocated enough memory for this array to hold 30 elements in the studentGrades array. You can also define a new array with a single line of code:

```
int[] studentGrades = new int[30];
```

I don't know about you, but I enjoy writing beautiful code like this. I get a chill when writing code like this because my imagination starts to take off with visions of scrolling backgrounds and spaceships and bullets and explosions, all of which are made possible with arrays. But the real power of an array is made obvious when you start iterating through an array with a loop. If you need to update the values of this array, you might access the array elements individually like this:

```
studentGrades[0] = 90;
...
studentGrades[29] = 100;
```

If you truly need to set each element in an array individually, then an array can still help to cut down on the clutter in your program. And an array will always benefit from processing in a loop when it comes to things such as printing out the contents of the array or storing it in a data file, or for any other purpose you may have for the array. Let's set all of the elements in an array to a starting value of zero (this is good programming practice):

```
long[] speed = new long[100];
for (int i = 0; i < 100; i++) {
    speed[i] = 0;
}
```

There is another way to create an array by setting the initial values of the array right at the definition. This array of five floats is defined and initialized in memory with starting values at the same time.

```
float[] radioStations = { 88.5, 91.3, 97.7, 101.5, 103.0 };
```

You can also create multidimensional arrays. An array with more than one dimension will have a multiplicative number of elements (based on the number of elements in each dimension) because for every one element in the first dimension, there are N elements in the next dimension (based on the size of the next dimension). In my own experience writing games, I seldom use more than one dimension for an array because it is possible (and more efficient) to use a single-dimensioned array, and then index into it creatively to deal with multiple dimensions.

Here is an example two-dimensional array that stores the values for a game level. The pound characters (#) represent walls (or any other object you want in your game) while the periods (.) represent dirt, grass, or any other type of image. I presume that this is a level for a tile-based game, where each character in the array is drawn to the screen as a tile from a bitmap file.

```
char[][] gameLevel = {
    {'#','#','#','#','#','#','#','#','#','#'},
    {'#','.','.','.','.','.','.','.','.','#'},
    {'#','.','.','.','.','.','.','.','.','#'},
    {'#','.','.','.','.','.','.','.','.','#'},
    {'#','.','.','.','.','.','.','.','.','#'},
    {'#','.','.','.','.','.','.','.','.','#'},
    {'#','#','#','#','#','#','#','#','#','#'}
};
```

Another common practice is to create a game level with just numbers (such as 0 to 9). Some programmers prefer to use character-based levels because they sort of *look* more like a game level, and are, therefore, easier to edit. I tend to prefer integer-based game levels using a level editor such as Mappy, which exports levels as a comma-delimited array of numbers. Here is how Mappy might export the same level with numeric data:

```
2, 2, 2, 2, 2, 2, 2, 2, 2, 2,
2, 1, 1, 1, 1, 1, 1, 1, 1, 2,
2, 1, 1, 1, 1, 1, 1, 1, 1, 2,
2, 1, 1, 1, 1, 1, 1, 1, 1, 2,
2, 1, 1, 1, 1, 1, 1, 1, 1, 2,
2, 1, 1, 1, 1, 1, 1, 1, 1, 2,
2, 2, 2, 2, 2, 2, 2, 2, 2, 2
```

Tip

You can download Mappy from www.tilemap.co.uk. The subject of tiled scrolling is not covered in this book. For an exhaustive guide to the subject, I refer you to *Visual Basic Game Programming for Teens, 3rd Edition* (Course PTR, 2010) (or the sister book *Visual C# Game Programming for Teens*). Although this book covers Basic, it is one of the few books that explains how to build a level editor from scratch, and the concepts can be applied to Java should you wish to create such a game.

Can you make out the similarity between the two game levels shown here? It's all the same data, just represented differently. When Mappy exports a level like this, it sends the data to a text file that you can then open and paste into your game's source code. To make it work, you would define an array to handle the data like this:

```
int[][] gameLevel = {
    {2, 2, 2, 2, 2, 2, 2, 2, 2, 2},
    {2, 1, 1, 1, 1, 1, 1, 1, 1, 2},
    {2, 1, 1, 1, 1, 1, 1, 1, 1, 2},
    {2, 1, 1, 1, 1, 1, 1, 1, 1, 2},
    {2, 1, 1, 1, 1, 1, 1, 1, 1, 2},
    {2, 1, 1, 1, 1, 1, 1, 1, 1, 2},
    {2, 2, 2, 2, 2, 2, 2, 2, 2, 2}
};
```

Tip

Don't forget the semicolon at the end of an array declaration, or you will get some very strange errors from the Java compiler.

I prefer to treat a game level (or other array-based data sequence) as a single-dimensioned array because data like this is easier to work with as a one-dimensional array. Here is how I would define it:

```
int[] gameLevel = {
    2, 2, 2, 2, 2, 2, 2, 2, 2, 2,
    2, 1, 1, 1, 1, 1, 1, 1, 1, 2,
    2, 1, 1, 1, 1, 1, 1, 1, 1, 2,
    2, 1, 1, 1, 1, 1, 1, 1, 1, 2,
    2, 1, 1, 1, 1, 1, 1, 1, 1, 2,
    2, 1, 1, 1, 1, 1, 1, 1, 1, 2,
    2, 2, 2, 2, 2, 2, 2, 2, 2, 2
};
```

Do you see the subtle difference between this 1D array and the 2D array defined before? All I need to know are the width and height of the array data, and then I don't need multiple dimensions. In this example, this game level is 10 tiles wide and 10 tiles deep, for a total of 100 tiles. (A *tile* is a small bitmap used to build a game world in a 2D scrolling game, and it very closely resembles the analogy of floor tiles in the way it is used.)

The Essence of Class

In case you haven't noticed, I've been talking about classes a lot. That's because you can't really get around the subject when writing a Java program. The main part of a Java source code file itself is a class. You might have seen a C program before and you might already be familiar with the main() function. Here is a simple C program:

```
int main(int argc, char argv[]) {
    printf("I am a C program.\n");
    return 0;
}
```

Let's take a look at the same program written in pure C++:

```
#include <iostream>
int main(int argc, char argv[]) {
    std::cout << "I am a C++ program." << std::endl;
    return 1;
}
```

Now take a look at the same program written in Java:

```
import java.io.*;
public class SampleJava {
    public static void main(String args[]) {
        System.out.println("I am a Java program.");
    }
}
```

Do you see any similarities among these programs? You should, because they are listed in evolutionary order. Now, I don't want to get into an argument with anyone about whether Java is truly an evolutionary leap ahead of C++ because I'm not sure if I believe that in the strictest sense (with a feature comparison). But I do like to think of Java as the next logical step above C++; it is easier, less prone to error, but not as powerful. Doesn't that describe any system that tends to evolve over time? Take the computer industry itself, for instance. The earliest computers were built with thousands of vacuum tubes, which were difficult to maintain and very prone to error; and as far as power consumption goes, I think the computers of old were definitely more powerful than the computers we commonly use today—but let's not talk about performance, which is no contest.

The C program is quite simple and maybe even readable by a non-programmer (who may not understand anything other than the printf line, and even then with much confusion). The C++ program is so much gobbledygook to anyone but a programmer. But those of us with a C++ background often describe C++ code as beautiful and elegant, with a powerful, perhaps even *intimidating*, lure. The Java program is very similar to the C and C++ programs. Like the C++ program, the Java program must "get something" from "somewhere else" in the form of the import java.io.* statement. This java.io is a library that provides access to the System.out class, which is used for printing out text (as you probably guessed). But the biggest difference is that the Java program is located inside a *class*. This class is called SampleJava, and inside this class (enclosed with curly braces) is a main function very similar to the main functions found in the C and C++ programs.

What is this SampleJava class, you may ask? The truth is, *everything* in Java is a class, and it is not possible to do anything useful in Java without using a class. All source code that you write in Java will be enclosed inside a class definition.

The main Function

The core of a Java application is the main function. (Note that applets typically don't have a main function, as I'll explain shortly.) The main function has this basic format:

```
public static void main(String args[]) { }
```

The parameter (String args[]) allows you to pass information to the Java program and is only practical when developing a Java application (rather than an applet) to which you can pass parameters, presumably from a command prompt or shell. You *can* pass parameters to a Java applet, but that is not done very often. I once worked for a company that built vehicle tracking systems using GPS (*global positioning system*), and my job was to maintain the Java program that displayed a map with all the vehicles in the state of Arizona moving along their routes. This Java program received vehicle tracking information from a server, and then displayed it in an applet.

Caution

Java applets don't need a main function because there are several *events* that are found in an applet instead (such as init and paint).

Let's dissect the main function to help you better understand what it does. The term public specifies that this function is visible outside the class. (Remember, every Java program runs inside a class.) The static term specifies that the function definition never changes and is not to be inherited (borrowed for use in another function). The static keyword is optional and not often used in an applet. The void term means that the function does not return a value. Every Java application you write will have a main function, just like every C and C++ program. However, a Java applet, which runs in a web browser, contains events instead and is not in complete control in the same way that a standalone Java application (with a main method) is.

However, you *can* write Java classes that *don't* have a main function. Why would you want to do that? A class is usually created to perform a specific task, such as the handling of sprites in a game. You might write a sprite class that knows how to load a bitmap file and draw a sprite on the screen; then the main Java program (with the main function) will *consume* or use the sprite class, which itself has no main function. A class has its own variables and functions, some of which are hidden inside the class itself and invisible outside the class. What I'm describing here are some of the key aspects of object-oriented programming, or OOP. In some cases, as when developing an applet, you may just use the paint event rather than using a main function. (More on that later.)

Object-Oriented Programming

There are four main concepts involved in OOP, though you may not use all of them in every class you write:

- Data hiding
- Encapsulation
- Inheritance
- Polymorphism

I'll briefly talk about each of these concepts because you will be dealing with these throughout the book. I don't spend a lot of time discussing advanced concepts like these while writing Java games, and this book is not intended as a primer on the Java language. Hundreds of books have been written about Java programming, including some very complex textbooks on the subject used in college courses.

Data Hiding

Data hiding is a key concept of OOP because it provides a way to protect data within an object at runtime from direct manipulation. Instead of providing access to certain pieces of data, a class definition will include functions (often called *methods* or *accessors/mutators* in OOP lore) for retrieving and changing data (often called *properties*) that is hidden within the class definition. An accessor function retrieves a hidden variable; a mutator changes a hidden variable.

This way, the programmer can specify exactly what changes can be made to a private variable through the built-in mutator functions and return custom-formatted data through the accessor functions. For instance, if you want to make sure that a birth date is valid, the mutator function can restrict changes to a certain range (such as 0 to 120). The following source code demonstrates the concept of data hiding. I have intentionally kept the code listing simpler by not including any comments.

```java
public class vehicle {
    private String make;
    private int numwheels;

    public String getMake() {
        return make;
    }
    public boolean setMake(String newmake) {
        if (newmake.length() > 0) {
            make = newmake;
            return true;
        } else {
            return false;
        }
    }

    public int getNumWheels() {
        return numwheels;
    }
    public boolean setNumWheels(int count) {
        if (count > 0 && count < 20)
        {
            numwheels = count;
            return true;
        } else {
            return false;
```

```
            }
        }
}
```

Encapsulation

Encapsulation is related to data hiding in that it describes how information and processes are both handled internally by a class. These two concepts are often used interchangeably, depending on the opinion of the programmer. (I prefer to use the term *encapsulation* rather than *data hiding*.) I would suggest that encapsulation involves modeling a real-world entity, whereas data hiding describes the ability to use private variables in a class. It's common to encapsulate a real-world entity by writing a class that describes the data and functions for working with that data. In the vehicle class example, I have encapsulated the specifications for a basic vehicle inside a class with hidden (or private) data members and public functions (or methods).

Inheritance

Inheritance describes the ability to reuse class definitions and to make changes to a subclass that relies on a base class. For instance, the vehicle class might be used as a basis for many subclasses covering a wide range of vehicles, from two-wheel motorcycles to 18-wheel semi trucks. When you are writing the code for a class, it is best to put each class inside its own source code file. Java allows you to inherit from a single base class.

Note

Although C++ allows you to inherit from multiple base classes, this feature often causes more problems than it solves, so it is seldom used. Instead of multiple inheritance, Java allows you to use multiple interfaces—which are guidelines for the properties and methods that should be found within a particular class.

For instance, the SimpleClass program includes the source code listing for the vehicle class, and it is stored in a file called vehicle.java. Also included in the SimpleClass project is the main source code file called SimpleClass.java—and this file "consumes" or uses the vehicle class defined in the vehicle.java file. Additional classes can be written and saved in their own source files.

Tip

To add a new class to your project, just create a new text file with a .java extension and compile it separately from your main program file. This is very easy to do using TextPad by pressing Ctrl+1 to compile your Java code.

A *constructor* is a method that is called whenever you create a new class in your program. I'm not talking about typing in a new class, but when a class is instantiated into an object at runtime. When a new class is created (with the new operator), the class definition is used to construct an object. See where the keyword comes in here? The new object is "constructed" when it is being created at runtime; the class is a blueprint used to build or construct the object at runtime.

Definition

Instantiate means to create or to construct. Within the context of object-oriented programming, new objects are instantiated when they are created at runtime from the blueprint specified in a class definition (such as the vehicle class).

When I click the OK button on the Class Wizard dialog box, a new file called truck.java is added to my project, and it contains this source code:

```java
public class truck extends vehicle {
    public truck() {
    }
}
```

This is a nice, clean starting point for a new class. Note that this class inherits from the vehicle class (extends vehicle), and it includes a simple constructor (public truck()). This constructor is called whenever you use new to create a new truck object, using code like this:

```java
truck silverado = new truck();
```

The constructor is specified after the new operator in this line of code, and this is called an *empty constructor*. If you want to pass parameters to a constructor, you can do so by defining another version of the constructor, which is a topic that needs to be covered in the next section on polymorphism.

Polymorphism

Polymorphism is a complex word that, when broken down, equates to *poly* ("many") and *morph* ("shape"); therefore, polymorphism means "many shape" or "many shapes." Java allows you to write many versions of a function (or method) with different sets of parameters. When you write more than one version of a method, you have overloaded that method. *Overloading* is a technical programming term that describes polymorphism at work.

Tip

I have been using the terms *function* and *method* together up to this point. I will refer to *method* from this point forward. Just note that a method is the same as a function, and this applies to accessor/mutator functions (terms that are used by C++ programmers). Just remember: A *property* is a variable, and a *method* is a function.

The complete truck class source code listing demonstrates polymorphism. Note the constructor, truck(), which has been overloaded once with an alternative version with the following syntax:

```
public truck(String make, String model, String engine, int towing)
```

You will probably not pass all of the data to a class in this manner all at once, as it is not usually very practical. You may pass any values to the constructor that you think will help with the initialization of the object that is being instantiated, but keep in mind that there are methods available for reading and changing those variables (or properties) as well.

Do you see how the default constructor includes several method calls to set the private variables to some initial values? This is a good practice to do when creating a class definition, because it eliminates the chance of a null-pointer runtime error from occurring—which is common when working with strings that have not yet been set to a value. I've decided not to include a string length check in the set functions to make the source code easier to read, but this sort of built-in error handling is a good idea.

```
public class truck extends vehicle {
    private String model;
```

```java
    private String engine;
    private int towingcapacity;

    public truck() {
        setMake("make");
        setNumWheels(4);
        setModel("model");
        setEngine("engine");
        setTowingCapacity(0);
    }

    public truck(String make, String model, String engine, int towing) {
        setMake(make);
        setModel(model);
        setEngine(engine);
        setTowingCapacity(towing);
    }

    public String getModel() {
        return model;
    }
    public void setModel(String newmodel) {
        model = newmodel;
    }

    public String getEngine() {
        return engine;
    }
    public void setEngine(String newengine) {
        engine = newengine;
    }

    public int getTowingCapacity() {
        return towingcapacity;
    }
    public void setTowingCapacity(int value) {
        towingcapacity = value;
    }
}
```

Now let's make some changes to the main source code in the SimpleClass.java file. This is the part of the program that consumes, or uses, the `vehicle` and `truck` classes. Here is the complete listing:

```java
import java.lang.*;
import javax.swing.*;
import java.awt.*;

public class SimpleClass extends JFrame {
    vehicle car;
    truck lightning;

    public SimpleClass() {
        super("SimpleClass");
        setSize(600,400);
        setVisible(true);
        setDefaultCloseOperation(JFrame.EXIT_ON_CLOSE);

        //initialize a vehicle object
        car = new vehicle();
        car.setMake("Ford");
        car.setNumWheels(4);
        //initialize a truck object using a constructor
        lightning = new truck("Ford SVT", "F-150 Lightning",
            "5.4L Triton V8", 7700);
        lightning.
    }

    public void paint(Graphics g) {
        //let's use a nice big font
        g.setFont(new Font("Verdana", Font.BOLD, 12));

        //display the car info
        g.drawString("Car make: " + car.getMake(), 20, 50);
        g.drawString("Number of wheels: " + car.getNumWheels(), 20, 70);

        //display the truck info
        g.drawString("Truck make: " + lightning.getMake(), 20, 90);
        g.drawString("Truck model: " + lightning.getModel(), 20, 110);
        g.drawString("Truck engine: " + lightning.getEngine(), 20, 130);
```

```
        g.drawString("Truck towing capacity: " +
                lightning.getTowingCapacity(), 20, 150);
    }

    public static void main(String[] args) {
        new SimpleClass();
    }
}
```

What is the most significant part of this program that might seem unusual or surprising? Well, take a look at those last few lines of code where the truck information is displayed on the screen. The truck is using a method called getMake() that is not even defined in the truck class; this is a method found only in the vehicle class, from which the truck class was inherited. That is the real power of inheritance—the ability to reuse functionality while enhancing existing classes.

I have added the truck class to the SimpleClass program, which is where the vehicle class may also be found. You can open the SimpleClass project from the companion website materials (www.courseptr.com/downloads) in the \sources\chapter02 folder. Figure 2.3 shows the output from the current version of the program up to this point.

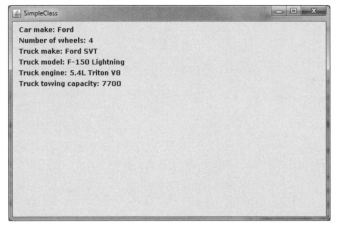

Figure 2.3
The SimpleClass program now demonstrates inheritance with the truck class.

What You Have Learned

This chapter provided an overview of the basics of Java programming. You learned about the differences between a Java application and a Java applet, and how to write programs of each type and then compile and run them. You learned the basics of object-oriented programming and many other Java programming issues that will be helpful in later chapters. Specifically, this chapter covered:

- How to write a Java application
- How to write a Java applet
- How to compile a Java program

Review Questions

The following questions will help you to determine how well you have learned the subjects discussed in this chapter. The answers are provided in Appendix A, "Chapter Quiz Answers."

1. What is the name of the JDK tool used to compile Java programs?
2. Which JDK command-line tool is used to run a Java application?
3. Which JDK command-line tool is used to run a Java applet?
4. What are two good, free Java IDEs recommended in this chapter?
5. Encapsulation, polymorphism, and inheritance are the keys to what programming methodology?
6. What's the main difference between a Java application and an applet?
7. Which method of the Graphics class can you use to print a text message on the screen?
8. How many bits make up a Java integer (the int data type)?
9. How many bits are there in a Java long integer (the long data type)?
10. What programming language was Java based on?

On Your Own

Use the following exercises to test your grasp of the material covered in this chapter.

Exercise 1

Write your own Java class and then use it to extend an inherited class to try out the concepts of inheritance and encapsulation.

Exercise 2

Modify your new class by adding some methods that demonstrate the concept of polymorphism by writing several versions of the same method with different sets of parameters.

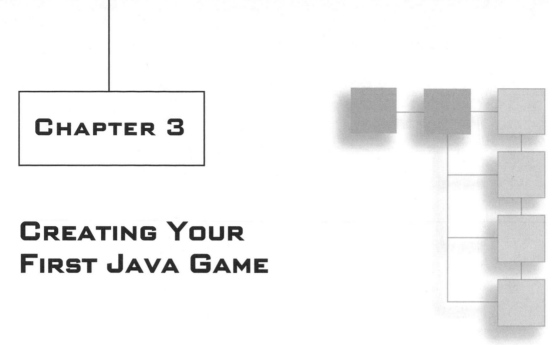

CHAPTER 3

CREATING YOUR
FIRST JAVA GAME

This chapter will give you a glimpse of what's coming in the next few chapters while teaching you some of the basics of game creation. The game featured here was inspired by the classic Atari game of *Asteroids*. My first video game system was an Atari 2600, and I spent many hours with it. In this chapter, you'll learn how to create a variation of this classic game, which will be the basis of a more advanced game later on when we get to Part III. This will also be our first really big *applet* chapter—learning how to build a Java applet–based game, and the specific source code features of an applet. We will return to using JFrame as well in upcoming chapters rather than focusing on just one or the other.

Here are the key topics in this chapter:

- Creating an *Asteroids*-style game
- Writing key classes: `BaseVectorShape`, `Ship`, `Asteroid`, and `Bullet`
- Writing the main source code
- Calculating velocities on the fly

ABOUT THE GAME PROJECT

Our game project in this chapter will run in a web browser window with a resolution of 640×480 and will be done entirely using vector graphics. It will have some features that you have not yet learned about, but the exposure to this code will be helpful to you. I want to introduce you to some of the concepts early

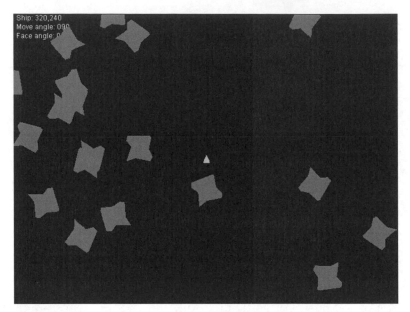

Ship: 320,240
Move angle: 090
Face angle: 0

Figure 3.1
This *Asteroids* clone is the basis for a much more ambitious game.

on, before you have learned all of the prerequisites (otherwise, we wouldn't be able to create a game until about halfway through the book!). You may not understand everything in the source code for the game at this point, but you will learn how it works in time. Figure 3.1 shows the completed game you will build in this chapter.

As mentioned, the game is entirely based on vector graphics. The player's ship, the asteroids, and the bullets are all rendered as polygons, as shown in Figure 3.2.

Definition

Vector graphic displays are different from our modern monitors in that they draw shapes based on entire lines. On the other hand, our modern displays draw *raster graphics* based on pixels.

All of the objects in the game are moved using an algorithm that calculates the X and Y velocity values, which are used to update the object's position on the screen. All of these values use floating-point math, and the result is fluid 2D rotation animation and realistic movement. Each of the vector shapes in the game has a built-in bounding rectangle that is used to simplify collision testing, which is a crucial aspect of the game (see Figure 3.3). Without it, the bullets

Figure 3.2
The objects in the game are all rendered as vector graphics.

Figure 3.3
Bounding rectangles are used to detect when collisions occur.

would not destroy the asteroids, and the ship would be invulnerable! Collision testing is what makes gameplay possible in a game.

The goal is to modify this game concept later on to come up with a high-quality, polished game with a lot of interesting gameplay features (such as power-ups) by the time you've finished the book. The final version of Galactic War is an arcade-style game with many different types of asteroids, animated explosions, and power-ups for the player's ship. When we start working in earnest on Galactic War, we'll make a transition from vector graphics (based on polygons) to rasterized graphics (based on bitmaps). But before you can run, as the old saying goes, you have to learn how to walk. This chapter teaches you how to walk, and you will gradually improve the game a little at a time, starting with the next chapter.

CREATING THE GAME

This game is divided into five classes. Does that seem like a lot of classes for just your first game? I thought about that for a while, considering this might be too much code all at once. But I think you will enjoy it. This is a complete game, for the most part, so you can examine it—pore over the lines of code in Holmesian style (with a magnifying glass, if you wish)—to learn the secrets of how a game is made. You are presented with a mystery of sorts—a complete game. Your task is to reverse engineer the situation to determine, step by step, what events led up to the complete game. The main class, Asteroids, contains the main source code for the game. Four additional classes are used:

- BaseVectorShape
- Ship
- Bullet
- Asteroid

Creating the Project

You can type in the code for each of the classes (and the main source code file, Asteroids.java) and then compile each file into a .class file using the Java Development Kit (JDK) command-line tools. The compiler is called javac.exe. You can compile a file by simply typing:

```
javac Asteroids.java
```

and likewise for the other source code files. I recommend using TextPad if you are a Windows user because of its very convenient support for the JDK, where you can compile your Java program with Ctrl+1 and run it with Ctrl+3.

The BaseVectorShape Class

The three main objects in the game (the asteroids, the bullets, and the player's ship) are all derived from the BaseVectorShape class. I originally wrote this game without the base class, and in the end, all three of the game objects (the player's ship, the bullets, and the asteroids) ended up sharing most of their properties and methods, so the BaseVectorShape class was a way to clean up the code. In the end, I put a lot of useful methods in this class for handling the needs of this vector graphics game. By doing this, I have used the object-oriented feature called *inheritance*. The Asteroid, Ship, and Bullet classes are all derived from BaseVectorShape, which contains code that is shared by all three. As a result, the code for the three subclasses is quite short in each case.

This game detects collisions between the asteroids, bullets, and player's ship, so each vector shape in the game includes its own bounding rectangle. While the getBounds() method is not found in the BaseVectorShape class for reasons I'll explain in a moment, this method does use the getX() and getY() methods from the base class to calculate the bounding rectangle. This class basically contains all the variables that will be used to move the objects around on the screen, such as the X and Y position, the velocity, the facing and moving angles, and the shape itself (which is a polygon).

Tip

What is bounding rectangle collision detection? This phrase describes the process of detecting when objects collide with each other in the game (such as a bullet hitting an asteroid) using rectangular shapes that surround or contain the shape. As a result, the shape is bound within that rectangle, so to speak.

```
import java.awt.Shape;
// Base vector shape class for for polygonal shapes
public class BaseVectorShape {
    //variables
    private Shape shape;
    private boolean alive;
```

```java
    private double x,y;
    private double velX, velY;
    private double moveAngle, faceAngle;

    //accessor methods
    public Shape getShape() { return shape; }
    public boolean isAlive() { return alive; }
    public double getX() { return x; }
    public double getY() { return y; }
    public double getVelX() { return velX; }
    public double getVelY() { return velY; }
    public double getMoveAngle() { return moveAngle; }
    public double getFaceAngle() { return faceAngle; }

    //mutator and helper methods
    public void setShape(Shape shape) { this.shape = shape; }
    public void setAlive(boolean alive) { this.alive = alive; }
    public void setX(double x) { this.x = x; }
    public void incX(double i) { this.x += i; }
    public void setY(double y) { this.y = y; }
    public void incY(double i) { this.y += i; }
    public void setVelX(double velX) { this.velX = velX; }
    public void incVelX(double i) { this.velX += i; }
    public void setVelY(double velY) { this.velY = velY; }
    public void incVelY(double i) { this.velY += i; }
    public void setFaceAngle(double angle) { this.faceAngle = angle; }
    public void incFaceAngle(double i) { this.faceAngle += i; }
    public void setMoveAngle(double angle) { this.moveAngle = angle; }
    public void incMoveAngle(double i) { this.moveAngle += i; }

    //default constructor
    BaseVectorShape() {
        setShape(null);
        setAlive(false);
        setX(0.0);
        setY(0.0);
        setVelX(0.0);
        setVelY(0.0);
        setMoveAngle(0.0);
        setFaceAngle(0.0);
    }
}
```

The Ship Class

The Ship class handles the shape, position, and velocity of the player's ship in the game. It includes its own bounding rectangle, which is calculated based on the custom polygon shape for the ship. The Ship class inherits all of the public properties and methods from the BaseVectorShape class.

```
import java.awt.Polygon;
import java.awt.Rectangle;
// Ship class - polygonal shape of the player's ship
public class Ship extends BaseVectorShape {
    //define the ship polygon
    private int[] shipx = { -6, -3, 0, 3, 6, 0 };
    private int[] shipy = { 6, 7, 7, 7, 6, -7 };

    //bounding rectangle
    public Rectangle getBounds() {
        Rectangle r;
        r = new Rectangle((int)getX() - 6, (int) getY() - 6, 12,12);
        return r;
    }

    Ship() {
        setShape(new Polygon(shipx, shipy, shipx.length));
        setAlive(true);
    }
}
```

The Bullet Class

The Bullet class defines the bullets fired from the ship. It is also derived from the BaseVectorShape class, so most of the functionality of this class is provided by the base class. All we really need to do for bullets in this game is to define a rectangle that is one pixel in width and height to create a tiny rectangle. This small shape is used to calculate the bounding rectangle returned in the getBounds() method. While we're only drawing a rectangle the size of a single pixel, we will still treat it as a rectangle, but when it's time to check to see whether the bullet has hit an asteroid (using collision detection), then we'll do it slightly differently than the way in which we compare collisions between the player's ship and the asteroids. Instead of checking for an intersection, we'll see whether the bullet is "contained within" an asteroid.

```java
import java.awt.*;
import java.awt.Rectangle;

// Bullet class - polygonal shape of a bullet
public class Bullet extends BaseVectorShape {

    //bounding rectangle
    public Rectangle getBounds() {
        Rectangle r;
        r = new Rectangle((int)getX(), (int) getY(), 1, 1);
        return r;
    }

    Bullet() {
        //create the bullet shape
        setShape(new Rectangle(0, 0, 1, 1));
        setAlive(false);
    }
}
```

The Asteroid Class

The Asteroid class also inherits from BaseVectorShape and provides three of its own new methods: getRotationVelocity, setRotationVelocity, and getBounds. The rotation velocity value is used to rotate the asteroids (which is a cool effect in the game). The getBounds method returns the bounding rectangle for the asteroid and is similar to the same method found in the Ship and Bullet classes.

```java
import java.awt.Polygon;
import java.awt.Rectangle;

// Asteroid class - for polygonal asteroid shapes
public class Asteroid extends BaseVectorShape {
    //define the asteroid polygon shape
    private int[] astx = {-20,-13, 0,20,22, 20, 12, 2,-10,-22,-16};
    private int[] asty = { 20, 23,17,20,16,-20,-22,-14,-17,-20, -5};
```

```
//rotation speed
protected double rotVel;
public double getRotationVelocity() { return rotVel; }
public void setRotationVelocity(double v) { rotVel = v; }

//bounding rectangle
public Rectangle getBounds() {
    Rectangle r;
    r = new Rectangle((int)getX() - 20, (int) getY() - 20, 40, 40);
    return r;
}

//default constructor
Asteroid() {
    setShape(new Polygon(astx, asty, astx.length));
    setAlive(true);
    setRotationVelocity(0.0);
}
}
```

The Main Source Code File

The main source code file for this game is found in a file called Asteroids.java. I am providing the complete source code listing here so you can examine it in detail while reading my explanations of each method along the way. The first thing you'll notice with the main source code for our Asteroids clone is the implements keywords. This program implements two interfaces: Runnable and KeyListener. Runnable gives us an extremely powerful new capability—*threads*! With a thread, our program can run in real time, with things moving on the screen automatically. This really brings the game to life compared to prior examples! The next interface is pretty obvious: KeyListener "listens" for key presses, and notifies us when a key is pressed. The next major feature of this game over previous examples is that it's *double buffered*, which is a second buffer representing the dimensions of the game window, giving the game a very smooth refresh without any flicker or artifacts. Without the second buffer, the window would flicker like crazy as the window is cleared and the graphics are drawn over and over again. Everything else in the code is just support for these three major concepts.

```java
import java.applet.*;
import java.awt.*;
import java.awt.event.*;
import java.awt.geom.*;
import java.awt.image.*;
import java.util.*;

//Primary class for the game
public class Asteroids extends Applet implements Runnable, KeyListener {
    //the main thread becomes the game loop
    Thread gameloop;

    //use this as a double buffer
    BufferedImage backbuffer;

    //the main drawing object for the back buffer
    Graphics2D g2d;

    //toggle for drawing bounding boxes
    boolean showBounds = false;

    //create the asteroid array
    int ASTEROIDS = 20;
    Asteroid[] ast = new Asteroid[ASTEROIDS];

    //create the bullet array
    int BULLETS = 10;
    Bullet[] bullet = new Bullet[BULLETS];
    int currentBullet = 0;

    //the player's ship
    Ship ship = new Ship();

    //create the identity transform (0,0)
    AffineTransform identity = new AffineTransform();

    //create a random number generator
    Random rand = new Random();
```

Applet init() Event

The applet init() event is run when the applet first starts up and is used to initialize the game. The code first creates a double buffer, upon which all graphics will be rendered in order to produce a smooth screen refresh without flicker. The player's ship and the asteroids are initialized, and then the key listener is started.

```
// applet init event
public void init() {
    //create the back buffer for smooth graphics
    backbuffer = new BufferedImage(640, 480,
        BufferedImage.TYPE_INT_RGB);
    g2d = backbuffer.createGraphics();

    //set up the ship
    ship.setX(320);
    ship.setY(240);

    //set up the bullets
    for (int n = 0; n<BULLETS; n++) {
        bullet[n] = new Bullet();
    }

    //create the asteroids
    for (int n = 0; n<ASTEROIDS; n++) {
        ast[n] = new Asteroid();
        ast[n].setRotationVelocity(rand.nextInt(3)+1);
        ast[n].setX((double)rand.nextInt(600)+20);
        ast[n].setY((double)rand.nextInt(440)+20);
        ast[n].setMoveAngle(rand.nextInt(360));
        double ang = ast[n].getMoveAngle() - 90;
        ast[n].setVelX(calcAngleMoveX(ang));
        ast[n].setVelY(calcAngleMoveY(ang));
    }

    //start the user input listener
    addKeyListener(this);
}
```

Applet update() Event

The applet's `update()` event is triggered whenever the screen needs to be refreshed. This game does not call the `update()` method from the game loop yet, although a future version of the game will make this change, which provides better control over the screen refresh process. This method does all of the drawing to the applet window by first drawing graphics to the back buffer. This buffer is then copied to the applet window during the `paint()` event.

The identity transform is the *starting point* of a vector-based transform that allows vector-based shapes to be rotated and moved around in the game. First, you start at the *identity* and then move the shape and rotate it from there. If you don't start off with the identity before manipulating a shape, then it will be moved with the previous shape rather than on its own.

```
// applet update event to redraw the screen
public void update(Graphics g) {
    //start off transforms at identity
    g2d.setTransform(identity);

    //erase the background
    g2d.setPaint(Color.BLACK);
    g2d.fillRect(0, 0, getSize().width, getSize().height);

    //print some status information
    g2d.setColor(Color.WHITE);
    g2d.drawString("Ship: " + Math.round(ship.getX()) + "," +
        Math.round(ship.getY()) , 5, 10);
    g2d.drawString("Move angle: " + Math.round(
        ship.getMoveAngle())+90, 5, 25);
    g2d.drawString("Face angle: " + Math.round(
        ship.getFaceAngle()), 5, 40);

    //draw the game graphics
    drawShip();
    drawBullets();
    drawAsteroids();

    //repaint the applet window
    paint(g);
}
```

Drawing the Player's Ship

The drawShip() method is called by the update() event to draw the player's ship onto the back buffer at the correct X and Y location. Before drawing, the identity transform is set so that the ship's local coordinate system is used, rather than the previous vector's coordinates. Remember, a transform effects an object's X and Y position. The identity is the starting point (0,0).

When the ship is first drawn, it is actually centered at the origin, with the shape of the ship being drawn from −6 to +6 in the X and Y axes. So the ship is about 12 pixels square in size. If you don't draw a vector around the origin, then rotation will not work at all, because rotations occur at the origin—or rather, at the identity location.

```
// drawShip called by applet update event
public void drawShip() {
    g2d.setTransform(identity);
    g2d.translate(ship.getX(), ship.getY());
    g2d.rotate(Math.toRadians(ship.getFaceAngle()));
    g2d.setColor(Color.ORANGE);
    g2d.fill(ship.getShape());
}
```

Drawing the Bullets

The drawBullets() method goes through the array of bullets and draws any bullets that need to be drawn. This only occurs if a bullet is alive using the isAlive() method. Then the bullet is transformed to its position on the screen, and the shape is drawn (which is a tiny rectangle).

```
// drawBullets called by applet update event
public void drawBullets() {
    //iterate through the array of bullets
    for (int n = 0; n < BULLETS; n++) {
        //is this bullet currently in use?
        if (bullet[n].isAlive()) {
            //draw the bullet
            g2d.setTransform(identity);
            g2d.translate(bullet[n].getX(), bullet[n].getY());
            g2d.setColor(Color.MAGENTA);
            g2d.draw(bullet[n].getShape());
```

```
            }
        }
    }
```

Drawing the Asteroids

The drawAsteroids() method draws all of the asteroids in the ast[] array, depending on whether they are *alive*. When the player fires a bullet and it hits an asteroid, that asteroid's alive variable is set to false, so the asteroid is no longer drawn to the screen—and it is also ignored by the bullets after that. An interesting option in this method will draw the bounding rectangle around the asteroids if you have toggled bounding on by pressing the B key.

```
// drawAsteroids called by applet update event
public void drawAsteroids() {
    //iterate through the asteroids array
    for (int n = 0; n < ASTEROIDS; n++) {
        //is this asteroid being used?
        if (ast[n].isAlive()) {
            //draw the asteroid
            g2d.setTransform(identity);
            g2d.translate(ast[n].getX(), ast[n].getY());
            g2d.rotate(Math.toRadians(ast[n].getMoveAngle()));
            g2d.setColor(Color.DARK_GRAY);
            g2d.fill(ast[n].getShape());
        }
    }
}
```

Screen Refresh

The paint() event occurs when the applet window needs to be refreshed. This method is called by the update() method and simply serves the purpose of drawing the back buffer to the applet window.

```
// applet window repaint event--draw the back buffer
public void paint(Graphics g) {
    //draw the back buffer onto the applet window
    g.drawImage(backbuffer, 0, 0, this);
}
```

Thread Events and the Game Loop

There are three thread events that are part of a program when you implement the Runnable interface in a Java applet. Runnable tells Java that your applet will support more than one thread. A thread is sort of a mini program that can run on its own. You create a new thread in the start() event, and then destroy that thread in the stop() event to keep things running smoothly.

The most interesting thread event is called run(). This event method contains the code for the game loop, which is a while loop that sort of powers the game and keeps it running at a consistent frame rate. This event calls the gameUpdate() method, which processes the current frame of the game by moving objects around on the screen, testing for collisions, and so on.

```java
// thread start event - start the game loop running
public void start() {
    //create the gameloop thread for real-time updates
    gameloop = new Thread(this);
    gameloop.start();
}

// thread run event (game loop)
public void run() {
    //acquire the current thread
    Thread t = Thread.currentThread();

    //keep going as long as the thread is alive
    while (t == gameloop) {
        try {
            //update the game loop
            gameUpdate();

            //target framerate is 50 fps
            Thread.sleep(20);
        }
        catch(InterruptedException e) {
            e.printStackTrace();
        }
        repaint();
    }
}
```

```
// thread stop event
public void stop() {
    //kill the gameloop thread
    gameloop = null;
}
```

Game Loop Update

The gameUpdate() method is called by the game loop thread when it's time to process the game for the next applet window refresh. The game loop is timed to hit around 50 frames per second (fps), and the window refresh occurs after gameUpdate is run. Normally the game loop will run as fast as possible and only the screen refresh will be tied to a specific frame rate, but in this first game, that difference is not important.

```
// move and animate the objects in the game
private void gameUpdate() {
    updateShip();
    updateBullets();
    updateAsteroids();
    checkCollisions();
}
```

Updating the Ship

The updateShip() method updates the ship's X and Y position using the velocity variables. This method also "warps" the ship around when it crosses an edge of the screen (in which case the shape is moved to the opposite side of the screen). This is a technique used in many classic arcade games.

```
// Update the ship position based on velocity
public void updateShip() {
    //update ship's X position
    ship.incX(ship.getVelX());

    //wrap around left/right
    if (ship.getX() < -10)
        ship.setX(getSize().width + 10);
    else if (ship.getX() > getSize().width + 10)
        ship.setX(-10);
```

```
        //update ship's Y position
        ship.incY(ship.getVelY());

        //wrap around top/bottom
        if (ship.getY() < -10)
            ship.setY(getSize().height + 10);
        else if (ship.getY() > getSize().height + 10)
            ship.setY(-10);
    }
```

Updating the Bullets

The updateBullets() method updates the X and Y position for each bullet that is currently alive using the velocity variables. When a bullet hits the edge of the screen, it is disabled.

```
// Update the bullets based on velocity
public void updateBullets() {
    //move each of the bullets
    for (int n = 0; n < BULLETS; n++) {

        //is this bullet being used?
        if (bullet[n].isAlive()) {

            //update bullet's x position
            bullet[n].incX(bullet[n].getVelX());

            //bullet disappears at left/right edge
            if (bullet[n].getX() < 0 ||
                bullet[n].getX() > getSize().width)
            {
                bullet[n].setAlive(false);
            }

            //update bullet's y position
            bullet[n].incY(bullet[n].getVelY());

            //bullet disappears at top/bottom edge
            if (bullet[n].getY() < 0 ||
                bullet[n].getY() > getSize().height)
```

```
            {
                bullet[n].setAlive(false);
            }
        }
    }
}
```

Updating the Asteroids

The updateAsteroids() method updates the X and Y position of each asteroid that is currently alive based on the velocity variables. These X and Y values and velocities are all set to random values when the game starts up. The asteroids are warped around the edges of the screen. One interesting thing about the asteroids that differs from the ship and bullets is that the asteroids are rotated by a random number of degrees each frame, causing them to spin on the screen. This is a pretty nice effect that adds to the quality of the game.

```
// Update the asteroids based on velocity
public void updateAsteroids() {
    //move and rotate the asteroids
    for (int n = 0; n < ASTEROIDS; n++) {

        //is this asteroid being used?
        if (ast[n].isAlive()) {

            //update the asteroid's X value
            ast[n].incX(ast[n].getVelX());

            //warp the asteroid at screen edges
            if (ast[n].getX() < -20)
                ast[n].setX(getSize().width + 20);
            else if (ast[n].getX() > getSize().width + 20)
                ast[n].setX(-20);

            //update the asteroid's Y value
            ast[n].incY(ast[n].getVelY());

            //warp the asteroid at screen edges
            if (ast[n].getY() < -20)
                ast[n].setY(getSize().height + 20);
            else if (ast[n].getY() > getSize().height + 20)
                ast[n].setY(-20);
```

```
        //update the asteroid's rotation
        ast[n].incMoveAngle(ast[n].getRotationVelocity());

        //keep the angle within 0-359 degrees
        if (ast[n].getMoveAngle() < 0)
            ast[n].setMoveAngle(360 - ast[n].getRotationVelocity());
        else if (ast[n].getMoveAngle() > 360)
            ast[n].setMoveAngle(ast[n].getRotationVelocity());
    }
  }
}
```

Testing for Collisions

We haven't discussed collision detection yet, but I think you will get the hang of it here because this checkCollisions() method is straightforward. First, there is a loop that goes through the asteroid array (ast[]). Inside this loop, if an asteroid is alive, it is tested for collisions with any active bullets, then it is tested for a collision with the ship. If a collision occurs, then an explosion sound effect is played, and the asteroid is disabled. If it collided with a bullet, the bullet is also disabled. When the player's ship is hit, it is reset at the center of the screen with zero velocity. A collision occurs when one shape overlaps another shape, which is why we use the intersects() and contains() methods to determine when a collision occurs. Specifically, contains() is used to see whether the bullet has hit an asteroid, while intersects() is used to see whether an asteroid has hit the ship.

The key to the collision code here is a method in the Shape object called contains() that accepts a Rectangle or a Point and returns true if there is an overlap. This method makes it possible to perform bounding rectangle collision detection with just a few lines of code because the shapes already have built-in getBounds() methods available.

```
// Test asteroids for collisions with ship or bullets
public void checkCollisions() {

    //iterate through the asteroids array
    for (int m = 0; m<ASTEROIDS; m++) {
```

```
                //is this asteroid being used?
                if (ast[m].isAlive()) {

                    // check for collision with bullet
                    for (int n = 0; n < BULLETS; n++) {

                        //is this bullet being used?
                        if (bullet[n].isAlive()) {

                            //perform the collision test
                            if (ast[m].getBounds().contains(
                                bullet[n].getX(), bullet[n].getY()))
                            {
                                bullet[n].setAlive(false);
                                ast[m].setAlive(false);
                                continue;
                            }
                        }
                    }

                    // check for collision with ship
                    if (ast[m].getBounds().intersects(ship.getBounds())) {
                        ast[m].setAlive(false);
                        ship.setX(320);
                        ship.setY(240);
                        ship.setFaceAngle(0);
                        ship.setVelX(0);
                        ship.setVelY(0);
                        continue;
                    }
                }
            }
        }
```

Keyboard Events

This game only uses the keyPressed() event to detect key presses, while keyReleased() and keyTyped() are ignored (although they must be in the source code listing because of the KeyListener interface). The most important parts of this method are found in the code following the thrust and fire keys, which are mapped to the Up arrow and Ctrl keys. (The Enter key and spacebar can also be used to fire.) When the Up arrow is pressed, this adds thrust to the ship, causing it to move.

Definition

An *algorithm* is a mathematical expression that causes one of the variables in the expression to change in a consistent way. A movement algorithm, for instance, causes the x variable on an x–y coordinate plane to change so that it consistently increases in value, moving whatever object it represents horizontally across the screen.

An advanced movement algorithm is used to move the objects in the game, which is covered in the next section. Moving the ship must look as realistic as possible—so you can apply thrust to the ship, rotate to a new direction, then apply thrust, and that new angle of movement is added to the current velocity values. The result is a very realistic zero-gravity motion for the ship. Some programmers like to use a mass/acceleration algorithm to move a spaceship. That is a good method, where the mass (or weight) of the ship affects how fast it can move. I have simulated this effect using a velocity algorithm instead, which, again, is covered in the next section.

```
// key listener events
public void keyReleased(KeyEvent k) { }
public void keyTyped(KeyEvent k) { }
public void keyPressed(KeyEvent k) {
    int keyCode = k.getKeyCode();
    switch (keyCode) {
    case KeyEvent.VK_LEFT:
        //left arrow rotates ship left 5 degrees
        ship.incFaceAngle(-5);
        if (ship.getFaceAngle() < 0) ship.setFaceAngle(360-5);
        break;
    case KeyEvent.VK_RIGHT:
        //right arrow rotates ship right 5 degrees
        ship.incFaceAngle(5);
        if (ship.getFaceAngle() > 360) ship.setFaceAngle(5);
        break;
    case KeyEvent.VK_UP:
        //up arrow adds thrust to ship (1/10 normal speed)
        ship.setMoveAngle(ship.getFaceAngle() - 90);
```

```
        ship.incVelX(calcAngleMoveX(ship.getMoveAngle()) * 0.1);
        ship.incVelY(calcAngleMoveY(ship.getMoveAngle()) * 0.1);
        break;
    //Ctrl, Enter, or Space can be used to fire weapon
    case KeyEvent.VK_CONTROL:
    case KeyEvent.VK_ENTER:
    case KeyEvent.VK_SPACE:
        //fire a bullet
        currentBullet++;
        if (currentBullet > BULLETS - 1) currentBullet = 0;
        bullet[currentBullet].setAlive(true);

        //point bullet in same direction ship is facing
        bullet[currentBullet].setX(ship.getX());
        bullet[currentBullet].setY(ship.getY());
        bullet[currentBullet].setMoveAngle(ship.getFaceAngle() - 90);

        //fire bullet at angle of the ship
        double angle = bullet[currentBullet].getMoveAngle();
        double svx = ship.getVelX();
        double svy = ship.getVelY();
        bullet[currentBullet].setVelX(svx + calcAngleMoveX(angle) * 2);
        bullet[currentBullet].setVelY(svy + calcAngleMoveY(angle) * 2);
        break;
    }
}
```

Calculating Realistic Motion

The most fascinating part of this game is how the movement of the player's ship, the bullets, and the asteroids are all controlled by two methods that return floating-point values for the X and Y update for the object. In order to move an object in any direction, we need to calculate it's *linear velocity* at the given angle.

Definition

Velocity is a rate of change of position calculated in pixels per second.

The `calcAngleMoveX()` method uses cosine to calculate the update value for X, returned as a double. The `calcAngleMoveY()` method uses sine to calculate the update value for Y, also returned as a double. These small methods accept a single parameter (the angle that a game object is facing) and return an estimated X and Y update value in pixels based on that angle. I can't stress enough how wonderful these two methods are! In the past, I have relied mainly on the brute force (and imprecise) method to move game objects (usually called *sprites*) on the screen. I would set the `velocityX` to 1 and `velocityY` to 0 to cause an object to move to the right. Or, I would set `velocityX` to 0 and `velocityY` to −1 to cause the game object to move up on the screen. These velocity variables, along with an object's X and Y values, would cause the object to move around on the screen in a certain way.

I have written many games that used this type of movement code. Invariably, these games include a lot of `switch` statements to account for each of the directions that an object might be facing. For instance, if a spaceship sprite has eight directions of travel, then I would write a `switch` statement that considered the case for each direction (0 to 7, where 0 is north and 4 is south), and then update the X and Y values based on the ship's direction.

No longer! These wonderful methods now calculate the velocity for X and Y based on an object's orientation as an angle (from 0 to 360). Not only does this result in a more realistic game, but the source code is actually cleaner and shorter! As far as realism goes, this code supports every angle from 0 to 359 (where a circle is composed of 360 degrees). You can point the spaceship in this game at an angle of 1, then fire a weapon, and that bullet will travel just slightly off from due north.

The biggest difference between this new method of sprite movement from my previous game is that I previously used integers, but now I am using floating-point variables (doubles). This allows the `velocityX` and `velocityY` variables to reflect any of the 360 degrees of movement. For an angle of 45 degrees, `velocityX` is set to 1 pixel, while `velocityY` is set to 0. The cardinal directions (north, south, east, and west) are similarly predictable. But when dealing with an angle such as 17 degrees, the velocity variables will be set to some very unusual numbers. For instance, `velocityX` might be set to something like 0.01, while velocityY is set to something like 1.57. These numbers don't equate to actual pixel-level movements on the screen in a single frame, but when you consider that the game is running at 50 fps or more, then these values add up, and the ship or other game object is moved over time in the correct direction. Since the vector transform method expects floating-point values for X and Y, these velocity values work just fine with the part of the program that draws things on the screen. It is fascinating to watch, and we will be using this technique throughout the book.

Now, without further ado, here are the velocity calculation methods in all their simplistic glory:

```
// calculate X movement value based on direction angle
public double calcAngleMoveX(double angle) {
    return (double) (Math.cos(angle * Math.PI / 180));
}

// calculate Y movement value based on direction angle
public double calcAngleMoveY(double angle) {
    return (double) (Math.sin(angle * Math.PI / 180));
}
}
```

WHAT YOU HAVE LEARNED

This chapter threw a lot of new concepts your way without fully explaining all of them, but with the goal of giving you an opportunity to examine a nearly complete game to see how it was created from start to finish. This *Asteroids*-style game will be enhanced in subsequent chapters into an exciting arcade-style game with a scrolling background. Specifically, you learned:

- How to use the Graphics2D class
- How to use a thread as a game loop
- How to draw vector graphics to make game objects
- How to move an object based on its velocity
- How to test for collisions between game objects

REVIEW QUESTIONS

The following questions will help you to determine how well you have learned the subjects discussed in this chapter. The answers are provided in Appendix A, "Chapter Quiz Answers."

1. What is the name of the method that calculates the velocity for X?

2. What is the base class from which `Ship`, `Asteroid`, and `Bullet` are inherited?

3. Which classic Atari game inspired the game developed in this chapter?

4. Which type of collision testing does this game use?

5. Which method of the `Shape` class does this game use for collision testing?

6. Which geometric shape class do the `Ship` and `Asteroid` classes use?

7. Which geometric shape class does the `Bullet` class use?

8. Which applet event actually draws the screen?

9. What is the name of the interface class used to add threading support to the game?

10. What math function does `calcAngleMoveX` use to calculate the X velocity?

ON YOUR OWN

Although this game will be enhanced in future chapters, you will learn a lot by making changes to the source code to add some of your own ideas to the game right now. Use the following exercises to test your grasp of the material covered in this chapter.

Exercise 1

If you apply a lot of thrust to the ship so that it is moving very quickly across the screen, and then rotate around backward and fire a bullet, that bullet will seem to stand still or move very slowly. This is because the bullet is based on the ship's velocity. This isn't very realistic. Modify the weapon firing code in the `keyPressed` event method to fire bullets at a fixed rate regardless of the ship's velocity.

Exercise 2

The ship tends to rotate rather slowly when you press the Left or Right arrow keys, making it difficult to hit asteroids that are closing in on the ship from all directions. The rotation angle is adjusted by 5 degrees each time the keys are pressed. Modify the game so that the ship rotates much more quickly without changing this 5-degree value. In other words, you want it to rotate by the same value, but do these rotations more quickly.

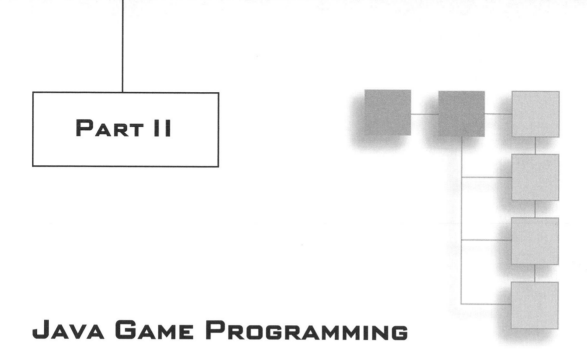

PART II

JAVA GAME PROGRAMMING

The second part of the book will cover the important topics you need to know in order to write an applet-based game in Java, including graphics, sound, music, keyboard and mouse input, timing, and so on. These subjects will be a mix of JFrame-based applications and applet-based projects for the first few chapters, after which the focus shifts primarily over to JFrame. Here are the chapters in Part II:

- Chapter 4: Vector-Based Graphics
- Chapter 5: Bitmap-Based Graphics
- Chapter 6: Simple Sprites
- Chapter 7: Sprite Animation
- Chapter 8: Keyboard and Mouse Input
- Chapter 9: Sound Effects and Music
- Chapter 10: Timing and the Game Loop

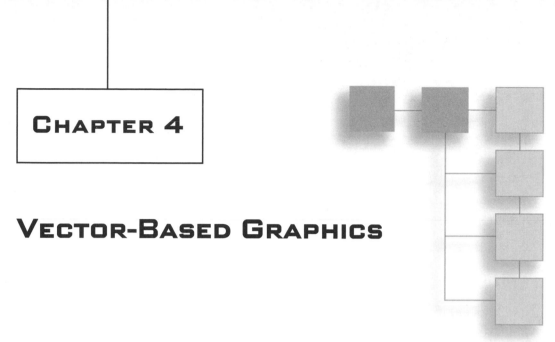

CHAPTER 4

VECTOR-BASED GRAPHICS

The previous chapter really pushed the limits as far as the amount of information covered without thorough explanations beforehand. I wanted to immerse you in the source code for a game right up front before fully explaining all of the concepts to give you a feel for what is involved in creating a real game. The *Asteroids* clone was not a great game, and not even very good looking, but it was functional. Java has a robust and feature-rich set of classes for working with 2D vector graphics and bitmaps (explained in the next chapter), making it possible to draw rectangles, polygons, and other shapes very easily. The examples in this chapter again are applets rather than JFrame-based applications. Aside from initialization code, there's very little difference in the two types of projects, and I want you to become comfortable with both types. Here are the key topics in this chapter:

- Drawing and manipulating vector graphics
- Using the `AffineTransform` class
- Applying the translation, rotation, and scaling of shapes

PROGRAMMING VECTOR GRAPHICS

You have already been exposed to a significant number of features in `Graphics2D` and other classes in `java.awt` (the Abstract Window Toolkit), such as `Rectangle` and `Polygon`. The core of Java's 2D graphics engine is the `Graphics2D` class. This

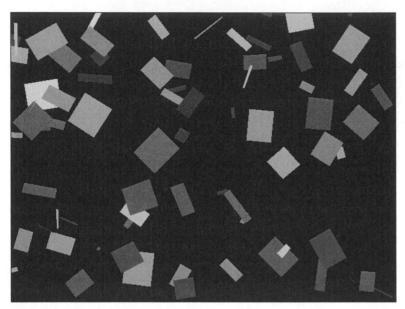

Figure 4.1
The RandomShapes program demonstrates the Graphics2D class.

class is incredibly versatile for working with vector graphics and bitmapped graphics. For instance, Graphics2D has many methods for drawing images in a variety of ways! In my opinion, this is somewhat of an overkill just to draw images on the screen. But Java is well known for its versatility and convenience. This class knows how to draw rectangles and many other shapes. But it can do a lot more than just draw—it can also move, rotate, and scale shapes!

Working with Shapes

Let's write a short program to demonstrate. The RandomShapes program is shown in Figure 4.1, and the source code listing follows. I have highlighted all of the important lines of code in bold text, and you'll learn about the classes, properties, and methods that have been highlighted.

```
// RandomShapes program
import java.awt.*;
import java.applet.*;
import java.awt.geom.*;
import java.util.*;
```

```java
public class RandomShapes extends Applet {
    //here's the shape used for drawing
    private Shape shape;

    //applet init event
    public void init() {
        shape = new Rectangle2D.Double(-1.0, -1.0, 1.0, 1.0);
    }

    //applet paint event
    public void paint(Graphics g) {
        //create an instance of Graphics2D
        Graphics2D g2d = (Graphics2D)g;

        //save the identity transform
        AffineTransform identity = new AffineTransform();

        //create a random number generator
        Random rand = new Random();

        //save the window width/height
        int width = getSize().width;
        int height = getSize().height;

        //fill the background with black
        g2d.setColor(Color.BLACK);
        g2d.fillRect(0, 0, width, height);

        for (int n = 0; n < 300; n++) {
            //reset Graphics2D to the identity transform
            g2d.setTransform(identity);

            //move, rotate, and scale the shape randomly
            g2d.translate(rand.nextInt() % width, rand.nextInt() % height);
            g2d.rotate(Math.toRadians(360 * rand.nextDouble()));
            g2d.scale(60 * rand.nextDouble(), 60 * rand.nextDouble());

            //draw the shape with a random color
            g2d.setColor(new Color(rand.nextInt()));
            g2d.fill(shape);
        }
    }
}
```

This program used the Graphics2D class to translate, rotate, and scale a Shape object randomly, which results in the screen being filled with random rectangles of varying sizes and orientations. This simple program illustrates the base concept behind the *Asteroids*-style game from Chapter 3—that Java provides the toolset for manipulating 2D graphics, and it's up to you how you will use these versatile tools.

The RandomShapes program defines a Shape object (called shape) and then uses that basic object to create a Rectangle2D like so:

```
shape = new Rectangle2D.Double(-1.0, -1.0, 1.0, 1.0);
```

This works, even though the shape object was originally created as a Shape because Rectangle2D is derived from the Shape class. In other words, Rectangle2D inherits from Shape. This makes it possible to use the Graphics2D method fill to draw a filled rectangle, even though it was defined originally as a basic Shape. For each class, such as Rectangle, there is a floating-point version, such as Rectangle2D. Classes such as Rectangle utilize integer values, while Rectangle2D uses floats and doubles. You can also use the Point and Polygon classes in similar fashion.

Working with Polygons

The Polygon class is a bit different from Point and Rectangle because it allows you to define the shape yourself using X and Y value pairs. You can construct a polygon with just a single point or a polygon with four points to duplicate the Point and Rectangle classes yourself. Or you can define custom polygons, such as the asteroids and ship in Chapter 3. The asteroid shape (shown in Figure 4.2) was defined like this:

```
private int[] astx = {-20,-13, 0,20,22, 20, 12, 2,-10,-22,-16};
private int[] asty = { 20, 23,17,20,16,-20,-22,-14,-17,-20, -5};
```

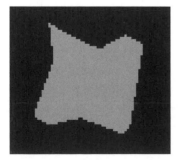

Figure 4.2
The asteroid shape.

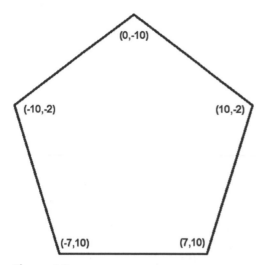

Figure 4.3
This five-sided polygon will be modeled in the RandomPolygons program.

These two arrays define the X and Y points for the polygon. We call a point a *vertex*, and the plural form is *vertices*. When you are creating a polygon in this manner, keep in mind that the X and Y arrays must pair up, since every X must go with a Y value to make a vertex.

When you're ready to draw a shape, whether it is a rectangle, a polygon, or something else, you have two choices. You can use the fill() method to draw the shape with a filled-in color. Or you can use the draw() method to draw the outline or border of the shape in the current color. The color is set with the setColor() method beforehand. Sometimes it can be confusing when you are trying to define the shape of a polygon using the two arrays of X and Y points, so you may want to design the polygon on paper or in a graphics editor first. Figure 4.3 shows the design of a five-sided star-shaped polygon.

Seeing a diagram of the image can really help, especially when you have a complex polygon in the works. Here are the arrays for defining this polygon. Note how the points directly correspond to the values in the figure.

```
private int[] xpoints = { 0,-10, -7, 7, 10 };
private int[] ypoints = {-10, -2, 10, 10, -2 };
```

Let's write a program to demonstrate how to create and draw polygons. The RandomPolygons program will use the five-sided star polygon with random rotation and scaling. The output of the program is shown in Figure 4.4.

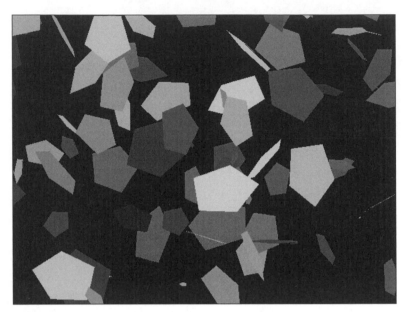

Figure 4.4
The RandomPolygons program draws star-shaped polygons.

```
// RandomPolygons program
import java.awt.*;
import java.applet.*;
import java.util.*;
import java.awt.geom.*;

public class RandomPolygons extends Applet {
    private int[] xpoints = { 0,-10, -7, 7, 10 };
    private int[] ypoints = {-10, -2, 10, 10, -2 };

    //here's the shape used for drawing
    private Polygon poly;

    //applet init event
    public void init() {
        poly = new Polygon(xpoints, ypoints, xpoints.length);
    }

    //applet paint event
    public void paint(Graphics g) {
```

```
    //create an instance of Graphics2D
    Graphics2D g2d = (Graphics2D) g;

    //save the identity transform
    AffineTransform identity = new AffineTransform();

    //create a random number generator
    Random rand = new Random();

    //save the window width/height
    int width = getSize().width;
    int height = getSize().height;

    //fill the background with black
    g2d.setColor(Color.BLACK);
    g2d.fillRect(0, 0, width, height);

    for (int n = 0; n < 300; n++) {
      //reset Graphics2D to the identity transform
      g2d.setTransform(identity);

      //move, rotate, and scale the shape randomly
      g2d.translate(rand.nextInt() % width, rand.nextInt() % height);
      g2d.rotate(Math.toRadians(360 * rand.nextDouble()));
      g2d.scale(5 * rand.nextDouble(), 5 * rand.nextDouble());

      //draw the shape with a random color
      g2d.setColor(new Color(rand.nextInt()));
      g2d.fill(poly);
    }
  }
}
```

Rotating and Scaling Shapes

The preceding programs have used vector rotation to rotate rectangles and polygons by a random value. Now I want to give you a little more direct exposure to this feature by writing a program that rotates a single polygon on the screen using the arrow keys and, alternately, the mouse buttons. The scale factor is set to a fixed value of 20, which you can change if you want. Figure 4.5 shows the output of the RotatePolygon program.

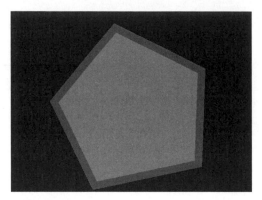

Figure 4.5
The RotatePolygon program rotates a star-shaped polygon.

There are a couple of notable differences between this program and the last one. This program just draws a single shape, so there is no need to set the identity transform before drawing. This program implements the KeyListener and MouseListener interfaces, which means that the program must use all of the methods defined in these interface classes, even if you don't plan to use them. It's an odd quirk that is inherent to how interface classes work because they are abstract.

```
// RotatePolygon program
import java.awt.*;
import java.awt.event.*;
import java.applet.*;
import java.util.*;
import java.awt.geom.*;

public class RotatePolygon extends Applet
        implements KeyListener, MouseListener {
    private int[] xpoints = { 0, -10, -7, 7, 10 };
    private int[] ypoints = {-10, -2, 10, 10, -2 };

    //here's the shape used for drawing
    private Polygon poly;

    //polygon rotation variable
    int rotation = 0;
```

```java
//applet init event
public void init() {
    //create the polygon
    poly = new Polygon(xpoints, ypoints, xpoints.length);

    //initialize the listeners
    addKeyListener(this);
    addMouseListener(this);
}

//applet paint event
public void paint(Graphics g) {
    //create an instance of Graphics2D
    Graphics2D g2d = (Graphics2D) g;

    //save the identity transform
    AffineTransform identity = new AffineTransform();

    //save the window width/height
    int width = getSize().width;
    int height = getSize().height;

    //fill the background with black
    g2d.setColor(Color.BLACK);
    g2d.fillRect(0, 0, width, height);

    //move, rotate, and scale the shape randomly
    g2d.translate(width / 2, height / 2);
    g2d.scale(20, 20);
    g2d.rotate(Math.toRadians(rotation));

    //draw the shape with a random color
    g2d.setColor(Color.RED);
    g2d.fill(poly);
    g2d.setColor(Color.BLUE);
    g2d.draw(poly);
}

//handle keyboard events
public void keyReleased(KeyEvent k) { }
```

```java
public void keyTyped(KeyEvent k) { }
public void keyPressed(KeyEvent k) {
    switch (k.getKeyCode()) {
    case KeyEvent.VK_LEFT:
        rotation--;
        if (rotation < 0) rotation = 359;
        repaint();
        break;
    case KeyEvent.VK_RIGHT:
        rotation++;
        if (rotation > 360) rotation = 0;
        repaint();
        break;
    }
}

//handle mouse events
public void mouseEntered(MouseEvent m) { }
public void mouseExited(MouseEvent m) { }
public void mouseReleased(MouseEvent m) { }
public void mouseClicked(MouseEvent m) { }
public void mousePressed(MouseEvent m) {
    switch(m.getButton()) {
    case MouseEvent.BUTTON1:
        rotation--;
        if (rotation < 0) rotation = 359;
        repaint();
        break;
    case MouseEvent.BUTTON3:
        rotation++;
        if (rotation > 360) rotation = 0;
        repaint();
        break;
    }
}
}
```

WHAT YOU HAVE LEARNED

This chapter provided a bridge from the material you were immersed into in the previous chapter to the new concepts you will learn in the next chapter, covering the basics of vector graphics programming. The next step in graphics is to draw bitmaps, and then regular sprites, followed by animated sprites. We have much to learn in upcoming chapters! Here is what we covered in this chapter:

- How to use the Graphics2D class to manipulate vector graphics
- How to translate, rotate, and scale vector shapes

REVIEW QUESTIONS

The following questions will help you to determine how well you have learned the subjects discussed in this chapter. The answers are provided in Appendix A, "Chapter Quiz Answers."

1. What is the primary class we've been using to manipulate vector graphics in this chapter?
2. What is the name of the Applet event that refreshes the screen?
3. What is the name of the Graphics2D method that draws a filled rectangle?
4. Define the words comprising the acronym "AWT."
5. What class makes it possible to perform translation, rotation, and scaling of shapes?
6. Which Graphics2D method draws a polygon?
7. Which transform method moves a shape to a new location?
8. What method initializes the keyboard listener interface?
9. What method in the Random class returns a double-precision floating-point value?
10. Which KeyListener event detects key presses?

ON YOUR OWN

Use the following exercises to test your grasp of the material covered in this chapter.

Exercise 1

There are many example programs in this chapter that could be modified and experimented upon. Let's tweak the RandomPolygons program—modify the program so that it draws two different polygons instead of just a single one.

Exercise 2

Modify the RotatePolygon program so that it will rotate based on mouse movement instead of button clicks. You will need to implement the Mouse-MotionListener interface (and events) and call the addMouseMotionListener method to gain access to the mouseMoved event. In this event, you can track mouse movement and rotate the polygon accordingly.

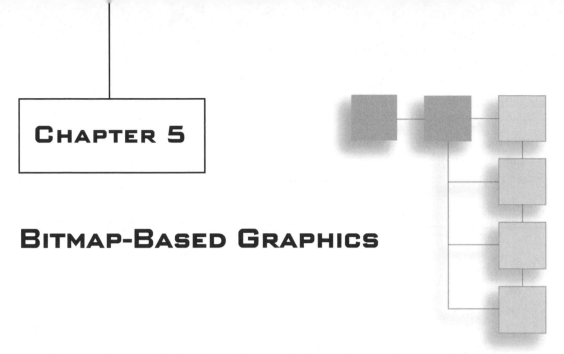

CHAPTER 5

BITMAP-BASED GRAPHICS

Java has a robust and feature-rich set of classes for working with 2D bitmap-based graphics (also known as *raster graphics*), allowing you to load and draw bitmaps very easily. Bitmaps are the keys to building a good 2D game with images rather than vector shapes.

Here are the key topics in this chapter:

- Loading and drawing bitmap images
- Applying transformations to bitmap images
- Drawing opaque and transparent images

PROGRAMMING BITMAPPED GRAPHICS

I mentioned before that there are many methods for drawing bitmap images in Java. Actually, most of those methods are found in the base Graphics class, while several more are found in Graphics2D. I think you will find the Graphics2D methods more useful, so we won't spend any time working with the legacy versions. The great thing about the Graphics2D class is how its methods for manipulating 2D graphics work equally well with vectors *and* bitmaps. This means you will be able to translate, rotate, and scale bitmap images just as easily as you have manipulated vector graphics thus far. This awesome functionality will translate well into the subsequent chapters on sprite and animation programming. The real difference when working with images is that you will need to create a separate AffineTransform class to manipulate the Image object, rather than going directly through Graphics2D. This strangely named class allows us to rotate, scale, and move bitmaps.

Note

The online documentation for the Java API can be found at this website: http://download.oracle .com/javase/6/docs/api.

Loading and Drawing Images

To load an image from a file, we have to use a helper class called Toolkit:

```
Toolkit tk = Toolkit.getDefaultToolkit();
```

Toolkit includes a method called getImage() that can load a bitmap file (the most common format for Java is PNG, the Portable Network Graphics format). This method is found in Toolkit, which is why we have to create a Toolkit object to load the artwork for a game. The method for drawing a bitmap is found in Graphics2D and is similarly easy to use: just call drawImage() with the appropriate parameters.

Let's write a program that demonstrates how to load and draw a bitmap image. We can use the getImage() method to load an image file, and then use draw-Image() to draw it onto the applet window. Figure 5.1 shows the output from the DrawImage program. I have highlighted the important lines of code.

Note

This high-quality castle image was rendered by Reiner Prokein using Caligari trueSpace. He offers a large amount of royalty-free game artwork, such as this castle, at his website, www.reinerstileset.de (a German site with an English version).

```
// DrawImage program
import java.awt.*;
import java.util.*;
import javax.swing.*;
import java.net.*;

public class DrawImage extends JFrame {
    private Image image;
```

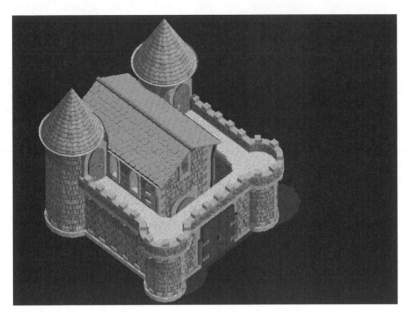

Figure 5.1
The DrawImage program loads and draws a bitmap file.

```
public static void main(String[] args) {
    new DrawImage();
}

public DrawImage() {
    super("DrawImage");
    setSize(600,600);
    setVisible(true);
    setDefaultCloseOperation(JFrame.EXIT_ON_CLOSE);
    Toolkit tk = Toolkit.getDefaultToolkit();
    image = tk.getImage(getURL("castle.png"));
}

private URL getURL(String filename) {
    URL url = null;
    try {
        url = this.getClass().getResource(filename);
    }
    catch (Exception e) { }
    return url;
}
```

```
public void paint(Graphics g) {
    //create an instance of Graphics2D
    Graphics2D g2d = (Graphics2D) g;

    //fill the background with black
    g2d.setColor(Color.BLACK);
    g2d.fillRect(0, 0, getSize().width, getSize().height);

    //draw the image
    g2d.drawImage(image, 0, 40, this);
}
}
```

Applying Transforms to Images

Now I'll demonstrate how to apply a transform to a simple bitmap image. Remember, a transform affects the position, rotation, or scale. Transforms will make our sprite code in the upcoming chapters really fun because the sprite images will be manipulated with these transforms as well. Since this code is similar to the code for transforming vectors, it should look at least somewhat familiar even if you don't fully understand it. One difference when working with an image is that you must define a separate AffineTransform object for manipulating the Image object because the Graphics2D transforms are designed to work only with vectors. Figure 5.2 shows the output of the RandomImages program, showing a spaceship image being moved, rotated, and scaled.

```
// RandomImages program
import java.awt.*;
import javax.swing.*;
import java.util.*;
import java.awt.geom.*;
import java.net.*;

public class RandomImages extends JFrame {
    private Image image;

    public static void main(String[] args) {
        new RandomImages();
    }
```

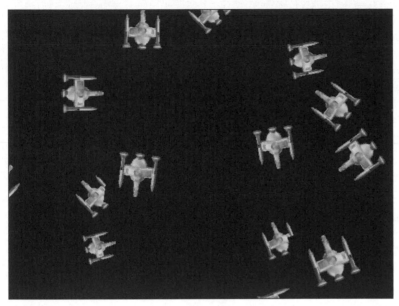

Figure 5.2
The RandomImages program draws images at random locations, with random rotation and scaling.

```
//applet init event
public RandomImages() {
    super("RandomImages");
    setSize(600,500);
    setVisible(true);
    setDefaultCloseOperation(JFrame.EXIT_ON_CLOSE);

    Toolkit tk = Toolkit.getDefaultToolkit();
    image = tk.getImage(getURL("spaceship.png"));
}

//identity transformation
AffineTransform identity = new AffineTransform();

private URL getURL(String filename) {
    URL url = null;
    try {
        url = this.getClass().getResource(filename);
    }
```

```
        catch (Exception e) { }
        return url;
    }

    //applet paint event
    public void paint(Graphics g) {
        //create an instance of Graphics2D
        Graphics2D g2d = (Graphics2D) g;

        //working transform object
        AffineTransform trans = new AffineTransform();

        //random number generator
        Random rand = new Random();

        //applet window width/height
        int width = getSize().width;
        int height = getSize().height;

        //fill the background with black
        g2d.setColor(Color.BLACK);
        g2d.fillRect(0, 0, getSize().width, getSize().height);

        //draw the image multiple times
        for (int n = 0; n < 50; n++) {
            trans.setTransform(identity);
            //move, rotate, scale the image randomly
            trans.translate(rand.nextInt()%width, rand.nextInt()%height);
            trans.rotate(Math.toRadians(360 * rand.nextDouble()));
            double scale = rand.nextDouble()+1;
            trans.scale(scale, scale);

            //draw the image
            g2d.drawImage(image, trans, this);
        }
    }
}
```

TRANSPARENCY

Although you can load and draw a bitmap at this point, the code you've seen so far is very limited. For one thing, the getImage() method can't load a bitmap file out of a Java Archive (JAR) file. JAR files will become very important later in Part III, when we build the Galactic War game. Since the game is so large, with so many bitmap and sound files, it takes a long time for the game to load over the web (unless you have a broadband connection). You'll learn how to create and use a JAR file soon enough. All I'm concerned about right now is that we are using code that will be compatible with a JAR, so that Java can read files out of the JAR as easily as it reads the raw files from the web server (or the directory in which your program is located if you are running it locally).

The Abstract Window Toolkit, known as AWT, provides a class called Toolkit that knows how to load a bitmap file. It's smart enough to look in the current URL path where the applet is located (something that you must pass to the getImage() method). You can use Toolkit in your own programs or you can instantiate a global Toolkit object and then use it throughout the game; there are many options. Let's take a look at how this class works:

```
Toolkit tk = Toolkit.getDefaultToolkit();
Image ship = tk.getImage("star_destroyer.png");
```

First, I created a Toolkit object by returning the object passed back from Toolkit.getDefaultToolkit(). This method returns a Toolkit object that represents the state of the Java program or applet. You can then use this Toolkit object's getImage() method to load a bitmap file. Since we want our applets to be JAR-friendly so games will run on the web as efficiently as possible, I will use the getURL() method again:

```
Image ship = tk.getImage(getURL("star_destroyer.png"));
```

Opaque Images

Let's start with what you have already learned up to this point—how to load and draw a bitmap without any transparency. At this point, it doesn't matter whether you use the Applet or the Toolkit to load a bitmap file because the end result will be the same. I leave it to you to decide which method you prefer, and I will use them both interchangeably. Let's write a short program to serve as a basis for discussing this topic. The output from the BitmapTest program is

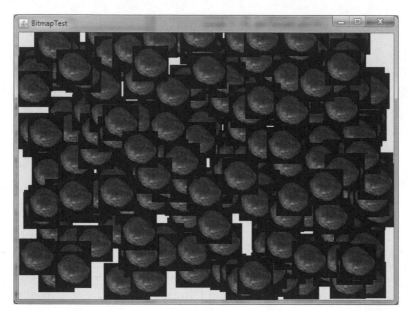

Figure 5.3
The BitmapTest program demonstrates the loading and drawing of opaque images.

shown in Figure 5.3. I have highlighted the key portions of code in bold in the listing that follows.

```
// BitmapTest program
import java.awt.*;
import java.util.*;
import java.net.*;
import javax.swing.*;

public class BitmapTest extends JFrame implements Runnable {
    Image image;
    Thread gameloop;
    Random rand = new Random();

    public static void main(String[] args) {
        new BitmapTest();
    }

    public BitmapTest() {
        super("Opaque Bitmap Test");
        setSize(640,480);
```

```java
            setVisible(true);
            setDefaultCloseOperation(JFrame.EXIT_ON_CLOSE);
            Toolkit tk = Toolkit.getDefaultToolkit();
            image = tk.getImage(getURL("asteroid2.png"));
            gameloop = new Thread(this);
            gameloop.start();
        }

        private URL getURL(String filename) {
            URL url = null;
            try {
                url = this.getClass().getResource(filename);
            }
            catch (Exception e) { }
            return url;
        }

        public void run() {
            Thread t = Thread.currentThread();
            while (t == gameloop) {
                try {
                    Thread.sleep(20);
                }
                catch (InterruptedException e) {
                    e.printStackTrace();
                }
                repaint();
            }
        }

        public void update(Graphics g) {
            paint(g);
        }

        public void paint(Graphics g) {
            Graphics2D g2d = (Graphics2D) g;
            int width = 640 - image.getWidth(this);
            int height = 480 - image.getHeight(this);
            g2d.drawImage(image, rand.nextInt(width), rand.nextInt(height), this);
        }
    }
```

Figure 5.4
This opaque bitmap image contains no transparency information.

This short program loads the bitmap image shown in Figure 5.4. In many programming languages and graphics libraries, you must specify a transparent pixel color to be used for transparency. In the example shown here, the black region around the edges of the asteroid would be considered the "tranparent zone" of the image. This transparent color is black in the example shown here (with an RGB value of 0,0,0), but other colors can be used for the transparent color too—the color pink (255,0,255) is often used for the transparent color because it stands out so well.

Java uses a more advanced method to handle transparency, as the next section explains.

Transparent Images

Java is a smart language that handles a lot of things for the programmer automatically, including the drawing of transparent images. This really makes life easier for a Java game programmer because many game libraries use a transparent pixel for transparency instead of a mask layer. So instead of dealing with transparency in code, it's handled in the source artwork. If you supply Java with a transparent bitmap file, it will draw that image transparently.

Most Java programs use the PNG format because it offers decent compression and transparency information without sacrificing image quality. You will need to use a graphics editor such as GIMP to convert images from whatever source format they are in (most likely the BMP format) to the PNG format, along with the mask layer that makes transparency possible.

Figure 5.5
The asteroid image is drawing with transparency due to its alpha channel.

Tip

I have used many graphic editors, including Paint Shop Pro, GIMP, and Photoshop. Although they are functionally different, they all share a similar toolset, including the ability to create an alpha channel. The instructions given here for GIMP will be similar to the steps in most other graphic editors.

Let's take the same program you just typed in for BitmapTest and run it again. Only this time, it will load up a new version of the asteroid1.png file that has been edited to support transparency. Figure 5.5 shows the output from the TransparentTest program. The source code has not changed (refer earlier to the BitmapTest program listing), but the PNG file has changed, which accounts for the difference!

Working Some Masking Magic

Let's take a look at how you actually create a masked PNG image. I'm using GIMP because it's very easy to use and free. If you want to use this program, you can download it from www.gimp.org. To add a transparency layer to an image,

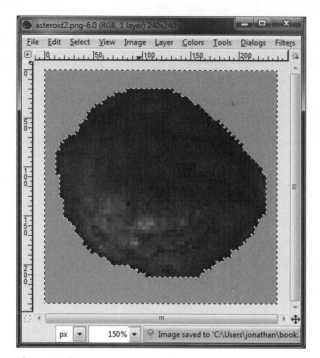

Figure 5.6
The outer edge of the asteroid image has been selected with the Magic Wand tool.

you need to locate the Magic Wand tool available in most graphics editors. After selecting the Magic Wand icon with your mouse, click somewhere in the black region (or on any pixel that isn't part of the game object). This should locate the edges of the game object and highlight everything around it (see Figure 5.6). Another more precise way to select a background is with the Color Picker or Select By Color tool.

Now that you have a selection available, you can create a Layer Mask to invert it because this selection will exclude the image. Click on the Selections menu and choose Invert (see Figure 5.7). This brings up the dialog shown in Figure 5.8. Choose the Selection option and check the Invert mask option.

Tip

If you have a complex image and would like to exclude many portions of it in order to select the boundary of the real image, you can hold down the Shift key while clicking with the Fuzzy Select (or Magic Wand) tool inside portions of the image to add new selections.

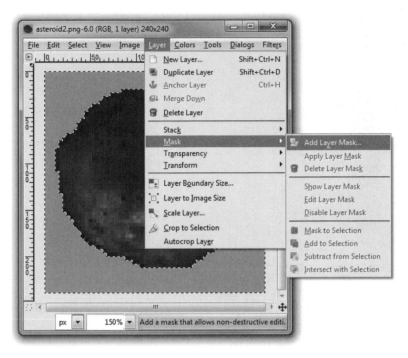

Figure 5.7
Preparing to add a layer mask.

Figure 5.8
The Add Layer Mask dialog is used to choose options for the new layer mask.

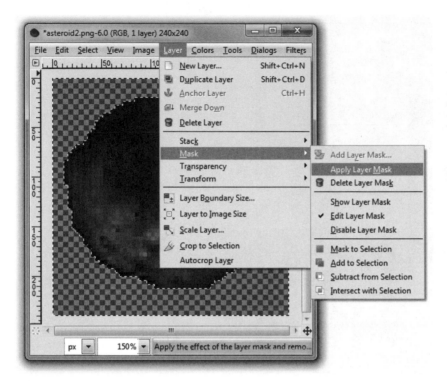

Figure 5.9
Applying the new layer mask makes it permanent.

The next step is to create a new mask layer in the image to represent the transparent portion. You can tell GIMP to generate a mask based on the selection you've made in the image. To do this, open the Layers menu, select Apply Layer Mask, and then Show Selection, as shown in Figure 5.9.

Tip

GIMP is a freeware graphic editor for multiple platforms with many good features found in costly commercial graphic editors. Download GIMP (GNU Image Manipulation Program) from www.gimp.org.

In Figure 5.10, the alpha channel has been created based on the masked selection. The checkerboard background behind the asteroid image shows the transparent region. The result looks very nice; this asteroid is ready for rendering! You can load this image into your Java applet and draw it, and it will automatically be drawn with transparency so the outer edges of the image (where the black pixels used to be) will not overwrite the background of the screen.

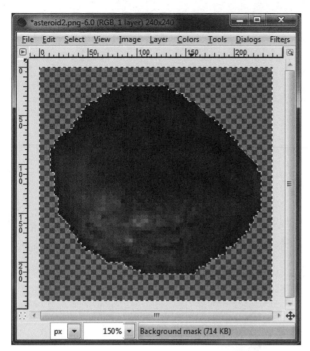

Figure 5.10
The asteroid image now has a masked transparency layer.

What You Have Learned

We will continue to work with transparent images from this point forward, so you have learned a very important tool in this chapter that will make it possible to create extremely attractive games. Specifically, you learned:

- How to draw bitmap images
- How to translate, rotate, and scale bitmap images
- How to draw bitmaps with transparency

Review Questions

The following questions will help you to determine how well you have learned the subjects discussed in this chapter. The answers are provided in Appendix A, "Chapter Quiz Answers."

1. What is the primary class we've been using to manipulate bitmapped graphics in this chapter?

2. What method initializes the keyboard listener interface?

3. What `Graphics2D` method is used to draw an image?

4. Which Java class contains the `getImage()` method?

5. What class makes it possible to perform translation, rotation, and scaling of images?

6. Which `Graphics2D` method draws an image?

7. Which transform method moves an image to a new location?

8. What is the name of the "transparency" channel in a 32-bit PNG image?

9. What is the `Applet` class method used to load a resource from a JAR?

10. Which `KeyListener` event detects key presses?

ON YOUR OWN

Use the following exercises to test your grasp of the material covered in this chapter.

Exercise 1

There are many example programs in this chapter that could be modified and experimented upon. Tweak the RandomImages program. Modify the program so that it loads and draws two different images randomly instead of just a single image.

Exercise 2

Modify the DrawImage program so that it will scale the image larger or smaller with the use of the keyboard plus (+) and minus (−) keys.

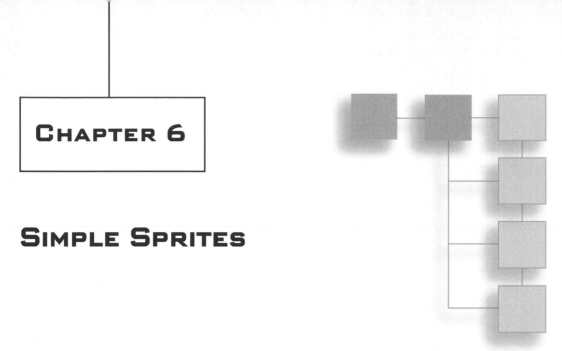

CHAPTER 6

SIMPLE SPRITES

Up to this point you have learned about a lot of Java classes that are useful for making a game, particularly the Graphics2D class. The previous two chapters provided the groundwork for this chapter by showing you how to tap into the Graphics2D class to draw vectors and bitmaps. At this point, the source code for even a simple bitmap-based game will tend to be too complicated and too difficult to manage without a better way to handle the objects in a game. What you need at this point is a new class that knows how to work with game objects—something known as an *actor* or a *sprite*. The goal of this chapter is to develop a way to handle the game objects moving around on the screen.

Here are the specific topics covered in this chapter:

- Programming simple sprites
- Creating a Sprite class
- Learning about collision testing

PROGRAMMING SIMPLE SPRITES

A sprite usually represents an animated graphic image that moves around in a game and is involved with other images to form the gameplay of a game. The difference between a regular image and a sprite is often that a sprite will encapsulate the image data as well as the methods needed to manipulate it. We will create a new class later in this chapter called ImageEntity, which will be able to load and draw a bitmap, and we will then create a new Sprite class that will use ImageEntity. Animation will be held off until the next chapter.

I would like to build a pair of classes to simplify sprite programming. We will create the Sprite class in this chapter and then add the AnimatedSprite class in the next chapter to handle animation. The new Sprite class that I'm going to show you here might be described as a *heavy class*. What do I mean by "heavy"? This is not a simple, abstract class. Instead, it is tied closely to the JFrame and Graphics2D objects in our main program. You would not be able to use this Sprite class on its own in a Java applet (running in a web browser) without modifications, because it relies on the presence of the JFrame to work. Although it is possible to write a Java game that runs in a JFrame or a JApplet (which are both somewhat related), the code to support both applications and applets at the same time is messy. Our new Sprite class will work fine as a support class for an application-based Java game. If we want to use it in an applet, minor modifications can be made (they are trivial!).

A sprite cannot draw itself without the JFrame and Graphics2D objects in a main program. Although the Sprite class could use methods such as getGraphics() to pull information from the main applet, our examples use a double buffer (a back buffer image used to update graphics smoothly, without flickering the screen).

The BaseGameEntity class will handle all of the position, velocity, rotation, and other logistical properties, while ImageEntity will make use of them by providing methods such as transform() and draw(). I want to simplify the Sprite class so it doesn't expose all of these properties and methods, but provides a simpler means to load and draw images. This simplification will be especially helpful in the next chapter because animation tends to complicate things. Although we have three classes just to draw a single sprite, there's reason behind this apparent madness—I don't want to duplicate code in all of the game entities if it can be helped. In the next few chapters we'll be drawing vectors *and* sprites, and it is helpful if we can reuse some of the code.

A useful sprite class should handle its own *position* and *velocity* data, rather than individual X and Y values for these properties. The sprite's position and velocity will be handled by the BaseGameEntity class. The Sprite class will not inherit from ImageEntity; instead, it will *use* this class internally, like a regular variable.

I also want the get methods that return values to resemble simple properties, while the change methods will be in the usual "set" format. For instance, I want the Sprite class to have a position() method that returns the position of the Sprite object, but it will use a setPosition() method to change the X and Y values. We should be able to access position and velocity by writing code like this:

```
sprite.position().x
sprite.position().y
```

Whenever possible, we will forego *good* object-oriented design in favor of *simpler* source code. This is especially helpful for beginners who may have never seen a truly huge source code listing, and thus would not understand why such things are important.

On top of these requirements, we should not be concerned with numeric data types! I don't want to typecast integers, floats, and doubles! So, this Sprite class will need to deal with the differences in the data types automatically and not complain about it! These are minor semantic issues, but they tend to seriously clean up the code. The result will be a solidly built sprite handler. First, let's take a look at a support class that will make it possible.

Tip

An *accessor method* is a method that returns a private variable in a class. A *mutator method* is a method that changes a private variable in a class. These are also commonly called "get" and "set" methods.

Basic Game Entities

The BaseVectorShape class was introduced back in Chapter 3 for the *Asteroids*-style game. We will use a very similar class for sprite programming in a future version of Galactic War (beginning in Chapter 11). Here is the code for this class.

```
public class BaseGameEntity extends Object {
    //variables
    protected boolean alive;
    protected double x,y;
    protected double velX, velY;
    protected double moveAngle, faceAngle;
```

```
//accessor methods
public boolean isAlive() { return alive; }
public double getX() { return x; }
public double getY() { return y; }
public double getVelX() { return velX; }
public double getVelY() { return velY; }
public double getMoveAngle() { return moveAngle; }
public double getFaceAngle() { return faceAngle; }

//mutator methods
public void setAlive(boolean alive) { this.alive = alive; }
public void setX(double x) { this.x = x; }
public void incX(double i) { this.x += i; }
public void setY(double y) { this.y = y; }
public void incY(double i) { this.y += i; }
public void setVelX(double velX) { this.velX = velX; }
public void incVelX(double i) { this.velX += i; }
public void setVelY(double velY) { this.velY = velY; }
public void incVelY(double i) { this.velY += i; }
public void setFaceAngle(double angle) { this.faceAngle = angle; }
public void incFaceAngle(double i) { this.faceAngle += i; }
public void setMoveAngle(double angle) { this.moveAngle = angle; }
public void incMoveAngle(double i) { this.moveAngle += i; }

//default constructor
BaseGameEntity() {
    setAlive(false);
    setX(0.0);
    setY(0.0);
    setVelX(0.0);
    setVelY(0.0);
    setMoveAngle(0.0);
    setFaceAngle(0.0);
}
}
```

The ImageEntity Class

The ImageEntity class gives us the ability to use a bitmap image for the objects in the game instead of just vector-based shapes (such as the asteroid polygon). It's never a good idea to completely upgrade a game with some new technique, which is why some of the objects in the first version of Galactic War will still be vectors, while the player's ship will be a bitmap. When you reach Chapter 11, you will have an opportunity to examine the progression of the game from its meager beginning to a complete and complex game with sprite entity management. I always recommend making small, incremental changes, play-testing the game after each major change to ensure that it still runs. There's nothing more frustrating than spending two hours making dramatic changes to a source code file, only to find the changes have completely broken the program so that either it will not compile or it is full of bugs.

The ImageEntity class also inherits from the BaseGameEntity class, so it is related to VectorEntity. This class is awesome! It encapsulates all of the functionality we need to load and draw bitmap images, while still retaining the ability to rotate and move them on the screen!

```java
// Base game image class for bitmapped game entities
import java.awt.*;
import java.awt.geom.*;
import javax.swing.*;
import java.net.*;

public class ImageEntity extends BaseGameEntity {
    //variables
    protected Image image;
    protected JFrame frame;
    protected AffineTransform at;
    protected Graphics2D g2d;

    //default constructor
    ImageEntity(JFrame a) {
        frame = a;
        setImage(null);
        setAlive(true);
    }

    public Image getImage() { return image; }

    public void setImage(Image image) {
        this.image = image;
        double x = frame.getSize().width/2- width()/2;
```

```java
        double y = frame.getSize().height/2 - height()/2;
        at = AffineTransform.getTranslateInstance(x, y);
    }

    public int width() {
        if (image != null)
            return image.getWidth(frame);
        else
            return 0;
    }
    public int height() {
        if (image != null)
            return image.getHeight(frame);
        else
            return 0;
    }

    public double getCenterX() {
        return getX() + width() / 2;
    }
    public double getCenterY() {
        return getY() + height() / 2;
    }

    public void setGraphics(Graphics2D g) {
        g2d = g;
    }

    private URL getURL(String filename) {
        URL url = null;
        try {
            url = this.getClass().getResource(filename);
        }
        catch (Exception e) { }
        return url;
    }

    public void load(String filename) {
        Toolkit tk = Toolkit.getDefaultToolkit();
        image = tk.getImage(getURL(filename));
```

```
            while(getImage().getWidth(frame) <= 0);
            double x = frame.getSize().width/2- width()/2;
            double y = frame.getSize().height/2 - height()/2;
            at = AffineTransform.getTranslateInstance(x, y);
        }

        public void transform() {
            at.setToIdentity();
            at.translate((int)getX() + width()/2, (int)getY() + height()/2);
            at.rotate(Math.toRadians(getFaceAngle()));
            at.translate(-width()/2, -height()/2);
        }

        public void draw() {
            g2d.drawImage(getImage(), at, frame);
        }

        //bounding rectangle
        public Rectangle getBounds() {
            Rectangle r;
            r = new Rectangle((int)getX(), (int)getY(), width(), height());
            return r;
        }
    }
}
```

CREATING A REUSABLE SPRITE CLASS

Following is the source code for the new Sprite class. This class includes a *ton* of features! In fact, it's so loaded with great stuff that you probably won't even know what to do with it all at this point. I am not a big fan of inheritance, preferring to build core functionality into each class I use. We will peruse the properties and methods of this class as we need them. This highly reusable Sprite class will be a useful helper class for any future game project you work on! It is a bit daunting only because I wanted to provide a complete class now rather than give it to you in parts over time. This class resulted from work done on the Galactic War game.

Collision Testing

The `Sprite` class includes several methods for detecting collisions with other sprites, and it also provides tests for collision with `Rectangle` and `Point2D` objects as a convenience. Remember that I wanted this `Sprite` class to be intuitive and not cause the compiler to complain about silly things, such as data type conversions? Well, the same is true of the collision testing code. There are three versions of the `collidesWith()` method in the `Sprite` class, providing support for three different parameters:

- `Rectangle`
- `Sprite`
- `Point2D`

This should cover almost any game object that you would like to test for a collision. Since these methods are built into the `Sprite` class, you can call them with a single parameter, and the internal data in the sprite itself is used for the second parameter that would normally be passed to a collision routine.

Sprite Class Source Code

This new `Sprite` class does not inherit from anything other than the base `Object`, although it uses `ImageEntity` internally for access to that class' excellent support for image loading and drawing. Why doesn't this class inherit from `BaseGameEntity` or `ImageEntity`? Those classes followed a logical inheritance chain but also included a lot of features that do not need to be in the core of the `Sprite` class. We still have access to those properties and methods if we want to use them, by using an `ImageEntity` as a private variable, but we get around the problem of having to deal with private/public access and inheritance. Inheritance is a beautiful concept, but in practice too much of it can make a program too complicated.

```
// Sprite class
import java.awt.*;
import javax.swing.*;

public class Sprite extends Object {
    private ImageEntity entity;
    protected Point pos;
```

```java
protected Point vel;
protected double rotRate;
protected int currentState;

//constructor
Sprite(JFrame a, Graphics2D g2d) {
    entity = new ImageEntity(a);
    entity.setGraphics(g2d);
    entity.setAlive(false);
    pos = new Point(0, 0);
    vel = new Point(0, 0);
    rotRate = 0.0;
    currentState = 0;
}

//load bitmap file
public void load(String filename) {
    entity.load(filename);
}

//perform affine transformations
public void transform() {
    entity.setX(pos.x);
    entity.setY(pos.y);
    entity.transform();
}

//draw the image
public void draw() {
    entity.g2d.drawImage(entity.getImage(),entity.at,entity.frame);
}

//draw bounding rectangle around sprite
public void drawBounds(Color c) {
    entity.g2d.setColor(c);
    entity.g2d.draw(getBounds());
}

//update the position based on velocity
public void updatePosition() {
```

```
        pos.x += vel.x;
        pos.y += vel.y;
    }

    //methods related to automatic rotation factor
    public double rotationRate() { return rotRate; }
    public void setRotationRate(double rate) { rotRate = rate; }
    public void updateRotation() {
        setFaceAngle(faceAngle() + rotRate);
        if (faceAngle() < 0)
            setFaceAngle(360 - rotRate);
        else if (faceAngle() > 360)
            setFaceAngle(rotRate);
    }

    //generic sprite state variable (alive, dead, collided, etc)
    public int state() { return currentState; }
    public void setState(int state) { currentState = state; }

    //returns a bounding rectangle
    public Rectangle getBounds() { return entity.getBounds(); }

    //sprite position
    public Point position() { return pos; }
    public void setPosition(Point pos) { this.pos = pos; }

    //sprite movement velocity
    public Point velocity() { return vel; }
    public void setVelocity(Point vel) { this.vel = vel; }

    //returns the center of the sprite as a Point
    public Point center() {
        int x = (int)entity.getCenterX();
        int y = (int)entity.getCenterY();
        return(new Point(x,y));
    }

    //generic variable for selectively using sprites
    public boolean alive() { return entity.isAlive(); }
    public void setAlive(boolean alive) { entity.setAlive(alive); }
```

```
//face angle indicates which direction sprite is facing
public double faceAngle() { return entity.getFaceAngle(); }
public void setFaceAngle(double angle) {
    entity.setFaceAngle(angle);
}
public void setFaceAngle(float angle) {
    entity.setFaceAngle((double) angle);
}
public void setFaceAngle(int angle) {
    entity.setFaceAngle((double) angle);
}

//move angle indicates direction sprite is moving
public double moveAngle() { return entity.getMoveAngle(); }
public void setMoveAngle(double angle) {
    entity.setMoveAngle(angle);
}
public void setMoveAngle(float angle) {
    entity.setMoveAngle((double) angle);
}
public void setMoveAngle(int angle) {
    entity.setMoveAngle((double) angle);
}

//returns the source image width/height
public int imageWidth() { return entity.width(); }
public int imageHeight() { return entity.height(); }

//check for collision with a rectangular shape
public boolean collidesWith(Rectangle rect) {
    return (rect.intersects(getBounds()));
}
//check for collision with another sprite
public boolean collidesWith(Sprite sprite) {
    return (getBounds().intersects(sprite.getBounds()));
}
//check for collision with a point
public boolean collidesWith(Point point) {
    return (getBounds().contains(point.x, point.y));
}
```

```
    public JFrame frame() { return entity.frame; }
    public Graphics2D graphics() { return entity.g2d; }
    public Image image() { return entity.image; }
    public void setImage(Image image) { entity.setImage(image); }
}
```

Tip

Animation is a feature missing from the Sprite class at this point; we will go over that subject in the next chapter.

Testing the Sprite Class

Let's give the new classes we've developed in this chapter a test run. The following program (shown in Figure 6.1) draws a background image and then draws a sprite randomly on the screen. This test program uses a thread and the Runnable interface in order to draw a sprite repeatedly on the screen without user input. We'll study this feature more thoroughly in Chapter 10, when we learn more about threads and the game loop. Study this short demo program

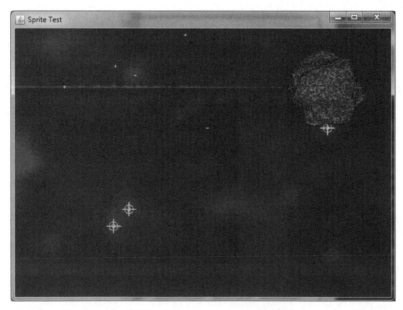

Figure 6.1
The SpriteTest program demonstrates how to use the Sprite class.

well, because it demonstrates perhaps the first high-speed example you've seen thus far.

```java
// SpriteTest program
import java.awt.*;
import java.awt.image.*;
import javax.swing.*;
import java.util.*;
import java.net.*;

public class SpriteTest extends JFrame implements Runnable {
    int screenWidth = 640;
    int screenHeight = 480;

    //double buffer objects
    BufferedImage backbuffer;
    Graphics2D g2d;

    Sprite asteroid;
    ImageEntity background;
    Thread gameloop;
    Random rand = new Random();

    public static void main(String[] args) {
        new SpriteTest();
    }

    public SpriteTest() {
        super("Sprite Test");
        setSize(640,480);
        setVisible(true);
        setDefaultCloseOperation(JFrame.EXIT_ON_CLOSE);

        //create the back buffer for smooth graphics
        backbuffer = new BufferedImage(screenWidth, screenHeight,
            BufferedImage.TYPE_INT_RGB);
        g2d = backbuffer.createGraphics();

        //load the background
        background = new ImageEntity(this);
        background.load("bluespace.png");
```

```
        //load the asteroid sprite
        asteroid = new Sprite(this, g2d);
        asteroid.load("asteroid2.png");

        gameloop = new Thread(this);
        gameloop.start();
    }

    public void run() {
        Thread t = Thread.currentThread();
        while (t == gameloop) {
            try {
                Thread.sleep(30);
            }
            catch (InterruptedException e) {
                e.printStackTrace();
            }

            //draw the background
            g2d.drawImage(background.getImage(), 0, 0, screenWidth-1,
                screenHeight-1, this);

            int width = screenWidth - asteroid.imageWidth() - 1;
            int height = screenHeight - asteroid.imageHeight() - 1;

            Point point = new Point(rand.nextInt(width),
                rand.nextInt(height));
            asteroid.setPosition(point);
            asteroid.transform();
            asteroid.draw();

            repaint();
        }
    }

    public void paint(Graphics g) {
        //draw the back buffer to the screen
        g.drawImage(backbuffer, 0, 0, this);
    }
}
```

WHAT YOU HAVE LEARNED

This significant chapter produced a monumental new version of Galactic War that is a foundation for the chapters to come. The final vestiges of the game's vector-based roots have been discarded, and the game is now fully implemented with bitmaps. In this chapter, you learned:

- How to create a new, powerful Sprite class
- How to detect sprite collision
- How to write reusable methods and classes

REVIEW QUESTIONS

The following questions will help you to determine how well you have learned the subjects discussed in this chapter. The answers are provided in Appendix A, "Chapter Quiz Answers."

1. What is the name of the support class created in this chapter to help the Sprite class manage position and velocity?

2. During which keyboard event should you disable a keypress variable, when detecting multiple key presses with global variables?

3. What are the three types of parameters you can pass to the collidesWith () method?

4. What Java class provides an alternate method for loading images that is not tied to the applet?

5. Which Java package do you need to import to use the Graphics2D class?

6. What numeric data type does the Point class use for internal storage of the X and Y values?

7. What data types can the Point class work with at the constructor level?

8. Which sprite property determines the angle at which the sprite will move?

9. Which sprite property determines at which angle an image is pointed, regardless of movement direction?

10. Which AffineTransform method allows you to translate, rotate, and scale a sprite?

ON YOUR OWN

Use the following exercises to test your understanding of the material covered in this chapter.

Exercise 1

The SpriteTest program demonstrates the use of the Sprite class. Modify the program so that it draws multiple instances of the asteroid sprite on the screen, each moving and animating differently.

Exercise 2

Modify the SpriteTest program even further by adding collision testing, such that the asteroids will rebound off one another when they collide.

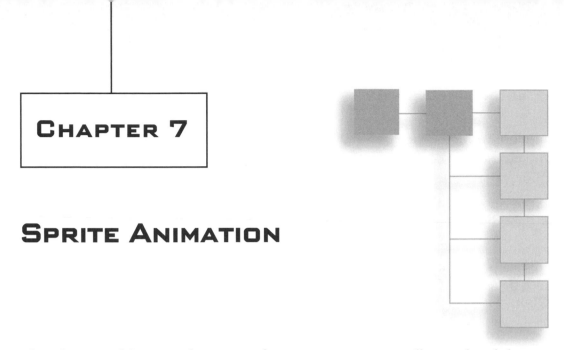

CHAPTER 7

SPRITE ANIMATION

This chapter adds a significant new feature to your Java toolbox—the ability to load and draw animated sprites and apply that knowledge to an enhanced new sprite class. You will learn about the different ways to store a sprite animation and how to access a single frame in an animation strip, and you will see a new class called AnimatedSprite with some serious new functionality that greatly extends the base Sprite class.

Here are the key topics we'll cover in this chapter:

- Sprite animation techniques
- Drawing individual sprite frames
- Keeping track of animation frames
- Encapsulating sprite animation in a class

SPRITE ANIMATION

Over the years I have seen many techniques for sprite animation. Of the many algorithms and implementations I've studied, I believe there are two essential ways to animate a graphic object on the screen—1) Loading individual frames, each stored in its own bitmap file (in sequence); or 2) Loading a single bitmap containing rows and columns of animation frames (as tiles).

Animation Techniques

First, there is the *sequence* method. This type of animation involves loading a bitmap image for each frame of the animation in sequence, and then animating them on the screen by drawing each image in order. This technique tends to take a long time to load all of the animation frames, especially in a large game with many sprites. There is also the system overhead required to maintain so many images in memory, even if they are small. Figure 7.1 shows an example.

Drawing an animation sequence is somewhat of a challenge when loading individual frames because of the logistics of it. How should you store the images—in an array or a linked list? I've seen some implementations using both methods, and neither is very friendly, so to speak, because the code is so complicated.

The second sprite animation technique is the *tiled* method. This type of animation involves storing an entire animation sequence inside a single bitmap file, also known as an *animation strip*. Inside this bitmap file are the many frames of the animation laid out in a single row or with many columns and rows. Figure 7.2 shows an animation strip on a single row, while Figure 7.3 shows a larger animation with multiple columns and rows.

CAT1.PNG   CAT2.PNG   CAT3.PNG   CAT4.PNG   CAT5.PNG   CAT6.PNG

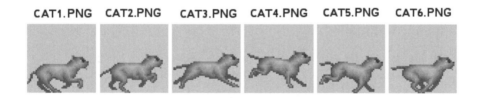

Figure 7.1
An animation sequence with frames stored in individual bitmap files.

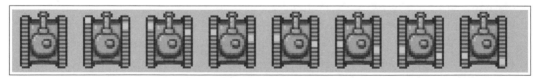

Figure 7.2
An animation strip with a single row. Courtesy of Ari Feldman.

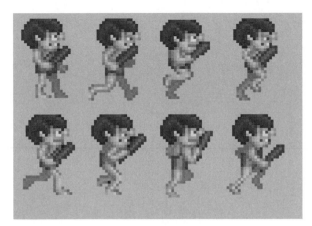

Figure 7.3
An animation strip with four columns and two rows. Courtesy of Ari Feldman.

Drawing Individual Frames

The key to drawing a single frame from an animation sequence stored in a tiled bitmap is to figure out where each frame is located *algorithmically*. It's impossible to manually code the X and Y position for each frame in the image; the very thought of it gives me hives. Not only would it take hours to jot down the X,Y position of every frame, but the bitmap file could easily be modified, thus rendering the manually calculated points irrelevant. This is computer science, after all, so there is an algorithm for almost everything.

You can calculate the column (that is, the number of frames *across*) by dividing the frame number by the number of columns and multiplying that by the height of each frame. This calculation focuses on the *quotient* as the answer we want.

```
frameY = (frameNumber / columns) * height;
```

This will give you the correct *row* down into the image where your desired frame is located, but it will not provide you with the actual *column*, or X value. For that, you need a similar solution. Instead of dividing the frame number by columns, we will use *modulus*. This calculation focuses on the *remainder* as the answer we want.

```
frameX = (frameNumber % columns) * width;
```

As you might have noticed, this looks almost exactly like the formula for calculating `frameY`. Now we're multiplying by width and using the *modulus*

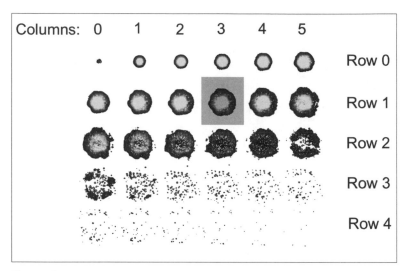

Figure 7.4
Illustration of a specific frame in the sprite sheet.

character instead of the *division* character. Modulus returns the *remainder* of a division, rather than the quotient itself. If you want the Y value, you look at the division *quotient*; if you want the X value, you look at the division *remainder*. Figure 7.4 illustrates how a desired frame is at a certain column and row position in the sprite sheet. See if you can use the division and modulus calculations to figure out where any random frame is located on the sheet on your own!

Here is a complete method that draws a single frame out of an animation sequence. There are a lot of parameters in this method! Fortunately, they are all clearly labeled with descriptive names. It's obvious that we pass it the source Image, the destination Graphics2D object (which does the real drawing), the destination location (X and Y), the number of columns across, the frame number you want to draw, and then the width and height of a single frame. What you get in return is the desired animation frame on the destination surface (which can be your back buffer or the applet window).

```
public void drawFrame(Image source, Graphics2D dest,
    int destX, int destY, int cols, int frame, int width, int height)
{
    int frameX = (frame % cols) * width;
    int frameY = (frame / cols) * height;
```

```
dest.drawImage(source, destX, destY, destX+width, destY+height,
    frameX, frameY, frameX+width, frameY+height, this);
}
```

Keeping Track of Animation Frames

Acquiring the desired animation frame is just the first step toward building an animated sprite in Java. After you have figured out how to grab a single frame, you must then decide what to do with it! For instance, how do you tell your program which frame to draw, and how does the program update the current frame each time through the game loop? I've found that the easiest way to do this is with a simple update method that increments the animation frame and then tests it against the bounds of the animation sequence. For instance:

```
currentFrame += 1;
if (currentFrame > 7) {
    currentFrame = 0;
}
else if (currentFrame < 0) {
    currentFrame = 7;
}
```

Take a close look at what's going on in the code here. First, the current frame is incremented by the value 1. To animate in the reverse order, this would be -1. Then, the next line checks the upper boundary (7) and loops back to 0 if the boundary is crossed. Similarly, the lower boundary is checked, setting currentFrame to the upper boundary value if necessary. Making this code reusable, we would need three variables:

- currentFrame
- totalFrames
- animationDirection

You would want to call this update code from the thread's run() event method. But, speaking of the thread, that does bring up an important issue—timing. Obviously, you don't want every sprite in the game to animate at exactly the same rate! Some sprites will move very slowly, while others will have fast animations. This is really an issue of fine-tuning the gameplay, but you must have some sort of mechanism in place for implementing timing for each animated sprite *separately*.

You can accomplish this by adding a couple more variables to the mix. First, you will need to increment a counter each time through the game loop. If that counter reaches a certain threshold value, then you reset the counter and go through the process of updating the animation frame as before. Let's use variables called frameCount and frameDelay. The frame delay is usually a smaller value than you would expect—such as 5 to 10, but usually not much more. A delay of 10 in a game loop running at 50 fps means that the object only animates at 5 fps, which is very slow indeed. I often use values of 1 to 5 for the frame delay. Here is the updated animation code with a delay in place:

```
frameCount++;
if (frameCount > frameDelay) {
    frameCount=0;
    currentFrame += animationDirection;
    if (currentFrame > totalFrames-1) {
        currentFrame = 0;
    }
    else if (currentFrame < 0) {
        currentFrame = totalFrames-1;
    }
}
```

The end result is a much *simplified* form of timed animation that assumes the update is taking place within a certain timed function already. If we did not call on this animation code from inside an already-timed function, then the animation would go too fast, and we would need to insert built-in timing into every sprite. We can get away with somewhat *lazy* timing code like this as long as we can assume timing is already handled.

Testing Sprite Animation

I'd like to go through a complete example with you so these concepts will feel more real to you, and so that you can see the dramatic result when a sprite is animated. The AnimationTest program loads a sprite sheet containing 30 frames of an explosion animation (shown in Figure 7.5) and animates it on the screen. Since we are sticking to the subject of animation in this chapter, the program doesn't attempt to do any transforms, such as rotation. But can you imagine the result of an animated sprite that can *also* be rotated? This program will help to determine what we need to do in the animation class coming up next.

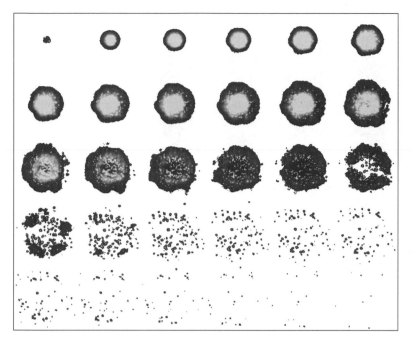

Figure 7.5
An animated explosion with 30 frames.

The output from the program is shown in Figure 7.6, where the single animated sprite is being drawn over a background image. Following is the code listing for the AnimationTest program. I have highlighted key portions of code that are new to this chapter in bold text.

```
// AnimationTest program
import java.awt.*;
import javax.swing.*;
import java.util.*;
import java.awt.image.*;
import java.net.*;

public class AnimationTest extends JFrame implements Runnable {
    static int ScreenWidth = 640;
    static int ScreenHeight = 480;
    Thread gameloop;
    Random rand = new Random();
```

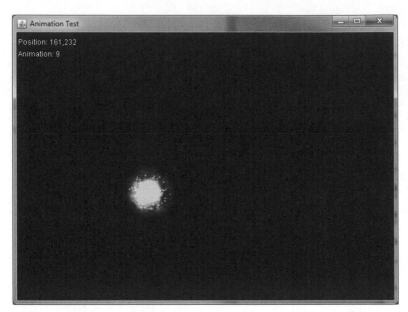

Figure 7.6
The AnimationTest program.

```
//double buffer objects
BufferedImage backbuffer;
Graphics2D g2d;

//sprite variables
Image image;
Point pos = new Point(300,200);

//animation variables
int currentFrame = 0;
int totalFrames = 30;
int animationDirection = 1;
int frameCount = 0;
int frameDelay = 10;

public static void main(String[] args) {
    new AnimationTest();
}
```

```
public AnimationTest() {
    super("Animation Test");
    setSize(ScreenWidth,ScreenHeight);
    setVisible(true);
    setDefaultCloseOperation(JFrame.EXIT_ON_CLOSE);

    //create the back buffer for smooth graphics
    backbuffer = new BufferedImage(ScreenWidth, ScreenHeight,
        BufferedImage.TYPE_INT_RGB);
    g2d = backbuffer.createGraphics();

    //load the ball animation strip
    Toolkit tk = Toolkit.getDefaultToolkit();
    image = tk.getImage(getURL("explosion.png"));

    gameloop = new Thread(this);
    gameloop.start();
}

private URL getURL(String filename) {
    URL url = null;
    try {
        url = this.getClass().getResource(filename);
    }
    catch (Exception e) {}
    return url;
}

public void run() {
    Thread t = Thread.currentThread();
    while (t == gameloop) {
        try {
            Thread.sleep(5);
        }
        catch (InterruptedException e) {
            e.printStackTrace();
        }
        gameUpdate();
    }
}
```

```java
public void gameUpdate() {
    //clear the background
    g2d.setColor(Color.BLACK);
    g2d.fill( new Rectangle(0, 0, ScreenWidth-1, ScreenHeight-1) );

    //draw the current frame of animation
    drawFrame(image, g2d, pos.x, pos.y, 6, currentFrame, 128, 128);

    g2d.setColor(Color.WHITE);
    g2d.drawString("Position: " + pos.x + "," + pos.y, 10, 50);
    g2d.drawString("Animation: " + currentFrame, 10, 70);

    //see if it's time to animate
    frameCount++;
    if (frameCount > frameDelay) {
        frameCount=0;
        //update the animation frame
        currentFrame += animationDirection;
        if (currentFrame > totalFrames - 1) {
            currentFrame = 0;
            pos.x = rand.nextInt(ScreenWidth-128);
            pos.y = rand.nextInt(ScreenHeight-128);
        }
        else if (currentFrame < 0) {
            currentFrame = totalFrames - 1;
        }
    }
    repaint();
}

public void paint(Graphics g) {
    //draw the back buffer to the screen
    g.drawImage(backbuffer, 0, 0, this);
}

//draw a single frame of animation
public void drawFrame(Image source, Graphics2D dest,
    int x, int y, int cols, int frame, int width, int height)
{
    int fx = (frame % cols) * width;
```

```
        int fy = (frame / cols) * height;
        dest.drawImage(source, x, y, x+width, y+height,
            fx, fy, fx+width, fy+height, this);
    }
}
```

Now, after reviewing this code, you might be wondering why we aren't using the ImageEntity and Sprite classes from the previous chapter, since they would cut down on so much of this code. That's a good question! While learning how to do animation, a single, self-contained example is helpful before we get into a class. Coming up next, we will do that.

Encapsulating Sprite Animation in a Class

There are some significant new pieces of code in the AnimationTest program that we'll definitely need for the upcoming Galactic War project (in Part III). All of the properties can be *stuffed* (that's slang for *encapsulated* or *wrapped*) into a class, and we can reuse that beautiful drawFrame() method as well. One really great thing about moving drawFrame() into a class is that most of the parameters can be eliminated, as they will be pulled out of the class internally. Setting up an animation will require a few steps up front when the game starts up, but after that, drawing an animated sprite will be an automatic process with just one or two method calls.

This new AnimatedSprite class will be completely self-contained. Now that we've seen how inheritance works and how useful it is for reusing code, and it works well for the existing Sprite class, we don't need to continue adding new levels to drive the point home. At this time, we will condense everything into just one class to cut down on any confusion that may arise as a result of using the three classes that have been written up to this point: BaseGameEntity, ImageEntity, and Sprite. The properties and methods in these three will be combined into the single AnimatedSprite class.

To improve performance, the AnimatedSprite class will *not* support affine transforms! This is because of a limitation in the Graphics2D.drawImage() function, which can either do animation *or* a transform, but not both in the same function call. So, there are two choices and we can only make one without writing a ton of code: 1) We can draw the current animation frame onto a scratch image and then apply the transforms to it before drawing it; or 2) We can draw frames of animation directly, but without the benefit of transforms. Since the Sprite class in the previous chapter works already with transforms, a good compromise is this: If you want transforms, use Sprite; otherwise, if you need animation, use AnimatedSprite (but without transforms). A compromise certainly could involve rendering each frame to a scratch image and then applying transforms to it, and perhaps more advanced sprite code would do just that.

Tip

The Sprite class supports transforms (rotation and scaling) and manual animation. The AnimatedSprite class does automatic animation but *cannot* do any transforms.

Here's the new source code listing for the AnimatedSprite class, which is completely self-contained. Probably the most obvious thing about this class is that most variables are declared as public, which exposes them to any program that uses the class without any get or set methods. In a game project, often those get and set methods just hurt productivity. The important thing is that the class works and is versatile, with variables that are used by the embedded methods in the class. This is not pure object-oriented programming (OOP) by any means—we give up some security for versatility and just count on programmers who use the class to know what they're doing. Getting the job done while writing good, clean code is often the rule in a programming team!

```
// AnimatedSprite class
import java.awt.*;
import java.awt.geom.*;
import java.awt.image.*;
import javax.swing.*;
import java.net.*;

public class AnimatedSprite {
    protected JFrame frame;
    protected Graphics2D g2d;
    public Image image;
    public boolean alive;
    public Point position;
    public Point velocity;
    public double rotationRate;
```

```
public int currentState;
public int currentFrame, totalFrames;
public int animationDirection;
public int frameCount, frameDelay;
public int frameWidth, frameHeight, columns;
public double moveAngle, faceAngle;

public AnimatedSprite(JFrame _frame, Graphics2D _g2d) {
    frame = _frame;
    g2d = _g2d;
    image = null;
    alive = true;
    position = new Point(0, 0);
    velocity = new Point(0, 0);
    rotationRate = 0.0;
    currentState = 0;
    currentFrame = 0;
    totalFrames = 1;
    animationDirection = 1;
    frameCount = 0;
    frameDelay = 0;
    frameWidth = 0;
    frameHeight = 0;
    columns = 1;
    moveAngle = 0.0;
    faceAngle = 0.0;
}

public JFrame getJFrame() { return frame; }
public Graphics2D getGraphics() { return g2d; }
public void setGraphics(Graphics2D _g2d) { g2d = _g2d; }

public void setImage(Image _image) { image = _image; }

public int getWidth() {
    if (image != null)
        return image.getWidth(frame);
    else
        return 0;
}
```

```java
public int getHeight() {
    if (image != null)
        return image.getHeight(frame);
    else
        return 0;
}

public double getCenterX() {
    return position.x + getWidth() / 2;
}
public double getCenterY() {
    return position.y + getHeight() / 2;
}
public Point getCenter() {
    int x = (int)getCenterX();
    int y = (int)getCenterY();
    return(new Point(x,y));
}

private URL getURL(String filename) {
    URL url = null;
    try {
        url = this.getClass().getResource(filename);
    }
    catch (Exception e) { }
    return url;
}

public Rectangle getBounds() {
    return (new Rectangle((int)position.x, (int)position.y, _
        getWidth(), getHeight()));
}

public void load(String filename, int _columns, int _totalFrames,
    int _width, int _height)
{
    Toolkit tk = Toolkit.getDefaultToolkit();
    image = tk.getImage(getURL(filename));
    while(image.getWidth(frame) <= 0);
    columns = _columns;
```

```
        totalFrames = _totalFrames;
        frameWidth = _width;
        frameHeight = _height;
    }

    protected void update() {
        //update position
        position.x += velocity.x;
        position.y += velocity.y;

        //update rotation
        if (rotationRate > 0.0) {
            faceAngle += rotationRate;
            if (faceAngle < 0)
                faceAngle = 360 - rotationRate;
            else if (faceAngle > 360)
                faceAngle = rotationRate;
        }

        //update animation
        if (totalFrames > 1) {
            frameCount++;
            if (frameCount > frameDelay) {
                frameCount = 0;
                currentFrame += animationDirection;
                if (currentFrame > totalFrames - 1) {
                    currentFrame = 0;
                }
                else if (currentFrame < 0) {
                    currentFrame = totalFrames - 1;
                }
            }
        }
    }

    //draw bounding rectangle around sprite
    public void drawBounds(Color c) {
        g2d.setColor(c);
        g2d.draw(getBounds());
    }
```

```java
public void draw() {
    update();
    //get the current frame
    int frameX = (currentFrame % columns) * frameWidth;
    int frameY = (currentFrame / columns) * frameHeight;
    //draw the frame
    g2d.drawImage(image, position.x, position.y,
        position.x+frameWidth, position.y+frameHeight,
        frameX, frameY, frameX+frameWidth, frameY+frameHeight,
        getJFrame());
}


//check for collision with a rectangular shape
public boolean collidesWith(Rectangle rect) {
    return (rect.intersects(getBounds()));
}
//check for collision with another sprite
public boolean collidesWith(AnimatedSprite sprite) {
    return (getBounds().intersects(sprite.getBounds()));
}
//check for collision with a point
public boolean collidesWith(Point point) {
    return (getBounds().contains(point.x, point.y));
}
}
```

Testing the New AnimatedSprite Class

Figure 7.7 shows the output of the program, which you can open up and run from the chapter's resource files if you wish (www.courseptr.com/downloads). Thanks to our new AnimatedSprite class, the source code here is quite short compared to previous sprite projects!

```java
import java.awt.*;
import javax.swing.*;
import java.util.*;
import java.awt.image.*;
import java.net.*;

public class AnimationClassDemo extends JFrame implements Runnable {
    static int ScreenWidth = 640;
```

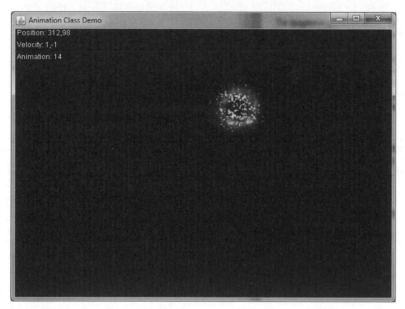

Figure 7.7
Testing the AnimatedSprite class.

```
static int ScreenHeight = 480;
Thread gameloop;
Random rand = new Random();

//double buffer objects
BufferedImage backbuffer;
Graphics2D g2d;

//sprite variables
AnimatedSprite sprite;

public static void main(String[] args) {
    new AnimationClassDemo();
}

public AnimationClassDemo() {
    super("Animation Class Demo");
    setSize(ScreenWidth,ScreenHeight);
    setVisible(true);
    setDefaultCloseOperation(JFrame.EXIT_ON_CLOSE);
```

```java
        //create the back buffer for smooth graphics
        backbuffer = new BufferedImage(ScreenWidth, ScreenHeight,
            BufferedImage.TYPE_INT_RGB);
        g2d = backbuffer.createGraphics();

        //load the explosion animation
        sprite = new AnimatedSprite(this, g2d);
        sprite.load("explosion.png", 6, 5, 128, 128);
        sprite.position = new Point(300,200);
        sprite.frameDelay = 10;
        sprite.totalFrames = 30;
        sprite.velocity = new Point(1,1);
        sprite.rotationRate = 1.0;

        gameloop = new Thread(this);
        gameloop.start();
    }

    public void run() {
        Thread t = Thread.currentThread();
        while (t == gameloop) {
            try { Thread.sleep(5); }
            catch (InterruptedException e)
            { e.printStackTrace(); }
            gameUpdate();
        }
    }

    public void gameUpdate() {
        //draw the background
        g2d.setColor(Color.BLACK);
        g2d.fill( new Rectangle(0, 0, ScreenWidth-1, ScreenHeight-1) );

        //draw the sprite
        sprite.draw();

        //keep the sprite in the screen boundary
        if (sprite.position.x < 0 || sprite.position.x>ScreenWidth-128)
            sprite.velocity.x *= -1;
        if (sprite.position.y < 0 || sprite.position.y>ScreenHeight-128)
            sprite.velocity.y *= -1;
```

```
    g2d.setColor(Color.WHITE);
    g2d.drawString("Position: " + sprite.position.x + "," +
        sprite.position.y, 10, 40);
    g2d.drawString("Velocity: " + sprite.velocity.x + "," +
        sprite.velocity.y, 10, 60);
    g2d.drawString("Animation: " + sprite.currentFrame, 10, 80);

    repaint();
}

public void paint(Graphics g) {
    //draw the back buffer to the screen
    g.drawImage(backbuffer, 0, 0, this);
}
}
```

What You Have Learned

This chapter tackled the difficult subject of sprite animation. Adding support for animation is not an easy undertaking, but this chapter provided you with the knowledge and a new class called AnimatedSprite that will make it possible for you to write your own games without reinventing the wheel every time you need to load an image and draw it. Here are the key topics you learned:

- How an animation is stored in a bitmap file
- How to load and draw an animation strip from a single bitmap file
- How to animate a sprite with timing
- How to put it all together into a reusable class

Review Questions

The following questions will help you to determine how well you have learned the subjects discussed in this chapter. The answers are provided in Appendix A, "Chapter Quiz Answers."

1. What is the name of the animation class created in this chapter?

2. From which class does the new animation class inherit?

3. How many frames of animation were there in the animated ball sprite?

4. What do you call an animation that is stored inside many files?

5. What do you call an animation that is all stored in a single file?

6. What type of parameter does the `AnimatedSprite.setVelocity` method accept?

7. What arithmetic operation is used to calculate an animation frame's Y position?

8. What arithmetic operation is used to calculate an animation frame's X position?

9. What is a good class to use when you need to create a bitmap in memory?

10. Which `AnimatedSprite` method draws the current frame of animation?

On Your Own

The following exercises will help you to determine how well you have understood the new material introduced in this chapter.

Exercise 1

Modify the AnimationTest program so that it draws 10 sprites, each with its own animation rate and random position on the screen. You can use a list or an array if you wish.

Exercise 2

Now that you can do full-blown animation, it's time to combine that awesome new capability with time-proven collision detection in order to add some actual functionality to the last project. Modify the program so that many sprites are moving on the screen and then cause the sprites to destroy each other when they collide.

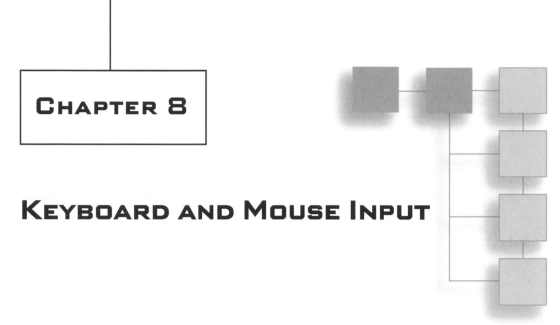

CHAPTER 8

KEYBOARD AND MOUSE INPUT

The keyboard and mouse are the only realistic devices for user input in a Java game, regardless of whether it's a web-based applet or a standalone application. But even when considering a standard Windows-based game developed in DirectX or another library, the keyboard and mouse are by far the most common forms of user interaction in a game. This chapter covers the important subject of handling user input.

Here are the key topics you will learn in this chapter:

- Listening for keyboard events
- Testing keyboard input
- Displaying key presses
- Reading mouse motion
- Detecting mouse buttons
- Testing mouse input

LISTENING TO THE USER

Java provides an interesting way to interact with users through a series of *listener* methods. You tell Java that you would like to listen to keyboard input events, and then Java sends keyboard events to your own listener methods, at which point you can check the key codes to figure out which keys have been pressed or released. The way Java tells your program that a key has been pressed (or that the mouse has moved) is through an interface that your program uses—or rather, *implements*. Your program must use the implements keyword to use an interface class. This is a type of class that just includes methods your program needs to use (or implement); the class doesn't really have any functionality on its own. This type of class is called an *interface* because it represents a blueprint of the methods your program must use.

KEYBOARD INPUT

The KeyListener interface listens for events generated by the keyboard and sends those events to the callback methods implemented in your program. These methods are called keyPressed, keyReleased, and keyTyped, and these three methods all have a single parameter called KeyEvent. When writing a program to use the KeyListener, you modify the class definition of your program using the implements keyword:

```
public class KeyboardTest extends JFrame implements KeyListener
```

Tip

> The interesting thing about the implements feature of Java classes is that you can implement multiple interfaces in your program by separating the interface class names with commas.

You may recall seeing the implements keyword used before with the Runnable interface (which added threading support). When you need to add more than one interface class, you can separate them with commas.

Listening for Keyboard Events

Your program needs to then call the addKeyListener method to initialize the keyboard listener so that key events will be sent to your program by the Java Runtime Environment. The sole parameter of this method is the instance of your program's class, represented by the keyword this. You use this as a way to identify the current class in a block of code without referring to that class specifically by name. It is usually best to call addKeyListener(this) in the init method within your program. (Recall that the constructor method is automatically called when your program starts running.)

Next, you must implement the three keyboard events in your program to satisfy the KeyListener interface:

```
public void keyPressed(KeyEvent e)
public void keyReleased(KeyEvent e)
public void keyTyped(KeyEvent e)
```

There are two ways to determine the key that has been pressed or released using the KeyEvent parameter. If you want to determine the character code of a key, you can use the getKeyChar method, which returns a char. If you want to know whether a key has been pressed based on the key code instead of the character, you can use the getKeyCode method instead. If your program is listening to the keyboard and you press the A key, then getKeyChar will return "a" (or "A" if you are holding down Shift), while getKeyCode will return a virtual key code called VK_A. All of the virtual key codes are contained in a class called KeyEvent. Table 8.1 shows a partial list of virtual key codes for the most commonly used keys for a game.

Table 8.1 Virtual Key Codes (Partial List)

Key Code	Description
VK_LEFT	Left arrow
VK_RIGHT	Right arrow
VK_UP	Up arrow
VK_DOWN	Down arrow
VK_0...VK_9	Numeric keys
VK_A...VK_Z	Alphabetic keys
VK_F1...VK_F12	Function keys
VK_KP_LEFT	Numeric keypad left
VK_KP_RIGHT	Numeric keypad right
VK_KP_UP	Numeric keypad up
VK_KP_DOWN	Numeric keypad down
VK_ENTER	Enter key
VK_BACK_SPACE	Backspace key
VK_TAB	Tab key

Figure 8.1
Output from the KeyboardTest program.

Note

When you want to get the keys being typed for use in a chat message, for instance, then you will want to use the keyTyped event, which returns ASCII characters. Most of your game's input will come from the keyPressed event, which provides key *codes*.

Testing Keyboard Input

Let's write a program to test keyboard input so you will have a complete example of how this works with Java code. I have highlighted the important code in bold. You can see the output of this program in Figure 8.1.

```java
import java.awt.*;
import java.awt.event.*;
import javax.swing.*;

public class KeyboardTest extends JFrame implements KeyListener {
    int keyCode;
    char keyChar;

    public static void main(String[] args) {
        new KeyboardTest();
    }
```

```
public KeyboardTest() {
    super("Keyboard Test");
    setSize(500,400);
    setVisible(true);
    setDefaultCloseOperation(JFrame.EXIT_ON_CLOSE);
    addKeyListener(this);
}

public void paint(Graphics g) {
    Graphics2D g2d = (Graphics2D)g;
    g2d.setColor(Color.WHITE);
    g2d.fill(new Rectangle(0,0,500,400));
    g2d.setColor(Color.BLACK);
    g2d.drawString("Press a key...", 20, 40);
    g2d.drawString("Key code: " + keyCode, 20, 60);
    g2d.drawString("Key char: " + keyChar, 20, 80);
}

public void keyPressed(KeyEvent e) {
    keyCode = e.getKeyCode();
    keyChar = ' ';
    repaint();
}

public void keyReleased(KeyEvent e) { }

public void keyTyped(KeyEvent e) {
    keyChar = e.getKeyChar();
    repaint();
}
}
```

This is the bare-minimum code you need to provide keyboard support to your Java programs, so you might want to jot down this page number for future reference (or save the code in a file that you can easily find).

Tip

A virtual key code is a platform-neutral value for a key. When you write code to work with a certain virtual key code (such as VK_LEFT), you can be certain that the key will be detected on any platform (Windows, Linux, Mac, Solaris, and so on).

Tip

The constructor method is a special method in a JFrame application. The constructor is the first method that runs when an application starts up. There are several other events generated by JFrame, such as `paint()`, that I will explain as we go along. The `paint()` event, for instance, refreshes the graphics in the window, so this is often where programmers will write much of the code for a game.

Mouse Input

Tapping into the mouse handler in Java is similar to the process of programming the keyboard, as you might have suspected. Java handles mouse input using events that are generated by the Java Runtime Environment (JRE) and passed to your program when you implement a mouse listener.

Tip

The Java Runtime Environment, or JRE, is a subset of the Java Development Kit (JDK) that is designed to allow you to have access to an essential set of classes that you can use to run Java programs. The JRE is also most commonly installed on end-user PCs when they want to run a Java program (including web applets). Both the JDK and JRE are included in the Java SE 6 download package.

The first step you must take to incorporate mouse event handling in your program is to call two functions that will tell the JRE to begin sending your program mouse events. Since we'll be dealing with two interfaces for the mouse, you must initialize both mouse handlers. This is similar to the function you learned about for initializing the keyboard handler. You put these functions in the constructor method so that they are sure to be called when the program starts up. You'll recall from the keyboard section earlier in this chapter that the `this` keyword represents the current program; in more technical terms, `this` represents the primary object that was created based on the class definition in your program.

Tip

An object is not a class; it is the result of a class. Think of a class as a blueprint for a product, and an object as the product itself that has been constructed.

```
addMouseListener(this);
addMouseMotionListener(this);
```

Reading Mouse Motion

Java provides an interface class for mouse motion and button press events that is similar to the keyboard interface. The `MouseListener` class is an *abstract* class that provides your program with an interface, or blueprint, with five methods that you must implement in your program (regardless of whether you will use all of them):

- `public void mouseClicked(MouseEvent e)`
- `public void mouseEntered(MouseEvent e)`
- `public void mouseExited(MouseEvent e)`
- `public void mousePressed(MouseEvent e)`
- `public void mouseReleased(MouseEvent e)`

The `MouseListener` interface keeps track of the mouse buttons, the mouse position in the window, and the mouse location when the mouse cursor moves *into* and *out of* the window.

There is another, completely different interface class for mouse *movement*. You can read the mouse's position during a button or enter/leave event with a `MouseListener`, but receiving events for actual mouse *motion* on the window requires another interface. To receive events for the mouse's movement across the window, you must use the `MouseMotionListener` interface. There are two events in this interface:

- `public void mouseDragged(MouseEvent e)`
- `public void mouseMoved(MouseEvent e)`

Detecting Mouse Buttons

Some of these events report when a mouse button is clicked, pressed, or released. The only methods that do not deal with the mouse buttons are `mouseEntered`, `mouseExited`, and `mouseMoved`, all of which deal with the mouse's position and motion, regardless of button status. The remaining events (`mouseClicked`, `mousePressed`, `mouseReleased`, and `mouseDragged`) all have to do with the buttons.

As you might have noticed, all of these events have a single parameter called `MouseEvent`. This parameter is actually a class, and the JRE fills it with information for each mouse event. You can look inside this class to get the mouse's position and button values. For the mouse's X and Y position values, you can use `MouseEvent.getX()` and `MouseEvent.getY()`. The parameter is usually defined as (`MouseEvent e`), so in actual practice you would use `e.getX()` and `e.getY()` to read the mouse's current position.

Likewise, `MouseEvent` tells you which button was pressed. Inside `MouseEvent` is a method called `getButton()` that will equal one of the following values depending on which button is being pressed:

- BUTTON1
- BUTTON2
- BUTTON3

The `getButton()` method is useful if you only care about detecting a single button press. If, for whatever reason, you need to know when two or three mouse buttons are being pressed at the same time, you can use a different method in the `MouseEvent` class called `getModifiers()`. This function will report multiple events in the `MouseEvent` class, such as the following:

- BUTTON1_MASK
- BUTTON2_MASK
- BUTTON3_MASK

There are many more masked values (that is, values that are bit-packed into a single variable) in the `MouseEvent` class that you can examine using the `getModifiers()` method. But if all you care about are the usual left-click and right-click events, you can make use of `getButton()`.

Testing Mouse Input

I would like to show you a program called MouseTest that demonstrates all of the mouse events that you have just learned about. To build this program, you should create a new project called MouseTest, and then remove all of the automatically generated code to be replaced with the following code listing instead. This program uses the `Graphics2D.drawString` method and a bunch of variables to display the status of all the mouse events individually. Figure 8.2

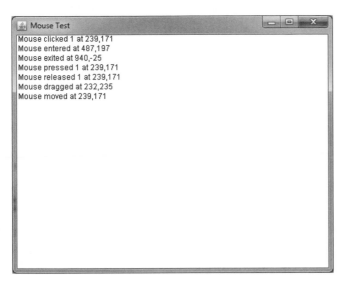

Figure 8.2
Output from the MouseTest program.

shows what the program output looks like. Note the important parts of the code listing in bold.

The first part of the program includes the class definition (with the needed interfaces following the implements keyword) and variable declarations.

```
import java.awt.*;
import java.awt.event.*;
import javax.swing.*;

public class MouseTest extends JFrame
        implements MouseListener, MouseMotionListener {

    //declare some mouse event variables
    int clickx, clicky;
    int pressx, pressy;
    int releasex, releasey;
    int enterx, entery;
    int exitx, exity;
    int dragx, dragy;
    int movex, movey;
    int mousebutton;
```

```
public static void main(String[] args) {
    new MouseTest();
}
```

The constructor is the first method that gets run in an application, and in this case, it's called public MouseTest(). So this is where you would initialize your game objects and variables, and this is also where you add the listeners for any input devices the program needs to use. If your program ever seems to be ignoring the keyboard or mouse, check this method to make sure you have added the appropriate listener.

```
public MouseTest() {
    super("Mouse Test");
    setSize(500,400);
    setVisible(true);
    setDefaultCloseOperation(JFrame.EXIT_ON_CLOSE);
    addMouseListener(this);
    addMouseMotionListener(this);
}
```

The paint() event method is called whenever the window needs to be refreshed. Since paint() comes with a parameter (Graphics g), we can use this object to draw onto the screen. In this program, I've used the Graphics.drawString() method to display text on the window. This code is messy in print due to the line wrapping, but it looks nice in the source code file included with this chapter's resource files (www.courseptr.com/downloads).

```
//redraw the window
public void paint(Graphics g) {
    Graphics2D g2d = (Graphics2D)g;
    g2d.setColor(Color.WHITE);
    g2d.fill(new Rectangle(0,0,500,400));
    g2d.setColor(Color.BLACK);
    g2d.drawString("Mouse clicked " + mousebutton + " at " + clickx +
        "," + clicky, 10, 40);
    g2d.drawString("Mouse entered at " + enterx + "," + entery,10,55);
    g2d.drawString("Mouse exited at " + exitx + "," + exity, 10, 70);
    g2d.drawString("Mouse pressed " + mousebutton + " at " + pressx +
        "," + pressy, 10, 85);
    g2d.drawString("Mouse released " + mousebutton + " at " +
        releasex + "," + releasey, 10, 100);
```

```
    g2d.drawString("Mouse dragged at " + dragx + "," + dragy, 10, 115);
    g2d.drawString("Mouse moved at " + movex + "," + movey, 10, 130);
}
```

The next portion of code includes the checkButton() method, which I have written to support the mouse event handler in the program. This checkButton() method checks the current button that is being pressed and sets a variable (mousebutton) to a value representing the pressed button.

```
//custom method called by mouse events to report button status
private void checkButton(MouseEvent e) {
    //check the mouse buttons
    switch(e.getButton()) {
    case MouseEvent.BUTTON1:
        mousebutton = 1;
        break;
    case MouseEvent.BUTTON2:
        mousebutton = 2;
        break;
    case MouseEvent.BUTTON3:
        mousebutton = 3;
        break;
    default:
        mousebutton = 0;
    }
}
```

The mouseClicked() event is part of the MouseListener interface. When you implement this interface, you must include all of the mouse events defined in the interface, or the compiler will generate some errors about the missing events. This event is called whenever you click the mouse button on the window—in which case both a press and release has occurred. This event is not usually needed when you program mousePressed() and mouseReleased() yourself.

```
public void mouseClicked(MouseEvent e) {
    //save the mouse position values
    clickx = e.getX();
    clicky = e.getY();

    //get an update on buttons
    checkButton(e);
```

```
        //refresh the screen (call the paint event)
        repaint();
    }
```

The next two mouse event methods, mouseEntered() and mouseExited(), are called whenever the mouse cursor enters or leaves the window. These events are not often needed in a game.

```
    public void mouseEntered(MouseEvent e) {
        enterx = e.getX();
        entery = e.getY();
        repaint();
    }
    public void mouseExited(MouseEvent e) {
        exitx = e.getX();
        exity = e.getY();
        repaint();
    }
```

The mousePressed() and mouseReleased() event methods are called whenever you click and release the mouse button, respectively. When these events occur, you can get the current position of the mouse as well as the button being pressed or released.

```
    public void mousePressed(MouseEvent e) {
        pressx = e.getX();
        pressy = e.getY();
        checkButton(e);
        repaint();
    }
    public void mouseReleased(MouseEvent e) {
        releasex = e.getX();
        releasey = e.getY();
        checkButton(e);
        repaint();
    }
```

The MouseMotionListener interface defines the next two events—mouseDragged() and mouseMoved(). These events are helpful when you just want to know when the mouse is moving over the window (and when it is moving while the button is being held down).

```
    public void mouseDragged(MouseEvent e) {
        dragx = e.getX();
        dragy = e.getY();
        repaint();
    }
    public void mouseMoved(MouseEvent e) {
        movex = e.getX();
        movey = e.getY();
        repaint();
    }
}
```

WHAT YOU HAVE LEARNED

This chapter explained how to tap into the keyboard and mouse listeners in order to add user input to your Java programs.

- You learned how to detect key presses.

- You learned about key codes and character values.

- You learned how to read the mouse's motion and buttons.

REVIEW QUESTIONS

The following questions will help you to determine how well you have learned the subjects discussed in this chapter. The answers are provided in Appendix A, "Chapter Quiz Answers."

1. What is the name of the method used to enable keyboard events in your program?

2. What is the name of the keyboard event interface?

3. What is the virtual key code for the Enter key?

4. Which keyboard event will tell you the code of a pressed key?

5. Which keyboard event will tell you when a key has been released?

6. Which keyboard event will tell you the character of a pressed key?

7. Which KeyEvent method returns a key code value?

8. What is the name of the method used to enable mouse motion events?

9. What is the name of the class used as a parameter for all mouse event methods?

10. Which mouse event reports the actual movement of the mouse?

On Your Own

Use the following exercises to test your grasp of the material covered in this chapter. Are you ready to put mouse and keyboard input to the test in a real game yet? These exercises will challenge your understanding of this chapter.

Exercise 1

Modify the KeyboardTest program so that pressing numeric keys 1 to 9 will change the font size used to display the key code and character values. To do this, use the Graphics class in the paint event, which has a method called setFont that you can implement like this:

```
g.setFont(new Font("Ariel", Font.NORMAL, value));
```

I will give you a hint: The key code for "1" is 49, so you can subtract 40 from the key code to arrive at a good font size.

Exercise 2

Modify the MouseTest program so that a point is drawn whenever the user presses a mouse button. You can use the Graphics class' fillRect method and the mouse position variables. (Just draw a rectangle with four corners that are one pixel apart.) If you are feeling confident with your new Java programming skills, try using the setColor method to change the color of the points.

CHAPTER 9

SOUND EFFECTS AND MUSIC

Java has a rich set of features for recording, mixing, and playing sound samples and MIDI sequences using a variety of classes that you will learn about in this chapter. You will learn about Java's rich set of sound support classes for loading and playing audio files in a variety of formats through Java's sound mixer. You will then learn about MIDI files and how to load and play them through Java's MIDI sequencer.

Here is a rundown of the key topics in this chapter:

- Loading and playing digital files
- Loading and playing MIDI files
- Writing some reusable audio classes

PLAYING DIGITAL SAMPLE FILES

Java's Sound API provides a package for working with digital sample files, which has methods for loading a sample file (AIFF, AU, or WAV) and playing it through the sound mixer. The package is called `javax.sound.sampled` and includes numerous classes, most of which we will ignore. Some of these classes provide support for recording sound and manipulating samples, so you could write a complete sound-editing program in Java that is similar to full-blown sound-editing programs. One good example is Audacity—a freeware, open-source sound editor that is available for download at http://audacity.sourceforge.net (see Figure 9.1).

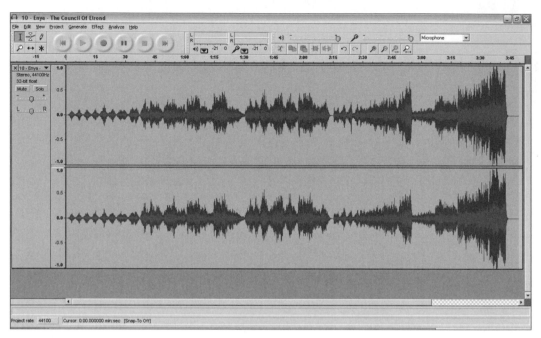

Figure 9.1
Audacity is an excellent freeware sound-editing program with many advanced features.

The Java Sound API supports the three main audio file formats used in web and desktop applications:

- AIFF
- AU
- WAV

The digital sample files can be 8-bit or 16-bit, with sample rates from 8 kHz to 48 kHz (which is CD quality). Java's Sound API includes a software sound mixer that supports up to 64 channels for both sound effects and background music for a Java program.

Tip

For the latest information about the Java Sound API, point your web browser to java.sun.com/products/java-media/sound.

Getting Started with Java Sound

The first step to writing some Java sound code is to include the `javax.sound.sampled` package at the top of your program:

```
import javax.sound.sampled.*;
```

If you are using an IDE such as NetBeans, you will see a pop-up menu appear to help you narrow down the class names within `javax`, which can be very educational. You'll see that when you type in `import javax.sound.`, the editor will show you the two classes available in `javax.sound.`, which are `sampled` and `midi`. By adding `.*` to the end of the `import` statement, you are telling the Java compiler to import every class within `javax.sound.sampled`, of which there are many.

In fact, when working with the sound system, you will need access to several classes, so it is convenient to import the associated packages at the start of a program so those classes are easier to use. For instance, without importing `javax.sound.sampled`, you would need to create a new sound sample variable using the full class path, such as:

```
javax.sound.sampled.AudioInputStream sample =
    javax.sound.sampled.AudioSystem.getAudioInputStream(
    new File("woohoo.wav"));
```

Could you imagine what it would look like if you had to write all of your code like this? It would be illegible for the most part. Here is what the code looks like after you have imported `javax.sound.sampled.*`:

```
AudioInputStream sample = AudioSystem.getAudioInputStream(new File("woohoo.
wav"));
```

`AudioSystem` and `AudioInputStream` are classes within the `javax.sound.sampled` package and are used to load and play a sample in your Java program. Later in this chapter, when I show you how to do background music, you'll get the hang of using some classes in a package called `javax.sound.midi`.

Caution

You may run into a problem with the audio portion of your game, where your source code seems to be well written, without bugs, but you still get unusual errors. One of the most common sources of problems when working with audio data is an unsupported file format error. This type of exception is called `UnsupportedAudioFileException` and will be discussed later in this chapter.

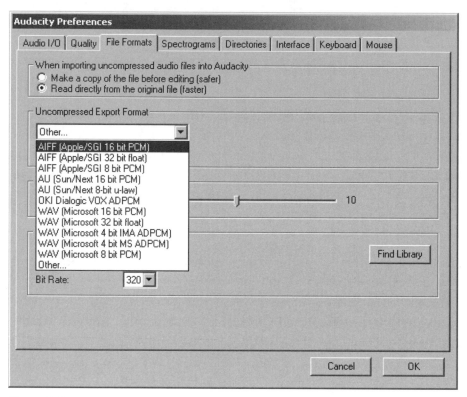

Figure 9.2
Changing the digital sample format settings in Audacity.

If the program's flow runs through the UnsupportedAudioFileException block in your error handler, then the audio file may be encoded with an unsupported file format. The other, more obvious, problem is that the file itself might be missing.

You can check and convert audio files using the freeware Audacity program that I mentioned earlier. Just load up a wary audio file that you suspect is encoded in a weird format, and then save the file to a new format. Figure 9.2 shows the File Formats tab in the Audacity Preferences dialog box. Here you can change the default file format for exporting audio files from the File menu. If you choose the Other option from the drop-down list, you will be presented with *even more* audio formats, but most of them are obsolete. (For instance, you can save to Creative Labs' old VOC format, which was popular in MS-DOS games many years ago.) Some of the custom formats require an additional download of a plug-in for that particular sound format.

The key to sound programming is a class called AudioInputStream. This class is used to load a sound file (which can be an AIFF, AU, or WAV file) from either a local file or from a remote URL anywhere on the Internet. An input stream is a source of data. You can create a new instance of the class like so:

```
AudioInputStream sample;
```

This statement is usually specified as a global variable within the class, defined up at the top of the class before any methods. You can define this variable as private, public, or protected. (The default, if you do not specify it, is public.) In object-oriented terms, *public* specifies that the variable is visible to other classes outside the current class, *private* means the variable is hidden to the outside world, and *protected* is similar to private, except that subclasses (through inheritance) have access to otherwise hidden variables defined as protected.

The code to load a sound from a file or URL is usually called from a program's constructor. The method used to load a sound is AudioSystem.getAudioInput-Stream. This method accepts a File, InputStream, or URL; there are two other ways to create an audio stream (AudioFormat and Encoding), neither of which is useful for our needs.

```
sample = AudioSystem.getAudioInputStream(new File("humbug.wav"));
```

Note that the return value of this method is an AudioInputStream. Also, since getAudioInputStream does not offer an overloaded version that just accepts a String for a filename, you must pass a File object to it instead. This is easy enough using a new File object, passing the filename to the File's constructor method. If you want to grab a file from a URL, your code might look something like this:

```
URL url = new URL("http://www.mydomain.com/test.wav");
sample = AudioSystem.getAudioInputStream(url);
```

Either way, you then have access to a sound file that will be loaded when needed. However, you can't just use an AudioInputStream to play a sound; as the class name implies, this is just a source of sample data without the ability to play itself. To play a sample, you use another class called Clip (javax.sound.sampled.Clip). This class is the return value of an AudioSystem method called getClip:

```
Clip clip = AudioSystem.getClip();
```

Loading Resources

The code presented here will load a sound file correctly when your Java program is running either on your local PC or in a web browser. However, we need to use a slightly different method to load a file out of a Java archive. This subject is covered in Chapter 16, which covers web deployment.

But I want to prepare you for distributing your Java programs on the web *now*, so that your programs will *already* be ready for deployment. To that end, you must replace the new File() and new URL() methods to load a resource (such as an image or sound file) with the following code instead: this.getClass().getResource(). The getResource() method is found in the current class instance, this.getClass(). You will find it most useful if you use this.getClass().getResource() anytime you need to build a URL. Here is a method I've written that accomplishes that goal:

```
private URL getURL(String filename) {
    URL url = null;
    try {
        url = this.getClass().getResource(filename);
    }
    catch (Exception e) { }
    return url;
}
```

Then, when you get to Chapter 16, the programs you've written will be ready for web deployment in a compressed Java archive (JAR)! During your explorations of the Java language while writing games and other programs, you will likely come up with many useful methods such as getURL(). You may want to store them in a reusable package of your own designation. The root package might be called jharbour, and then I would add subpackages to this, such as jharbour.graphics, jharbour.util, and so on. Since getURL() is the only custom reusable method repeatedly used in the book, it is more convenient to just include it in every class.

Since we don't need to pass a parameter to getClip, you might be wondering how this object knows what to play. There's actually one more step involved because at this point, all you have is a sound clip object with the *capability* to load and play an audio file or stream. This method actually returns a sound clip object from the default system mixer.

Loading the Sound Clip

At this point, you have an AudioInputStream and a Clip, so you just need to open the audio file and play it. These steps are both performed by the Clip class. First, let's open the sound file:

```
clip.open(sample);
```

Playing the Sound Clip

Next, there are two ways to play a clip, using the `Clip` class. You can use the `start()` method or the `loop()` method to play a sample. The `start()` method simply plays the sound clip.

```
narrator.start();
```

On the other hand, the `loop` method provides an option that lets you specify how many times the clip will repeat, either with a specific number of repeats or continuously. Here is how you might play a clip *one time* using the `loop` method:

```
explosion.loop(0);
```

Remember, the parameter specifies the number of times it will replay, as it's a given that the clip will always play at least once using the `loop` method. Here's how you can play a clip continuously:

```
thrusters.loop(Clip.LOOP_CONTINUOUSLY);
```

You might use this option if you have a music track that you would like to play repeatedly for the soundtrack of the game. Keep in mind, though, that sample files (AIFF, AU, and WAV) are quite large, so you wouldn't want the user to wait five minutes or longer (especially on dial-up) while the sound file is downloaded by your program from a URL (although it's not an issue when the program is running as an application). This happens when you call the `open()` method, so if you try to open a huge sound file it will force the user to sit there and wait for an indeterminate length of time while the clip downloads. This is why I recommend using a MIDI sequence rather than a digital soundtrack for your game's background music.

Tip

MIDI is the acronym for *Musical Instrument Digital Interface*. MIDI is a synthesized music format, not a sampled format, meaning that MIDI music was not recorded using an analog-to-digital converter (which is built into your computer's soundcard). Professional musical instruments use the MIDI format to record *notes* rather than *samples*.

You may feel free to use the `Clip` class' `start()` method to play a sound clip, but I recommend using `loop(0)` instead. This type of call will give you the same result, and it will be easy to modify the method call if you ever want to repeat a sound clip once or several times. For instance, you might use this technique to save some bandwidth. Instead of downloading a two-second explosion sound effect, go for a one-half-second clip, and then repeat it four times. Always keep your mind open to different ways to accomplish a task, and look for ways to optimize your game.

Tip

As you will learn in Chapter 16, the Java Runtime Environment (JRE) provides an attractive applet download screen with a progress bar when you use a Java archive (JAR) to store the applet and all of its media files.

Stopping the Sound Clip

Most of the time you will simply forget about a sound clip after it has started playing. After all, how often do you need to stop a sound effect from playing when there's a sound mixer taking care of all the details for you? Seldom, if ever. However, if you do need to stop a clip during playback, you can use the stop() method. I suspect the only time you will need this method is when you are looping a sample.

```
kaboom.stop();
```

Handling Errors

One interesting aspect of the sound classes is that they *require* that errors be caught. The compiler will refuse to build a program using some of the sound classes without appropriate try...catch error-handling blocks. Since this is a new concept, I'll quickly explain it.

Java errors are handled with a special error-handling feature called a try...catch block. This feature was simply borrowed from the C++ language, on which Java was based. Here is the basic syntax of a try...catch block:

```
try {
    //do something bad
} catch (Exception e) {
}
```

When you add error handling to your program, you are "wrapping" an error handler around your code by literally wrapping a try...catch block around a section of code that you need to track for errors. The Java sound classes require try...catch blocks with specific types of error checks. The generic Exception class is used to catch most errors that are not caught by a more specific type of error handler. You can have many catch blocks in your error handler, from the more specific down to the more generic in nature.

Tip

In some cases, a try...catch error handler is *required* to handle exception errors that a particular method throws (on purpose). In those cases, your program *must* implement the appropriate error handler (such as IOException).

Another available version of the error handler is called try...catch...finally. This type of error-handling block allows you to put code inside the finally section in order to perform any cleanup or closing of files. The code in a finally block will be run *regardless* of whether an error occurred. It gets executed if there *are* errors and if there are *no* errors.

For instance, if you are loading a file, you will first check for an IOException before providing a generic Exception handler. The AudioSystem, AudioInput-Stream, and Clip classes require the following error handlers:

- IOException
- LineUnavailableException
- UnsupportedAudioFileException

Let me show you how to implement an error handler for the audio code you're about to write for the PlaySound program. The following code is found in the constructor:

```
try {
    //source code lines clipped
} catch (MalformedURLException e) {
} catch (IOException e) {
} catch (LineUnavailableException e) {
} catch (UnsupportedAudioFileException e) {
}
```

I'll be the first person to admit that this is some ugly code. Error handling is notoriously ugly because it adds all kinds of unpleasant-looking management methods and events around your beautifully written source code. However, error handling is necessary and prevents your program from crashing and burning. I like to think of a try...catch block as a rev limiter that prevents a car engine from blowing itself up when a foolish driver hits the accelerator too hard.

Wrapping Sound Clips

Since error handling is a necessary evil, it supports the argument that you may want to put some oft-used code into reusable methods of your own. A couple of methods to load and play a sound file would be useful (and that error-handling code could be bottled up out of sight). It would be logical to encapsulate the AudioInputStream and Clip objects into a new class of your own design with your own methods to load and play a sound file or URL. Later in this chapter you will find source code for a class called SoundClip that does just that.

Playing Sounds

The Java sound classes are not quite a "turnkey" programming solution, because you must perform several steps to load and play a sound file. I think it would be convenient to write a class that has a collection of sound clips you can load and play at any time from that single class, but I hesitate to "wrap" any Java code inside another class when it is such a heavily object-oriented language in the first place. Let's just write an example program to see how to put all this code to work. The resulting program, called PlaySound, is shown in Figure 9.3. The relevant code to this chapter is highlighted in bold.

```java
import java.awt.*;
import javax.swing.*;
import java.io.*;
import java.net.*;
import javax.sound.sampled.*;

public class PlaySound extends JFrame {
    String filename = "gong.wav";
    AudioInputStream sample;

    public static void main(String[] args) {
        new PlaySound();
    }
```

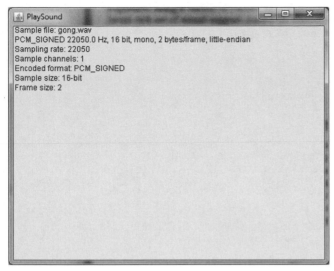

Figure 9.3
The PlaySound program demonstrates how to load and play a sound clip.

```
public PlaySound() {
    super("PlaySound");
    setSize(500,400);
    setVisible(true);
    setDefaultCloseOperation(JFrame.EXIT_ON_CLOSE);

    try {
        sample = AudioSystem.getAudioInputStream(getURL(filename));

        //create a sound buffer
        Clip clip = AudioSystem.getClip();

        //load the audio file
        clip.open(sample);

        //play sample
        clip.start();

    } catch (MalformedURLException e) {
    } catch (IOException e) {
```

```
        } catch (LineUnavailableException e) {
        } catch (UnsupportedAudioFileException e) {
        } catch (Exception e) { }

        repaint();
    }

    public void paint(Graphics g) {
        g.drawString("Sample file: " + filename, 10, 40);
        g.drawString(sample.getFormat().toString(), 10, 55);
        g.drawString("Sampling rate: " + (int)sample.getFormat().
            getSampleRate(), 10, 70);
        g.drawString("Sample channels: " + sample.getFormat().getChannels(),
            10, 85);
        g.drawString("Encoded format: " + sample.getFormat().getEncoding().
            toString(), 10, 100);
        g.drawString("Sample size: " + sample.getFormat().
            getSampleSizeInBits() + "-bit", 10, 115);
        g.drawString("Frame size: " + sample.getFormat().getFrameSize(),
            10, 130);
    }

    private URL getURL(String filename) {
        URL url = null;
        try {
            url = this.getClass().getResource(filename);
        }
        catch (Exception e) { e.printStackTrace(); }
        return url;
    }
}
```

PLAYING MIDI SEQUENCE FILES

Although using MIDI is not as popular as it used to be for background soundtracks in games, you have an opportunity to save a lot of bandwidth by using MIDI files for background music in a web-based game delivered as a Java applet. On the web, bandwidth is crucial, since a game that takes too long to load may cause a potential player to abandon the game and go elsewhere. For this reason, I would like to recommend the use of MIDI for in-game music when delivering a game via the web. Java supports three types of MIDI formats:

- MIDI Type 1
- MIDI Type 2
- Rich Music Format (RMF)

Loading a MIDI File

Loading a MIDI file in Java is just slightly more involved than loading a digital sample file because a MIDI file is played through a sequencer rather than being played directly by the audio mixer. The Sequence class is used to load a MIDI file:

```
Sequence song = MidiSystem.getSequence(new File("music.mid"));
```

Although this code does prepare a MIDI file to be played through the sequencer, we haven't actually created an instance of the sequencer yet, so let's do that now:

```
Sequencer seq = MidiSystem.getSequencer();
```

Note that the Sequencer class can be accessed through MidiSystem directly, but it requires less typing in of code to create a local variable to handle the setup of the MIDI sequencer. Next, let's tell the Sequencer class that we have a MIDI file available (via the Sequence class):

```
seq.setSequence(song);
```

This line of code establishes a link between the sequencer and this particular MIDI sequence file. Now all that remains to do is actually open the file and play it:

```
seq.open();
seq.start();
```

At this point, the MIDI sequence should start playing when the window comes up.

Playing Music

The following program listing demonstrates how to load and play a MIDI file in a Java window. The PlayMusic program is shown in Figure 9.4. As you can see, there are some minor details about the MIDI file that are displayed in the

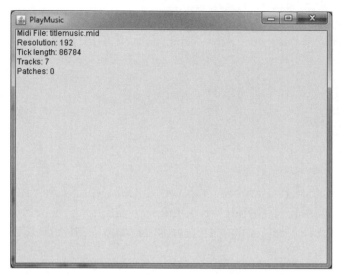

Figure 9.4
The PlayMusic program demonstrates how to load and play a MIDI sequence.

window, which is basically just an easy way to determine that the MIDI file has been loaded correctly. The key portions of code are highlighted in bold.

```java
import java.awt.*;
import javax.swing.*;
import java.io.*;
import java.net.*;
import javax.sound.midi.*;

public class PlayMusic extends JFrame {
    String filename = "titlemusic.mid";
    Sequence song;

    public static void main(String[] args) {
        new PlayMusic();
    }

    public PlayMusic() {
        super("PlayMusic");
        setSize(500,400);
        setVisible(true);
        setDefaultCloseOperation(JFrame.EXIT_ON_CLOSE);
```

```java
    try {
        song = MidiSystem.getSequence(getURL(filename));
        Sequencer sequencer = MidiSystem.getSequencer();
        sequencer.setSequence(song);
        sequencer.open();
        sequencer.start();

    } catch (InvalidMidiDataException e) {
    } catch (MidiUnavailableException e) {
    } catch (IOException e) { }

    repaint();
}

public void paint(Graphics g) {
    g.drawString("Midi File: " + filename, 10, 40);
    g.drawString("Resolution: " + song.getResolution(), 10, 55);
    g.drawString("Tick length: " + song.getTickLength(), 10, 70);
    g.drawString("Tracks: " + song.getTracks().length, 10, 85);
    g.drawString("Patches: " + song.getPatchList().length, 10, 100);
}

private URL getURL(String filename) {
    URL url = null;
    try { url = this.getClass().getResource(filename); }
    catch (Exception e) { e.printStackTrace(); }
    return url;
}
}
```

REUSABLE CLASSES

Now that you understand how to load and play sound clips and sequence files, let's put all of this useful (but scattered) code into two reusable classes that can be easily dropped into a project and used. Instead of dealing with all of the Java sound classes and packages, you will be able to simply create a new object from the SoundClip and MidiSequence classes, and then load up and play either a sample or sequence with a couple lines of code.

I should disclaim the usefulness of these classes for you, so you will know what to expect. Java's Sound API has a sound mixer that works very well, but we can't tap into the mixer directly using the Clip class that I've shown you in this chapter. The sound files that you load using the Clip class *do support mixing*, but a single clip will interrupt itself if played repeatedly. So, in the case of Galactic War, when your ship fires a weapon, the weapon sound is restarted every time you play the sound. However, if you have another clip for explosions (or any other sound), then it *will be mixed* with any other sound clips currently playing.

In other words, a single Clip object cannot mix *with itself*, only *with other sounds*. This process works quite well if you use short sound effects, but can sound odd if your sound clips are one second or more in length. (They sound fine at up to about half a second, which is typical for arcade-game sound effects.) If you want to repeatedly mix a single clip, there are two significant options (and one other unlikely option):

- Load the sound file into multiple Clip objects (such as an array), and then play each one in order. Whenever you need to play this specific sound, just iterate through the array and locate a clip that has finished playing, and then start playing it again.

- Load the sound file into a single Clip object, then copy the sample bytes into multiple Clip objects in an array, and then follow the general technique described in the first option for playback. This saves time from loading the clip multiple times.

- Write a threaded sound playback class that creates a new thread for every sound that is played. The thread will terminate when the sound has completed playing. This requires some pretty complex code, and there is a lot of overhead involved in creating and destroying a thread for every single sound that is played. One way to get around this overhead is to create a *thread pool* at the start of the program and then reuse threads in the pool. Again, this is some very advanced code, but it is how professional Java games handle sound playback. If you write a great Java game suitable for publishing (such as Galactic War, which you will start in the next chapter and develop throughout the book), I would recommend one of the first two options as good choices for a simple game. You don't want to deal with the overhead (or weighty coding

requirements) of a threaded solution, and an array of five or so dupli-
cates of a sound clip can be played to good effect—with mixing.

The SoundClip Class

The SoundClip class encapsulates the AudioSystem, AudioInputStream, and Clip
classes, making it much easier to load and play an audio file in your programs.
On the chapter's resources there is a project called SoundClass that demonstrates this class. This class simply includes all of the code we've covered in the
last few pages, combined into a single entity. Note the key portions of code that
I've discussed in this section, which are highlighted in bold.

Tip

A complete project demonstrating this class is available in the chapter's resource files (www.
courseptr.com/downloads) in the chapter09\SoundClass folder.

```java
import javax.sound.sampled.*;
import java.io.*;
import java.net.*;

public class SoundClip {
    //the source for audio data
    private AudioInputStream sample;

    //sound clip property is read-only here
    private Clip clip;
    public Clip getClip() { return clip; }

    //looping property for continuous playback
    private boolean looping = false;
    public void setLooping(boolean _looping) { looping = _looping; }
    public boolean getLooping() { return looping; }

    //repeat property used to play sound multiple times
    private int repeat = 0;
    public void setRepeat(int _repeat) { repeat = _repeat; }
    public int getRepeat() { return repeat; }
```

```java
//filename property
private String filename = "";
public void setFilename(String _filename) { filename = _filename; }
public String getFilename() { return filename; }

//property to verify when sample is ready
public boolean isLoaded() {
    return (boolean)(sample != null);
}

//constructor
public SoundClip() {
    try {
        //create a sound buffer
        clip = AudioSystem.getClip();
    } catch (LineUnavailableException e) { }
}

//this overloaded constructor takes a sound file as a parameter
public SoundClip(String audiofile) {
    this(); //call default constructor first
    load(audiofile); //now load the audio file
}

 private URL getURL(String filename) {
    URL url = null;
    try {
        url = this.getClass().getResource(filename);
    }
    catch (Exception e) { }
    return url;
}
//load sound file
public boolean load(String audiofile) {
    try {

        //prepare the input stream for an audio file
        setFilename(audiofile);
        //set the audio stream source
        sample = AudioSystem.getAudioInputStream(getURL(filename));
```

```java
        //load the audio file
        clip.open(sample);
        return true;

    } catch (IOException e) {
        return false;
    } catch (UnsupportedAudioFileException e) {
        return false;
    } catch (LineUnavailableException e) {
        return false;
    }
}

public void play() {
    //exit if the sample hasn't been loaded
    if (!isLoaded()) return;

    //reset the sound clip
    clip.setFramePosition(0);

    //play sample with optional looping
    if (looping)
        clip.loop(Clip.LOOP_CONTINUOUSLY);
    else
        clip.loop(repeat);
}

public void stop() {
    clip.stop();
}
}
```

The MidiSequence Class

The MidiSequence class is another custom class that makes it easier to work with the Java sound code. This class encapsulates the MidiSystem, Sequencer, and Sequence classes, making it much easier to load and play a MIDI file with just two lines of code instead of many. Take note of the key portions of code, which have been highlighted in bold.

Tip

A complete project demonstrating this class is available in the chapter's resource files in the chapter09\MidiSequence folder.

```java
import java.io.*;
import java.net.*;
import javax.sound.midi.*;

public class MidiSequence {
    //primary midi sequencer object
    private Sequencer sequencer;

    //provide Sequence as a read-only property
    private Sequence song;
    public Sequence getSong() { return song; }

    //filename property is read-only
    private String filename;
    public String getFilename() { return filename; }

    //looping property for looping continuously
    private boolean looping = false;
    public boolean getLooping() { return looping; }
    public void setLooping(boolean _looping) { looping = _looping; }

    //repeat property for looping a fixed number of times
    private int repeat = 0;
    public void setRepeat(int _repeat) { repeat = _repeat; }
    public int getRepeat() { return repeat; }

    //returns whether the sequence is ready for action
    public boolean isLoaded() {
        return (boolean)(sequencer.isOpen());
    }

    //primary constructor
    public MidiSequence() {
        try {
            //fire up the sequencer
            sequencer = MidiSystem.getSequencer();
```

```
        } catch (MidiUnavailableException e) { }
    }
    //overloaded constructor accepts midi filename
    public MidiSequence(String midifile) {
        this(); //call default constructor first
        load(midifile); //load the midi file
    }

    private URL getURL(String filename) {
        URL url = null;
        try {
            url = this.getClass().getResource(filename);
        }
        catch (Exception e) { }
        return url;
    }

    //load a midi file into a sequence
    public boolean load(String midifile) {
        try {
            //load the midi file into the sequencer
            filename = midifile;
            song = MidiSystem.getSequence(getURL(filename));
            sequencer.setSequence(song);
            sequencer.open();
            return true;
        } catch (InvalidMidiDataException e) {
            return false;
        } catch (MidiUnavailableException e) {
            return false;
        } catch (IOException e) {
            return false;
        }
    }

    //play the midi sequence
    public void play() {
        if (!sequencer.isOpen()) return;
        if (looping) {
            sequencer.setLoopCount(Sequencer.LOOP_CONTINUOUSLY);
```

```
                sequencer.start();
            } else {
                sequencer.setLoopCount(repeat);
                sequencer.start();
            }
        }

        //stop the midi sequence
        public void stop() {
            sequencer.stop();
        }

    }
```

WHAT YOU HAVE LEARNED

This chapter explained how to incorporate sound clips and MIDI sequences into your Java programs. Game audio is a very important subject because a game is just no fun without sound. You learned:

■ How to load and play a digital sound file

■ How to load and play a MIDI sequence file

■ How to encapsulate reusable code inside a class

REVIEW QUESTIONS

The following questions will help you to determine how well you have learned the subjects discussed in this chapter. The answers are provided in Appendix A, "Chapter Quiz Answers."

1. What is the name of Java's digital sound system class?

2. What is the name of Java's MIDI music system class?

3. Which Java class handles the loading of a sample file?

4. Which Java class handles the loading of a MIDI file?

5. What type of exception error will Java generate when it cannot load a sound file?

6. Which method of the MIDI system returns the sequencer object?

7. What is the main Java class hierarchy for the audio system class?

8. What is the main Java class hierarchy for the MIDI system class?

9. What three digital sound file formats does Java support?

10. What rare exception error will occur when no MIDI sequencer is available?

ON YOUR OWN

Use the following exercises to test your grasp of the material covered in this chapter. Are you ready to put sound and music to the test in a real game yet? These exercises will challenge your understanding of this chapter.

Exercise 1

Write your own sound-effects generating program to try out a large list of sound files. You can acquire sound files of various types by searching the web. Have the program play a specific sound file by pressing keys on the keyboard.

Exercise 2

Write a similar program for playing back multiple MIDI music sequence files by pressing various keys on the keyboard. For an even greater challenge, try combining this program with the one in Exercise 1 so that you can try out playing music and sound effects at the same time!

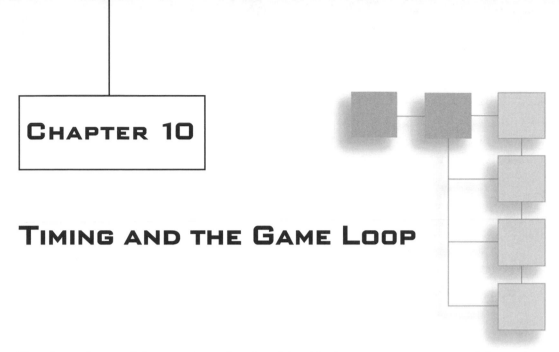

CHAPTER 10

TIMING AND THE GAME LOOP

You have learned how to use the Graphics2D class to program graphics using vector shapes and bitmap images, and you have even seen a nearly complete game written from scratch. You have learned how to load and play sound files and MIDI music files, and how to program the keyboard and mouse. By all accounts, you have the tools to create many different games already. But there are some tricks of the trade—secrets of the craft—that will help you to make your games stand out in the crowd and impress. This chapter discusses the game loop and its vital importance to a smooth-running game. You will learn about threads and timing, and you will take the *Asteroids*-style game created in Chapters 3 and 5 into completely new territory, as it is modified extensively in the following pages.

Here are the specific topics you will learn about:

- Using timing methods
- Starting and stopping a thread
- Using a thread for the game loop

THE POTENCY OF A GAME LOOP

The key to creating a game loop to facilitate the needs of a high-speed game is Java's multithreading capability. Threads are such an integral part of Java that it makes a special thread available to your program just for this purpose. This special thread is called `Runnable`, an interface class. However, it's entirely possible to write a Java game without threads by just using a simple game loop. I'll show you how to do this first, and then we'll take a look at threads as an even better form of game loop.

Tip

An *interface class* is an abstract class with properties and methods that are defined but not implemented. A program that uses an interface class is said to *consume* it, and must implement all of the public methods in the interface. Typical examples include `KeyListener` and `Runnable`.

A Simple Loop

The `Runnable` interface gives your program its own awareness. I realize this concept sounds a lot like artificial intelligence, but the term *awareness* is a good description of the `Runnable` interface. Before `Runnable`, your Java programs have been somewhat naive, capable of only processing during the screen refresh. Let's take a look at an example. Figure 10.1 shows the SimpleLoop program. As you can see, this program doesn't do anything in real time; it waits until you press a key or click the mouse before drawing a rectangle.

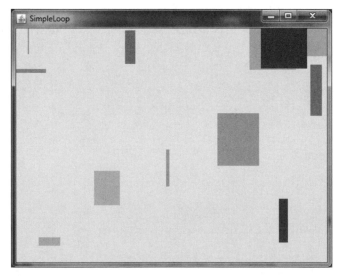

Figure 10.1
The SimpleLoop program.

```
// SimpleLoop program
import java.awt.*;
import java.awt.event.*;
import javax.swing.*;
import java.util.*;

public class SimpleLoop extends JFrame
        implements KeyListener, MouseListener {
    Random rand = new Random();

    public static void main(String[] args) {
        new SimpleLoop();
    }

    public SimpleLoop() {
        super("SimpleLoop");
        setSize(500,400);
        setVisible(true);
        setDefaultCloseOperation(JFrame.EXIT_ON_CLOSE);
        addKeyListener(this);
        addMouseListener(this);
    }

    public void paint(Graphics g) {
        Graphics2D g2d = (Graphics2D) g;

        //create a random rectangle
        int w = rand.nextInt(100);
        int h = rand.nextInt(100);
        int x = rand.nextInt(getSize().width - w);
        int y = rand.nextInt(getSize().height - h);
        Rectangle rect = new Rectangle(x,y,w,h);

        //generate a random color
        int red = rand.nextInt(256);
        int green = rand.nextInt(256);
        int blue = rand.nextInt(256);
        g2d.setColor(new Color(red,green,blue));
```

```
        //draw the rectangle
        g2d.fill(rect);
    }

    //handle keyboard events
    public void keyReleased(KeyEvent k) { }
    public void keyTyped(KeyEvent k) { }
    public void keyPressed(KeyEvent k) {
        repaint();
    }

    //handle mouse events
    public void mouseEntered(MouseEvent m) { }
    public void mouseExited(MouseEvent m) { }
    public void mouseReleased(MouseEvent m) { }
    public void mouseClicked(MouseEvent m) { }
    public void mousePressed(MouseEvent m) {
        repaint();
    }
}
}
```

Tip

The Random class is located in the java.awt.util class along with many other utility classes that provide commonly needed tools to your program. To use Random in your program, you must include this class with the following import statement:

```
import java.awt.util.*;
```

This program has no loop whatsoever, so it cannot process anything in real time—not spaceships, asteroids, jumping Italian plumbers, yellow dot-eaters, or female spelunkers packing dual Berettas. The only thing this program can do is draw a single rectangle at a time.

There are some ways you can make the program a little more interactive. The only problem with the mouse and keyboard listener interfaces is that you have to implement *all* of them or *none* of them. That reminds me of Yoda's famous saying, "Do, or do not. There is no 'try.'" An interface class is an all-or-nothing proposition that tends to junk up your source code, not to mention that it takes a lot of work to type in all of those interface event methods every time! But there's no real workaround for the unused event methods.

Note

I've been thinking about a way to use all of these interface classes (such as `Runnable` and the input listeners) by tucking them away into a class outside of the main program. This support class would provide my main program with real *events* when things happen, such as key presses, mouse movement, and other events. Perhaps this is the birth of an idea that will become some sort of game engine? Let's wait and see what Part III has in store.

Overriding Some Default Behaviors

There is a serious problem with this program because it was supposed to just *add* a new rectangle every time the user presses a key or mouse button, not *redraw* the entire window—with a single rectangle left over. There is definitely something odd going on because this program *should have* worked as expected.

Well, it turns out that Java has been screwing with the screen without permission—or rather, by *default*. The `JFrame` class, which is the basis for the SimpleLoop program, provides many default event methods that do certain things for you. You don't even need to implement `paint()` if you don't want to, and the `JFrame` base class will provide it for your program. Granted, nothing will be drawn on the window as a result, but the compiler won't give you an error. This differs from an interface class (such as `KeyListener`) that *mandates* that you must implement all of its abstract methods. So it's pretty obvious by this difference in functionality that `JFrame` is not an interface class, but a fully functioning class.

What happens, then, when you implement a `JFrame` class method such as `paint()`? These methods are essentially empty inside the `JFrame` class. Oh, they exist and are not abstract, but they don't *do anything*. The `JFrame` class defines these methods in such a way that you can *override* them in your program. For instance, in the SimpleLoop program, SimpleLoop is actually the name of the class, and it inherits from `JFrame`. Therefore, SimpleLoop has the opportunity to override any of the methods in `JFrame` that it wants to, including `paint()`.

Feeling Loopy

Now you finally have an opportunity to add a real loop to this program. But just for kicks, what do you think would happen if you added a `while()` loop to the constructor? I tried it, so you should try it too. Doing this will cause the window to quickly fill up with rectangles! The only problem with this kind of loop is that none of our program's other events will come up because we've trapped the program inside the while loop. The call to repaint the window is only the last step in a game. First, you move your game objects around on the screen, perform collision testing, and so forth. You can perform all of these steps in the paint() event, but that limits the program to a very low frame rate. The following is a suggestion on what we *might* try to do (note: this is *not* actual code that you should add to the SimpleLoop program—it's just an exploration of an idea).

```
//the game loop
while (true) {
    //move the game objects
    updateObjects();
    //perform collision testing
    testCollisions();
    //redraw the window
    repaint();
}
```

This would work, but we're still locking out processes that communicate with our program through events such as the keyboard and mouse handlers.

Stepping Up to Threads

We use the Runnable interface class to add threading support to a game. This interface has a single event method called run() that represents the thread's functionality. We can create this run() method in a game, and that will act like the game loop. The thread just calls run() once, so you must add a while loop to this method. The while loop will be running inside a thread that is separate from the main program. By implementing Runnable, a game becomes multithreaded. In that sense, it will support multiple processors or processor cores! For instance, if you have an Intel Core2 Duo or another multi-core processor, you should be able to see the applet running in a thread that is separate from the web browser or applet viewer program.

Starting and Stopping the Thread

To get a thread running in an applet, you have to create an instance of the Thread class, and then start it running using the applet's start() event. First, let's create the thread object:

```
Thread thread;
```

Next, create the thread in the constructor method:

```
thread = new Thread(this);
thread.start();
```

Then you can write the code for the thread's loop in the run() event method (part of Runnable). We'll take a look at what goes inside run() in a moment.

The ThreadedLoop Program

Let's take a look at the entire ThreadedLoop project, and then I'll explain the loop for the thread inside the run() method. The key portions of code have been highlighted in bold.

```
// ThreadedLoop program
import java.awt.*;
import java.lang.*;
import javax.swing.*;
import java.util.*;

public class ThreadedLoop extends JFrame implements Runnable {
    Random rand = new Random();

    //the main thread
    Thread thread;

    //count the number of rectangles drawn
    long count - 0, total = 0;

    public static void main(String[] args) {
        new ThreadedLoop();
    }

    public ThreadedLoop() {
        super("ThreadedLoop");
        setSize(500,400);
        setVisible(true);
        setDefaultCloseOperation(JFrame.EXIT_ON_CLOSE);
        thread = new Thread(this);
        thread.start();
    }
```

```
//thread run event
public void run() {
    long start = System.currentTimeMillis();

    //acquire the current thread
    Thread current = Thread.currentThread();

    //here's the new game loop
    while (current == thread) {
        try { Thread.sleep(0); }
        catch(InterruptedException e) { e.printStackTrace(); }

        //draw something
        repaint();

        //figure out how fast it's running
        if (start + 1000 < System.currentTimeMillis()) {
            start = System.currentTimeMillis();
            total = count;
            count = 0;
        }
    }
}

//JFrame paint event
public void paint(Graphics g) {
    Graphics2D g2d = (Graphics2D) g;

    //create a random rectangle
    int w = rand.nextInt(100);
    int h = rand.nextInt(100);
    int x = rand.nextInt(getSize().width - w);
    int y = rand.nextInt(getSize().height - h);
    Rectangle rect = new Rectangle(x,y,w,h);

    //generate a random color
    int red = rand.nextInt(256);
    int green = rand.nextInt(256);
    int blue = rand.nextInt(256);
    g2d.setColor(new Color(red,green,blue));
```

```
        //draw the rectangle
        g2d.fill(rect);

        //add another to the counter
        count++;

        g2d.setColor(Color.WHITE);
        g2d.fill(new Rectangle(0,360,500,400));
        g2d.setColor(Color.BLACK);
        g2d.drawString("Rectangles per second: " + total, 10, 380);
    }
}
```

Now let's examine this run() event that is called by the Runnable interface. There's a lot going on in this method. First, a variable called start gets the current time in milliseconds (System.currentTimeMillis()). This value is used to pause once per second to print out the total number of rectangles that have been drawn (see Figure 10.2).

Next, a local variable is set to the current thread, and then a while loop is created.

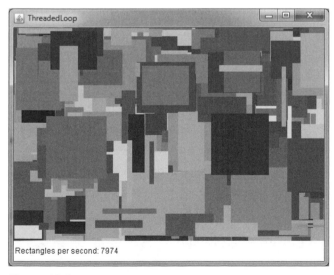

Figure 10.2
The ThreadedLoop program displays the number of rectangles drawn per second.

```
Thread current = Thread.currentThread();
```

This local thread makes sure that our loop only processes thread events intended for the game loop because you can use multiple threads in a program.

```
while (current == thread)
```

The core of the `thread` loop includes a call to `Thread.sleep(0)`, which is a placeholder for slowing the game down to a consistent frame rate. Right now it's running as fast as possible because the `sleep()` method is being passed a 0. This single method call requires an error handler because it throws an `Interrupted Exception` if the thread is ever interrupted by another thread. This is an advanced subject that doesn't concern us. If the thread is interrupted, it's not a big deal—we'll just ignore any such error that might crop up.

```
try {
    Thread.sleep(0);
}
catch(InterruptedException e) {
    e.printStackTrace();
}
```

After this call to sleep (which will slow the game to a consistent frame rate), then we can call game-related methods to update objects on the screen, perform collision testing, perform game logic to interact with enemies, and so on. In the block of code that follows, you can see some timing code inside an `if` statement. This code prints out the number of rectangles that have been drawn by the `paint()` event during the past 1,000 milliseconds (which equals 1 second).

```
//draw something
repaint();

//figure out how fast it's running
if (start + 1000 < System.currentTimeMillis()) {
    start = System.currentTimeMillis();
    count = 0;
}
```

The single call to `repaint()` actually makes this program *do something*; all of the rest of the code helps this method call to do its job effectively. The `run()` event contains the new threaded game loop.

Examining Multithreading

Aside from the sample game in Chapter 3, this program might have been your first exposure to multithreaded programming. Java makes the process very easy compared to other languages. I've used several threading libraries such as Posix threads, Boost threads, and Windows threads to add thread support in my C++ programs in Linux and Windows, and it's not very easy to use at all compared to Java's built-in support for threads. We will continue to use threads in every subsequent chapter, so you will have had a lot of exposure to this subject by the time you complete the book.

Note

Multi-Threaded Game Engine Design (Course Technology, 2010) covers thread libraries extensively with the C++ language while developing a fully featured game engine along the way.

WHAT YOU HAVE LEARNED

This was a heavyweight chapter that covered some very difficult subjects. But the idea is to get up the most difficult part of a hill so you can reach the peak, and then head on down the other side. That is what this chapter represents—the last few steps up to the peak. You have now learned the most difficult and challenging aspects of writing a Java game at this point, and you are ready to start heading down the hill at a more leisurely pace in the upcoming chapters. This chapter explained:

- How to create a threaded game loop
- How to override default applet methods
- How to manipulate a bitmap with transformations

REVIEW QUESTIONS

The following questions will help you to determine how well you have learned the subjects discussed in this chapter. The answers are provided in Appendix A, "Chapter Quiz Answers."

1. What is the name of the interface class that provides thread support?

2. What is the name of the thread execution method that you can use to run code inside the separate thread?

3. What is the name of the class that handles vector-based graphics?

4. What Thread method causes the thread to pause execution for a specified time?

5. What System method returns the current time in milliseconds?

6. What is the name of the method that returns the directory containing the applet (or HTML container) file?

7. What is the name of the method that returns the entire URL string including the applet (or HTML container) file?

8. What class do you use to store a bitmap image?

9. Which Graphics2D method is used to draw a bitmap?

10. Which class helps to improve gameplay by providing random numbers?

On Your Own

The following exercises will test your comprehension of the topics covered in this chapter by making some important changes to the projects.

Exercise 1

The ThreadedLoop program runs at breakneck speed with no delay. Modify the thread delay value to see whether you can slow down the number of rectangles being drawn to just 1,000 rectangles per second.

Exercise 2

The ThreadedLoop program just draws vector graphics. Modify the program so that it draws animated sprites instead.

PART III

THE GALACTIC WAR PROJECT

This final part of the book is devoted to the development of a complete game called Galactic War, built entirely in Java as a web applet. We have spent the last several chapters focusing on JFrame-based applications for the sake of convenience, but now we can return to the subject of Java applets that run in a web browser, with the goal of building a casual game. By the time you have finished reading the book, you will have learned how to create this game from scratch and deploy it to your website. Here are the chapters in Part III:

- Chapter 11: Galactic War: From Vectors to Bitmaps
- Chapter 12: Galactic War: Sprites and Collision Boxes
- Chapter 13: Galactic War: Squashed by Space Rocks
- Chapter 14: Galactic War: Entity Management
- Chapter 15: Galactic War: Finishing the Game
- Chapter 16: Galactic War: Web Deployment

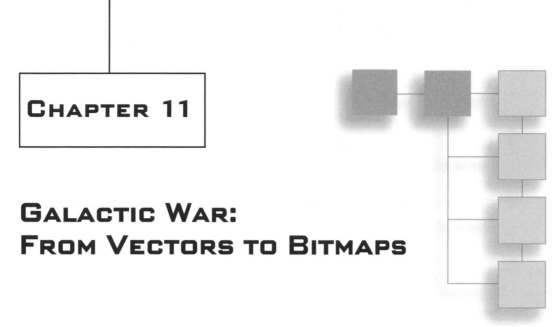

CHAPTER 11

GALACTIC WAR:
FROM VECTORS TO BITMAPS

The Galactic War project will demonstrate just one type of game that can be created in Java. This game is complex, but that complexity is hidden inside a game engine that, once written, does not need to be opened again. You will write an applet that will inherit from the game engine, and then the vast majority of the core code for the game will be handled behind the scenes. We'll build the game step by step, beginning with the simplistic *Asteroids*-style game from Chapter 3, gradually improving the game until it is finished and ready to be put up on your website. The first step to building Galactic War is to begin converting the original project from an entirely vector-based game into a bitmap-based game. We'll start with a partial conversion in this chapter, retaining some of the vector shapes but replacing the player's ship with a bitmap.

Here are the key topics:

- Improving the game
- Generalizing the vector classes

IMPROVING THE GAME

Chapter 3 gave you an example of a semi-complete *Asteroids*-style game to show you what would be covered in the upcoming chapters. You have now learned enough about game programming in Java to greatly enhance the game. That original game featured a class called BaseVectorShape, which contained all of the properties needed to manipulate game objects on the screen (the asteroids, bullets, and ship). In this chapter, we'll make a few changes to add sprite support, and in the next chapter we'll move the game entirely over to bitmaps.

By upgrading the spaceship to an image and doing away with the vector ship (which was little more than a filled triangle), the game is really starting to look more playable. There is no substitute for bitmapped graphics. But one of the goals I set out to achieve for this game is adding the ability to use an image instead of a shape, while still retaining the existing transformation features (most importantly, real-time rotation).

You can open up the project from Chapter 3 and continue using it or you can just copy the .java files from the old project to the new project. Here are the source code files you will want to bring over to the new game from previous chapters:

- BaseVectorShape.java
- Asteroid.java
- Bullet.java
- Ship.java
- SoundClip.java
- MidiSequence.java

Note that I did not include the main source code file, Asteroids.java. There are a few changes needed to add image support to the game, so I will just give you the complete source code listing for the main code file, which is now called GalacticWar.java.

Generalizing the Vector Classes

In the Asteroids project in Chapter 3, there were several classes to handle the ship, asteroids, and bullets in the game. Now we're going to generalize these three classes and make them more general purpose, since a lot of code is shared among these classes. The `Ship` class will be replaced entirely with an `ImageEntity` (covered back in Chapter 6). Let me show you what we're going to do with the `Asteroid` and `Bullet` classes.

Create a new source code file called VectorEntity.java. This class is very simple, as the following code suggests. Note that this class inherits from BaseGameEntity!

Note

> The BaseGameEntity and ImageEntity classes were created back in Chapter 6. Despite our having already created an awesome animation class in Chapter 7 called AnimatedSprite, we learned that this class does not support transformations. Since we desperately need transformations for Galactic War, we will have to rely primarily on the original Sprite class and a less capable AnimatedSprite class that uses a scratch pad image to support both transforms and animation. This is the *more advanced* class that was hinted about in Chapter 7! Despite sharing the name, this is not the same class anymore.

```
// Vector class for handling game entities
import java.awt.*;

public class VectorEntity extends BaseGameEntity {
    //variables
    private Shape shape;

    //accessor methods
    public Shape getShape() { return shape; }

    //mutator methods
    public void setShape(Shape shape) { this.shape = shape; }

    //default constructor
    VectorEntity() {
        setShape(null);
    }
}
```

The New Asteroid Class

The Asteroid class will be modified now to use VectorEntity as a base class. This frees up a lot of code that was previously duplicated in Asteroid and the other classes. The Asteroid class inherits from VectorEntity, which in turn inherits from BaseGameEntity. You can open up the Asteroid.java file that you copied over from the project in Chapter 3, or you can just add this as a new class to the Galactic War project.

```
// Asteroid class derives from BaseVectorShape
import java.awt.*;

public class Asteroid extends VectorEntity {
    //define the asteroid polygon shape
    private int[] astx = {-20,-13, 0,20,22, 20, 12, 2,-10,-22,-16};
    private int[] asty = { 20, 23,17,20,16,-20,-22,-14,-17,-20, -5};

    //rotation speed
    protected double rotVel;
    public double getRotationVelocity() { return rotVel; }
    public void setRotationVelocity(double v) { rotVel = v; }

    //bounding rectangle
    public Rectangle getBounds() {
        Rectangle r;
        r = new Rectangle((int)getX() - 20, (int) getY() - 20, 40, 40);
        return r;
    }

    //default constructor
    Asteroid() {
        setShape(new Polygon(astx, asty, astx.length));
        setAlive(true);
        setRotationVelocity(0.0);
    }
}
```

The New Bullet Class

Much of the code in the previous Bullet class has now been moved to VectorEntity as well, so we can just rewrite this class and give it the specific information relevant to a bullet object (most notably, that the getBounds() method returns a Rectangle that is one pixel wide and one pixel high).

```
// Bullet class derives from BaseVectorShape
import java.awt.*;

public class Bullet extends VectorEntity {

    //bounding rectangle
    public Rectangle getBounds() {
```

```
        Rectangle r;
        r = new Rectangle((int)getX(), (int) getY(), 1, 1);
        return r;
    }

    Bullet() {
        //create the bullet shape
        setShape(new Rectangle(0, 0, 1, 1));
        setAlive(false);
    }
}
```

The Main Source Code File: GalacticWar.java

The actual gameplay hasn't changed much in this new revision. Figure 11.1 shows the game with a new bitmap image being used for the player's spaceship. However, we have upgraded the core classes significantly in this update, which will be very useful in the next chapter, where ImageEntity will see a lot more use.

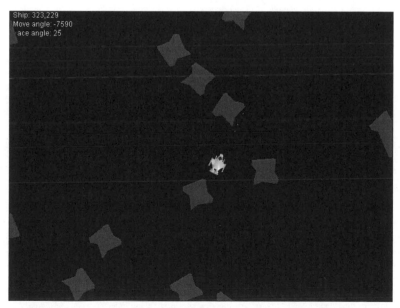

Figure 11.1
The player's spaceship is now a bitmap image rather than a polygon.

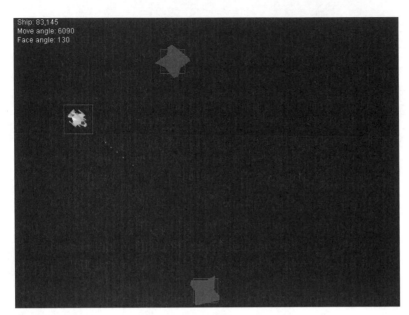

Figure 11.2
The bounding rectangles are used for collision testing.

The ImageEntity, which you learned about in Chapter 6, provides a getBounds() method to perform collision testing. You can still toggle the bounding rectangles on and off by pressing the B key. Figure 11.2 shows the rectangle around the player's ship. The collision code is a little too strict for a truly enjoyable game because the bounding rectangles are slightly too big. We'll correct this by fine-tuning the collision code in the next two chapters.

The majority of the code remains unchanged from the Asteroids.java file back in Chapter 3, so you can just open that file and modify it as indicated. But I'm going to list the entire program again because it's been a long time since we went over that code. I have highlighted in bold all of the lines of code that have changed. If the source code for a particular method has not changed at all, I simply commented out the code and inserted the statement //no changes needed, so keep an eye out for this comment and then reuse that code from the Chapter 3 project. It is a beautiful testament to object-oriented programming that so few changes are needed to this source code file!

```
// GALACTIC WAR, Chapter 11
import java.applet.*;
```

```java
import java.awt.*;
import java.awt.event.*;
import java.awt.geom.*;
import java.awt.image.*;
import java.util.*;

// Primary class for the game
public class GalacticWar extends Applet implements Runnable, KeyListener {
    //the main thread becomes the game loop
    Thread gameloop;
    //use this as a double buffer
    BufferedImage backbuffer;
    //the main drawing object for the back buffer
    Graphics2D g2d;
    //toggle for drawing bounding boxes
    boolean showBounds = false;

    //create the asteroid array
    int ASTEROIDS = 20;
    Asteroid[] ast = new Asteroid[ASTEROIDS];

    //create the bullet array
    int BULLETS = 10;
    Bullet[] bullet = new Bullet[BULLETS];
    int currentBullet = 0;

    //the player's ship
    ImageEntity ship = new ImageEntity(this);

    //create the identity transform
    AffineTransform identity = new AffineTransform();

    //create a random number generator
    Random rand = new Random();

    //load sound effects
    SoundClip shoot;
    SoundClip explode;
```

```java
    // applet init event
public void init() {
    //create the back buffer for smooth graphics
    backbuffer = new BufferedImage(640, 480, BufferedImage.TYPE_INT_RGB);
    g2d = backbuffer.createGraphics();

    //set up the ship
    ship.setX(320);
    ship.setY(240);
    ship.load("spaceship1.png");
    ship.setGraphics(g2d);

    //set up the bullets
    for (int n = 0; n<BULLETS; n++) {
        bullet[n] = new Bullet();
    }

    //set up the asteroids
    for (int n = 0; n<ASTEROIDS; n++) {
        ast[n] = new Asteroid();
        ast[n].setRotationVelocity(rand.nextInt(3)+1);
        ast[n].setX((double)rand.nextInt(600)+20);
        ast[n].setY((double)rand.nextInt(440)+20);
        ast[n].setMoveAngle(rand.nextInt(360));
        double ang = ast[n].getMoveAngle() - 90;
        ast[n].setVelX(calcAngleMoveX(ang));
        ast[n].setVelY(calcAngleMoveY(ang));
    }

    //load sound files
    shoot = new SoundClip("shoot.wav");
    explode = new SoundClip("explode.wav");

    //start the user input listener
    addKeyListener(this);
}

 // applet update event to redraw the screen
public void update(Graphics g) {
    //NO CHANGES HERE
}
```

```
// drawShip called by applet update event
public void drawShip() {
    //transform and draw the ship
    ship.transform();
    ship.draw();

     //draw bounding rectangle around ship
     if (showBounds) {
         g2d.setTransform(identity);
         g2d.setColor(Color.BLUE);
         g2d.draw(ship.getBounds());
     }
}
```

There are no changes beyond this point. Please double-check the source code listing in your new Galactic War project to ensure that all of the methods following this point are included (from the project in Chapter 3). If you prefer, you may open the completed project in the resource folder \sources\chapter11\ GalacticWar (found at www.courseptr.com/downloads).

```
// drawBullets called by applet update event
public void drawBullets() {
    //NO CHANGES HERE
}
// drawAsteroids called by applet update event
public void drawAsteroids() {
    //NO CHANGES HERE
}
// applet window repaint event--draw the back buffer
public void paint(Graphics g) {
    //NO CHANGES HERE
}
// thread start event - start the game loop running
public void start() {
    //NO CHANGES HERE
}
// thread run event (game loop)
public void run() {
    //NO CHANGES HERE
}
```

```java
// thread stop event
public void stop() {
    //NO CHANGES HERE
}
// move and animate the objects in the game
private void gameUpdate() {
    //NO CHANGES HERE
}
// Update the ship position based on velocity
public void updateShip() {
    //NO CHANGES HERE
}
// Update the bullets based on velocity
public void updateBullets() {
    //NO CHANGES HERE
}
// Update the asteroids based on velocity
public void updateAsteroids() {
    //NO CHANGES HERE
}
// Test asteroids for collisions with ship or bullets
public void checkCollisions() {
    //NO CHANGES HERE
}

// key listener events
public void keyReleased(KeyEvent k) { }
public void keyTyped(KeyEvent k) { }
public void keyPressed(KeyEvent k) {
    //NO CHANGES HERE
}

// calculate X movement value based on direction angle
public double calcAngleMoveX(double angle) {
    //NO CHANGES HERE
}

// calculate Y movement value based on direction angle
public double calcAngleMoveY(double angle) {
    //NO CHANGES HERE
}
}
```

WHAT YOU HAVE LEARNED

You have now learned the most difficult and challenging aspects of writing a Java game at this point, and you are ready to start heading down the hill at a more leisurely pace in the upcoming chapters. This chapter explained:

- How to add bitmaps to Galactic War
- How to support multiple key presses

REVIEW QUESTIONS

The following questions will help you to determine how well you have learned the subjects discussed in this chapter. The answers are provided in Appendix A, "Chapter Quiz Answers."

1. What is the name of the class that handles bitmaps?
2. Which class in Galactic War detects when bullets hit the asteroids?
3. What is the maximum number of sprites that can be supported by the game?
4. Which method in the Graphics2D class actually draws the image of a sprite?
5. What is the name of the Applet method that redraws the window?
6. How many key presses can the game detect at a single time?
7. What method do you use to track the mouse's movement?
8. What type of graphics entity does the game use for the asteroids?
9. Regarding ship rotation, by how many angles can the ship be rotated?
10. What method provides the game with support for collision detection?

ON YOUR OWN

The following exercise will test your comprehension of the topics covered in this chapter by making some important changes to the projects.

The Galactic War game is much more playable now than it was back in Chapter 3, thanks in part to the new keyboard handler. But we are completely ignoring a perfectly valid alternative to the keyboard—your trusty mouse. Devise a way to add mouse support to the game. You could rotate the ship when the mouse is moved left or right, and apply thrust when the mouse wheel is used, and fire when the button is pressed.

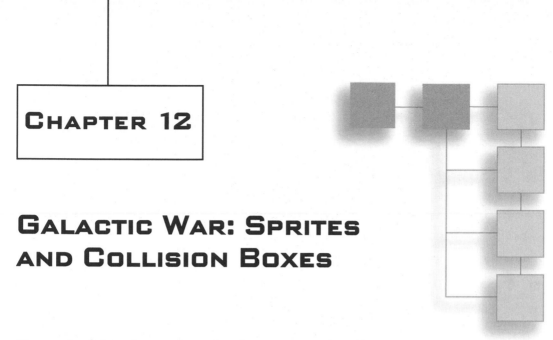

CHAPTER 12

GALACTIC WAR: SPRITES AND COLLISION BOXES

The goal of this chapter is to develop a way to handle the game objects moving around on the screen and to enhance the Galactic War game with some significant new gameplay features using sprites rather than just images and vectors.

Here are the specific topics you will learn about:

- Upgrading Galactic War to a sprite-based game
- Adding new artwork to the game
- Adding new functionality to the gameplay

CREATING THE PROJECT

The Galactic War game has so much potential that I'm eager to implement, but the game has been somewhat hobbled up to this point due to it being limited—first by vectors, then by simple bitmaps. Now that we have this useful new Sprite class available with some serious functionality built into it, the game will really start to resemble what I am envisioning for it.

The first thing I want to do is enlarge the applet window to 800 × 600. I realize that 640 × 480 provides better support for users of low-end PCs, but the truth of the matter is that most users run their PCs at 1024 × 768, while a similarly large percentage use 1280 × 960 or 1280 × 1024. Only a tiny minority of PC users run

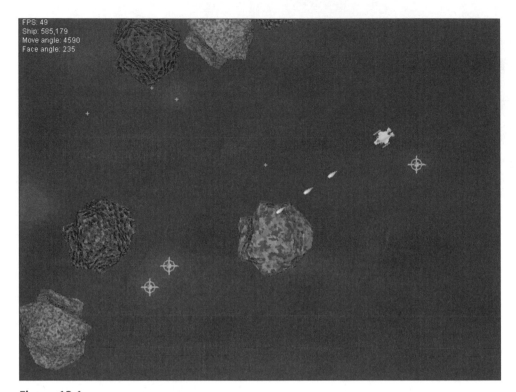

FPS: 49
Ship: 585,179
Move angle: 4590
Face angle: 235

Figure 12.1
The new version of Galactic War.

the system at the lower resolutions. A resolution of 800 × 600 will give the game more breathing room due to the large size of the asteroids.

As you can see in Figure 12.1, the game has been completely converted to bitmapped graphics, finally doing away with the vestiges of its vector graphics ancestry.

The Galactic War Bitmaps

There are a lot of high-quality bitmaps in the game now, giving it a sharp, catchy appearance. The first and most significant change to the game is that it now uses a background bitmap instead of a blank, black background. The bluespace.png background image was created by Reiner Prokein and is shown in Figure 12.2. This is one example of many backgrounds, sprites, and tiles you can find in the Reiner's Tileset collection at www.reinerstileset.de.

Figure 12.2
The background image used in Galactic War.

Figure 12.3
The five unique asteroids featured in the game.

There are five different types of asteroids of the *large* variety in this iteration of Galactic War. These gigantic rocks will be blasted into smaller pieces in later iterations of the game; at this point, shooting one of them simply causes it to disappear. I wanted to use very large starting asteroids to make the game more interesting by breaking them up into many smaller rocks. The asteroids shown in Figure 12.3 were rendered by a talented 3D artist by the name of Edgar Ibarra, who actually created these asteroid models for a project I was working on several

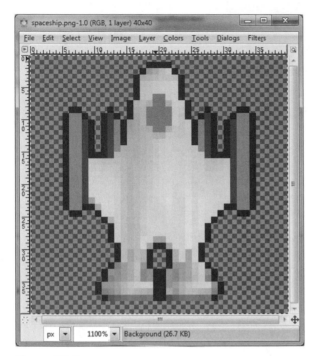

Figure 12.4
The player's spaceship used in Galactic War.

years ago. I have converted the asteroid bitmaps to the PNG format using Paint
Shop Pro, as well as applied a transparency mask in the process.

The spaceship has also been upgraded significantly from the version presented
in the previous chapter. I based the spaceship on a design by Reiner Prokein and
significantly modified it to give it a more distinct look with a pseudo-3D
appearance like an X-Wing from Star Wars. (Note the four guns, top and
bottom.) Figure 12.4 shows the ship sprite. This is a great-looking ship, if I do
say so myself. I'd like to add a small fire animation coming out of the engine
nozzles when you press the Up arrow key to apply thrust (future enhancement?).

The New and Improved Source Code

There's a *lot* of source code here for the new version of the game. This is
necessary because the game is now taking shape with a lot of functionality, and it
has room for new features in upcoming chapters. Future chapters will actually
involve additions and changes to the monumental work done in *this* chapter,

which is now a new foundational version of the game. The first thing I'd like to point out is that Galactic War no longer uses the VectorShape class, so you can remove it from the project. I have made no changes to BaseGameEntity or ImageEntity, so those can remain in the project. (ImageEntity is used by the Sprite class internally.) You can see the current state of the project by looking at the list of files now required by the project:

- BaseGameEntity.java

- GalacticWar.java

- ImageEntity.java

- Point2D.java

- Sprite.java

Tip

Two obviously glaring omissions from the game so far have been sound effects and music. We will add sound to the game in Chapter 15, "Galactic War: Finishing the Game."

The first code listing here includes the main class definition for the game, along with the global variables. I have highlighted key changes to the game in bold text.

```
/*************************************************
* GALACTIC WAR, Chapter 12
*************************************************/
import java.applet.*;
import java.awt.*;
import java.awt.event.*;
import java.awt.image.*;
import java.util.*;
import java.lang.System;


/*************************************************
* Primary class for the game
*************************************************/
public class GalacticWar extends Applet implements Runnable, KeyListener {
    //global constants
    static int SCREENWIDTH = 800;
```

```java
static int SCREENHEIGHT = 600;
static int CENTERX = SCREENWIDTH / 2;
static int CENTERY = SCREENHEIGHT / 2;
static int ASTEROIDS = 10;
static int BULLETS = 10;
static int BULLET_SPEED = 4;
static double ACCELERATION = 0.05;

//sprite state values
static int SPRITE_NORMAL = 0;
static int SPRITE_COLLIDED = 1;

//the main thread becomes the game loop
Thread gameloop;

//double buffer objects
BufferedImage backbuffer;
Graphics2D g2d;

//various toggles
boolean showBounds = true;
boolean collisionTesting = true;

//define the game objects
ImageEntity background;
Sprite ship;
Sprite[] ast = new Sprite[ASTEROIDS];
Sprite[] bullet = new Sprite[BULLETS];
int currentBullet = 0;

//create a random number generator
Random rand = new Random();

//define the sound effects objects
SoundClip shoot;
SoundClip explode;

//simple way to handle multiple keypresses
boolean keyDown, keyUp, keyLeft, keyRight, keyFire;
```

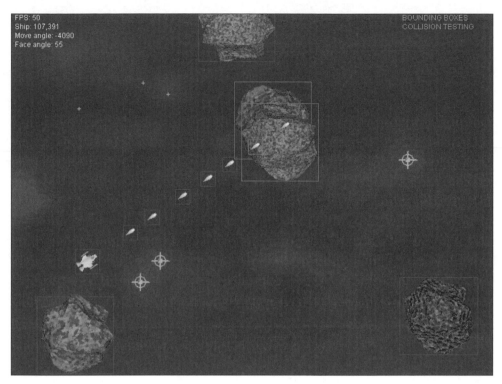

Figure 12.5
Bounding boxes and collisions are toggled with the B and C keys.

```
//frame rate counter
int frameCount = 0, frameRate = 0;
long startTime = System.currentTimeMillis();
```

The showBounds and collisionTesting variables are used to draw some helpful information on the screen, which is invaluable while developing a complex game. Figure 12.5 shows the game with bounding boxes and collision testing turned on. When a collision occurs, the bounding boxes of the two objects are drawn in red instead of blue. You can turn off collision testing altogether, if needed for testing.

This brings up an important point about the current state of the game. There are a lot of new features in the game, and it pretty much looks the way it will when it is finished—except for a scrolling background and a few other tidbits. The game really doesn't take any action at this point based on a collision. Instead, collisions are detected, and that status information is made available to the game through the sprite's state property (which is generic enough for use however you see fit). We'll revisit the process of responding to collisions in the next chapter.

Tip

We need a little more functionality out of the java.awt.Point class, so we'll be building our own Point2D class in this chapter. Try not to confuse this with java.awt.geom.Point2D, which is the base class for java.awt.Point, and has no relation to our custom Point2D class.

Next up is the init() event method of the applet.

```
/*******************************************************
 * applet init event
 *******************************************************/
public void init() {
    //create the back buffer for smooth graphics
    backbuffer = new BufferedImage(SCREENWIDTH, SCREENHEIGHT,
        BufferedImage.TYPE_INT_RGB);
    g2d = backbuffer.createGraphics();

    //load the background image
    background = new ImageEntity(this);
    background.load("bluespace.png");

    //set up the ship
    ship = new Sprite(this, g2d);
    ship.load("spaceship.png");
    ship.setPosition(new Point2D(CENTERX, CENTERY));
    ship.setAlive(true);

    //set up the bullets
    for (int n = 0; n<BULLETS; n++) {
        bullet[n] = new Sprite(this, g2d);
        bullet[n].load("plasmashot.png");
    }

    //set up the asteroids
    for (int n = 0; n<ASTEROIDS; n++) {
        ast[n] = new Sprite(this, g2d);
        ast[n].setAlive(true);
```

```
            //load the asteroid image
            int i = rand.nextInt(5)+1;
            ast[n].load("asteroid" + i + ".png");
            //set to a random position on the screen
            int x = rand.nextInt(SCREENWIDTH);
            int y = rand.nextInt(SCREENHEIGHT);
            ast[n].setPosition(new Point2D(x, y));
            //set rotation angles to a random value
            ast[n].setFaceAngle(rand.nextInt(360));
            ast[n].setMoveAngle(rand.nextInt(360));
            ast[n].setRotationRate(rand.nextDouble());
            //set velocity based on movement direction
            double ang = ast[n].moveAngle() - 90;
            double velx = calcAngleMoveX(ang);
            double vely = calcAngleMoveY(ang);
            ast[n].setVelocity(new Point2D(velx, vely));
        }

        //start the user input listener
        addKeyListener(this);
    }
```

The next section of code is the main game update portion of the game, including the applet update() event, the paint() event, and three methods to draw the game objects: drawShip(), drawBullets(), and drawAsteroids().

```
    /****************************************************
     * applet update event to redraw the screen
     ****************************************************/
    public void update(Graphics g) {
        //calculate frame rate
        frameCount++;
        if (System.currentTimeMillis() > startTime + 1000) {
            startTime = System.currentTimeMillis();
            frameRate = frameCount;
            frameCount = 0;
        }

        //draw the background
        g2d.drawImage(background.getImage(),0,0,
            SCREENWIDTH-1,SCREENHEIGHT-1,this);
```

```java
//draw the game graphics
drawAsteroids();
drawShip();
drawBullets();

//print status information on the screen
g2d.setColor(Color.WHITE);
g2d.drawString("FPS: " + frameRate, 5, 10);
long x = Math.round(ship.position().X());
long y = Math.round(ship.position().Y());
g2d.drawString("Ship: " + x + "," + y , 5, 25);
g2d.drawString("Move angle: " + Math.round(
    ship.moveAngle())+90, 5, 40);
g2d.drawString("Face angle: " + Math.round(
    ship.faceAngle()), 5, 55);

if (showBounds) {
    g2d.setColor(Color.GREEN);
    g2d.drawString("BOUNDING BOXES", SCREENWIDTH-150, 10);
}
if (collisionTesting) {
    g2d.setColor(Color.GREEN);
    g2d.drawString("COLLISION TESTING", SCREENWIDTH-150, 25);
}

//repaint the applet window
paint(g);
}


/****************************************************
 * drawShip called by applet update event
 ****************************************************/
public void drawShip() {
    // set the transform for the image
    ship.transform();
    ship.draw();
    if (showBounds) {
        if (ship.state() == SPRITE_COLLIDED)
            ship.drawBounds(Color.RED);
        else
```

```
            ship.drawBounds(Color.BLUE);
        }
    }

    /*****************************************************
     * drawBullets called by applet update event
     *****************************************************/
    public void drawBullets() {
        for (int n = 0; n < BULLETS; n++) {
            if (bullet[n].alive()) {
                //draw the bullet
                bullet[n].transform();
                bullet[n].draw();
                if (showBounds) {
                    if (bullet[n].state() == SPRITE_COLLIDED)
                        bullet[n].drawBounds(Color.RED);
                    else
                        bullet[n].drawBounds(Color.BLUE);
                }
            }
        }
    }

    /*****************************************************
     * drawAsteroids called by applet update event
     *****************************************************/
    public void drawAsteroids() {
        for (int n = 0; n < ASTEROIDS; n++) {
            if (ast[n].alive()) {
                //draw the asteroid
                ast[n].transform();
                ast[n].draw();
                if (showBounds) {
                    if (ast[n].state() == SPRITE_COLLIDED)
                        ast[n].drawBounds(Color.RED);
                    else
                        ast[n].drawBounds(Color.BLUE);
                }
            }
        }
    }
```

```
/*****************************************************
 * applet window repaint event--draw the back buffer
 *****************************************************/
public void paint(Graphics g) {
    g.drawImage(backbuffer, 0, 0, this);
}
```

The next section of code updates the game via the gameloop thread, which calls gameUpdate(). This method, in turn, calls methods to process user input; update the ship, bullets, and asteroids; and perform collision testing.

```
/*****************************************************
 * thread start event -- start the game loop running
 *****************************************************/
public void start() {
    gameloop = new Thread(this);
    gameloop.start();
}
/*****************************************************
 * thread run event (game loop)
 *****************************************************/
public void run() {
    //acquire the current thread
    Thread t = Thread.currentThread();
    //keep going as long as the thread is alive
    while (t == gameloop) {
        try {
            Thread.sleep(20);
        }
        catch(InterruptedException e) {
            e.printStackTrace();
        }
        //update the game loop
        gameUpdate();
        repaint();
    }
}
/*****************************************************
 * thread stop event
 *****************************************************/
```

```java
public void stop() {
    gameloop = null;
}

/*******************************************************
 * move and animate the objects in the game
 *******************************************************/
private void gameUpdate() {
    checkInput();
    updateShip();
    updateBullets();
    updateAsteroids();
    if (collisionTesting) checkCollisions();
}

/*******************************************************
 * Update the ship position based on velocity
 *******************************************************/
public void updateShip() {
    ship.updatePosition();
    double newx = ship.position().X();
    double newy = ship.position().Y();

    //wrap around left/right
    if (ship.position().X() < -10)
        newx = SCREENWIDTH + 10;
    else if (ship.position().X() > SCREENWIDTH + 10)
        newx = -10;

    //wrap around top/bottom
    if (ship.position().Y() < -10)
        newy = SCREENHEIGHT + 10;
    else if (ship.position().Y() > SCREENHEIGHT + 10)
        newy = -10;

    ship.setPosition(new Point2D(newx, newy));
    ship.setState(SPRITE_NORMAL);
}

/*******************************************************
 * Update the bullets based on velocity
 *******************************************************/
```

```java
public void updateBullets() {
    //move the bullets
    for (int n = 0; n < BULLETS; n++) {
        if (bullet[n].alive()) {

            //update bullet's x position
            bullet[n].updatePosition();

            //bullet disappears at left/right edge
            if (bullet[n].position().X() < 0 ||
                bullet[n].position().X() > SCREENWIDTH)
            {
                bullet[n].setAlive(false);
            }

            //update bullet's y position
            bullet[n].updatePosition();

            //bullet disappears at top/bottom edge
            if (bullet[n].position().Y() < 0 ||
                bullet[n].position().Y() > SCREENHEIGHT)
            {
                bullet[n].setAlive(false);
            }

            bullet[n].setState(SPRITE_NORMAL);
        }
    }
}


/******************************************************
 * Update the asteroids based on velocity
 ******************************************************/
public void updateAsteroids() {
    //move and rotate the asteroids
    for (int n = 0; n < ASTEROIDS; n++) {
        if (ast[n].alive()) {
            //update the asteroid's position and rotation
            ast[n].updatePosition();
            ast[n].updateRotation();
```

```
                    int w = ast[n].imageWidth()-1;
                    int h = ast[n].imageHeight()-1;
                    double newx = ast[n].position().X();
                    double newy = ast[n].position().Y();

                    //wrap the asteroid around the screen edges
                    if (ast[n].position().X() < -w)
                        newx = SCREENWIDTH + w;
                    else if (ast[n].position().X() > SCREENWIDTH + w)
                        newx = -w;
                    if (ast[n].position().Y() < -h)
                        newy = SCREENHEIGHT + h;
                    else if (ast[n].position().Y() > SCREENHEIGHT + h)
                        newy = -h;

                    ast[n].setPosition(new Point2D(newx,newy));
                    ast[n].setState(SPRITE_NORMAL);
                }
            }
        }

        /********************************************************
         * Test asteroids for collisions with ship or bullets
         ********************************************************/
        public void checkCollisions() {
            //check for collision between asteroids and bullets
            for (int m = 0; m<ASTEROIDS; m++) {
                if (ast[m].alive()) {
                    //iterate through the bullets
                    for (int n = 0; n < BULLETS; n++) {
                        if (bullet[n].alive()) {
                            //collision?
                            if (ast[m].collidesWith(bullet[n])) {
                                bullet[n].setState(SPRITE_COLLIDED);
                                ast[m].setState(SPRITE_COLLIDED);
                                explode.play();
                            }
                        }
                    }
                }
            }
```

```
        //check for collision asteroids and ship
        for (int m = 0; m<ASTEROIDS; m++) {
            if (ast[m].alive()) {
                if (ship.collidesWith(ast[m])) {
                    ast[m].setState(SPRITE_COLLIDED);
                    ship.setState(SPRITE_COLLIDED);
                    explode.play();
                }
            }
        }
    }
```

The next section of code processes keyboard input. The game has progressed to the point where the simplistic keyboard input from earlier chapters was insufficient, so I've added support to the game for multiple key presses now. This works through the use of several global variables: keyLeft, keyRight, and so on. These boolean variables are set to true during the keyPressed() event and set to false during the keyReleased() event method. This provides support for multiple keys at the same time in a given frame of the game loop. There is a practical limit to the number of keys you will be able to press at a time, but this code makes the game fluid-looking, and the input is smoother than the jerky input in the last chapter.

```
/**************************************************
 * process keys that have been pressed
 **************************************************/
public void checkInput() {
    if (keyLeft) {
        //left arrow rotates ship left 5 degrees
        ship.setFaceAngle(ship.faceAngle() - 5);
        if (ship.faceAngle() < 0) ship.setFaceAngle(360 - 5);
    }
    else if (keyRight) {
        //right arrow rotates ship right 5 degrees
        ship.setFaceAngle(ship.faceAngle() + 5);
        if (ship.faceAngle() > 360) ship.setFaceAngle(5);
    }
    if (keyUp) {
        //up arrow applies thrust to ship
        applyThrust();
```

```
    }
}

/*****************************************************
 * key listener events
 *****************************************************/
public void keyTyped(KeyEvent k) { }
public void keyPressed(KeyEvent k) {
    switch (k.getKeyCode()) {
    case KeyEvent.VK_LEFT:
        keyLeft = true;
        break;
    case KeyEvent.VK_RIGHT:
        keyRight = true;
        break;
    case KeyEvent.VK_UP:
        keyUp = true;
        break;
    case KeyEvent.VK_CONTROL:
        keyFire = true;
        break;
    case KeyEvent.VK_B:
        //toggle bounding rectangles
        showBounds = !showBounds;
        break;
    case KeyEvent.VK_C:
        //toggle collision testing
        collisionTesting = !collisionTesting;
        break;
    }
}
public void keyReleased(KeyEvent k) {
    switch (k.getKeyCode()) {
    case KeyEvent.VK_LEFT:
        keyLeft = false;
        break;
    case KeyEvent.VK_RIGHT:
        keyRight = false;
        break;
    case KeyEvent.VK_UP:
        keyUp = false;
```

```java
                break;
        case KeyEvent.VK_CONTROL:
            keyFire = false;
            fireBullet();
            break;
        }
    }

    public void applyThrust() {
        //up arrow adds thrust to ship (1/10 normal speed)
        ship.setMoveAngle(ship.faceAngle() - 90);

        //calculate the X and Y velocity based on angle
        double velx = ship.velocity().X();
        velx += calcAngleMoveX(ship.moveAngle()) * ACCELERATION;
        double vely = ship.velocity().Y();
        vely += calcAngleMoveY(ship.moveAngle()) * ACCELERATION;
        ship.setVelocity(new Point2D(velx, vely));
    }

    public void fireBullet() {
        //fire a bullet
        currentBullet++;
        if (currentBullet > BULLETS - 1) currentBullet = 0;
        bullet[currentBullet].setAlive(true);

        //set bullet's starting point
        int w = bullet[currentBullet].imageWidth();
        int h = bullet[currentBullet].imageHeight();
        double x = ship.center().X() - w/2;
        double y = ship.center().Y() - h/2;
        bullet[currentBullet].setPosition(new Point2D(x,y));

        //point bullet in same direction ship is facing
        bullet[currentBullet].setFaceAngle(ship.faceAngle());
        bullet[currentBullet].setMoveAngle(ship.faceAngle() - 90);

        //fire bullet at angle of the ship
        double angle = bullet[currentBullet].moveAngle();
        double svx = calcAngleMoveX(angle) * BULLET_SPEED;
```

```
        double svy = calcAngleMoveY(angle) * BULLET_SPEED;
        bullet[currentBullet].setVelocity(new Point2D(svx, svy));

        //play shoot sound
        shoot.play();
    }
```

The last section of code concludes the main code listing for this new version of Galactic War, implementing the now-familiar `calcAngleMoveX()` and `calc AngleMoveY()` methods.

```
    /***************************************************
     * Angular motion for X and Y is calculated
     ***************************************************/
    public double calcAngleMoveX(double angle) {
        double movex = Math.cos(angle * Math.PI / 180);
        return movex;
    }
    public double calcAngleMoveY(double angle) {
        double movey = Math.sin(angle * Math.PI / 180);
        return movey;
    }
}
```

WHAT YOU HAVE LEARNED

This significant chapter produced a monumental new version of Galactic War that is a foundation for the chapters to come. The final vestiges of the game's vector-based roots have been discarded, and the game is now fully implemented with bitmaps. In this chapter, you learned:

- How game entities can become unmanageable without a handler (such as the Sprite class).

- How the use of a sprite class dramatically cleans up the source code for a game.

REVIEW QUESTIONS

The following questions will help you to determine how well you have learned the subjects discussed in this chapter. The answers are provided in Appendix A, "Chapter Quiz Answers."

1. Which support class helps manage the position and velocity of sprites?

2. During which keyboard event should you disable a keypress variable, when detecting multiple key presses with global variables?

3. What is the name of the sprite collision detection routine used in Galactic War?

4. Which method in the Applet class provides a way to load images from a JAR file?

5. Which Java package do you need to import to use the Graphics2D class?

6. What three numeric data types does the Point2D class support for the X and Y values?

7. How does the use of a class such as Point2D improve a game's source code, versus using simple variables?

8. Which property in the Sprite class determines the angle at which the sprite will move?

9. Which property in the Sprite class determines the angle at which a sprite is pointed?

10. How many milliseconds must the game use as a delay in order to achieve a frame rate of 60 frames per second?

ON YOUR OWN

The Galactic War game is in a transition at this point, after having been upgraded significantly from vector-based graphics. At present, it does not perform any action due to collisions other than to report that a collision has occurred. We want to separate the *collision testing* code from the *collision response* code. Add a method that is called from gameUpdate() that displays the position (x,y) of any object that has collided with another object, for debugging purposes. You can do this by looking at a sprite's state property.

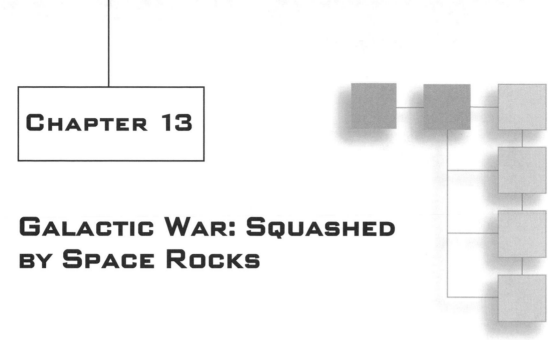

CHAPTER 13

GALACTIC WAR: SQUASHED BY SPACE ROCKS

We'll make a minor enhancement to Galactic War in this chapter by adding support for an animated explosion. To facilitate this, we'll have to write some new code to handle the timing and state properties for each sprite. The goal in this chapter is to add a handler for responding to ship-asteroid collisions. When a collision occurs, the game should animate an explosion over the ship, and then put the ship into a temporary invulnerability mode so the player can get the heck out of the way before another collision occurs.

Here are the key topics we'll cover in this chapter:

- Examining possible interactions among the game entities
- Adding collision detection between the player's ship and the asteroids

BEING CIVILIZED ABOUT COLLISIONS

Responding to collisions in a civilized manner is the first step toward adding realistic gameplay to any game. The next step is to add a sense of timing to the response code. We'll add explosions to show when the player gets hit by an asteroid! The new animated explosion in the game is a 16-frame sequence, which is shown in Figure 13.1.

When the explosion code is added to the game, the ship will literally blow up when it collides with an asteroid (see Figure 13.2).

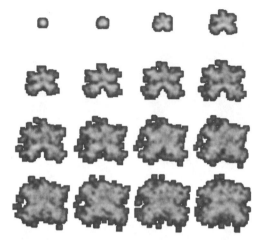

Figure 13.1
The 16-frame animated explosion (courtesy of Reiner Prokein).

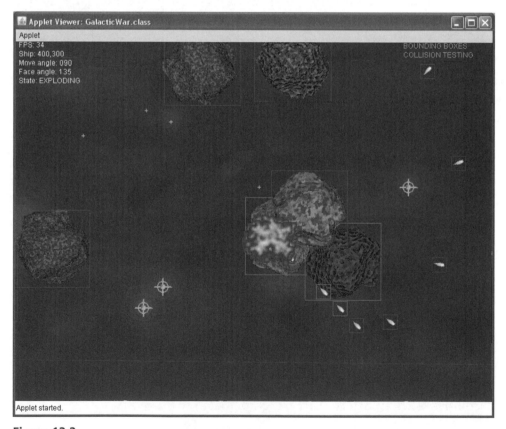

Figure 13.2
The new animated explosion is now part of the game.

Let's take a look at the changes required to update the game to support explosions. There's more involved here than just loading up the animation and drawing it because we have to account for timing and sprite state values. The first change is in the global section at the top of the class—note the changes in bold.

Tip

The static keyword defines a variable that does not change.

```
public class GalacticWar extends Applet
        implements Runnable, KeyListener {
    //global constants
    static int SCREENWIDTH = 800;
    static int SCREENHEIGHT = 600;
    static int CENTERX = SCREENWIDTH / 2;
    static int CENTERY = SCREENHEIGHT / 2;
    static int ASTEROIDS = 10;
    static int BULLETS = 10;
    static int BULLET_SPEED = 4;
    static double ACCELERATION = 0.05;

    //sprite state values
    static int STATE_NORMAL = 0;
    static int STATE_COLLIDED = 1;
    static int STATE_EXPLODING = 2;

    //the main thread becomes the game loop
    Thread gameloop;

    //double buffer objects
    BufferedImage backbuffer;
    Graphics2D g2d;

    //various toggles
    boolean showBounds = true;
    boolean collisionTesting = true;
    long collisionTimer = 0;
```

```
//define the game objects
ImageEntity background;
Sprite ship;
Sprite[] ast = new Sprite[ASTEROIDS];
Sprite[] bullet = new Sprite[BULLETS];
int currentBullet = 0;
AnimatedSprite explosion;

//create a random number generator
Random rand = new Random();

//sound effects
SoundClip shoot;
SoundClip explode;

//simple way to handle multiple keypresses
boolean keyDown, keyUp, keyLeft, keyRight, keyFire;

//frame rate counters and other timing variables
int frameCount = 0, frameRate = 0;
long startTime = System.currentTimeMillis();
```

Make the following changes near the top of the init() event method to switch the background object from an Image to an ImageEntity.

```
public void init() {
    //create the back buffer for smooth graphics
    backbuffer = new BufferedImage(SCREENWIDTH, SCREENHEIGHT,
        BufferedImage.TYPE_INT_RGB);
    g2d = backbuffer.createGraphics();

    //load the background image
    background = new ImageEntity(this);
    background.load("bluespace.png");
```

Next, scroll down inside the init() event method a bit more until you have found the call to addKeyListener(this) and insert the following code in bold. This code loads a 16-frame explosion animation.

```
    //load the explosion
    explosion = new AnimatedSprite(this, g2d);
    explosion.load("explosion96x96x16.png", 4, 4, 96, 96);
```

```
explosion.setFrameDelay(2);
explosion.setAlive(false);

//start the user input listener
addKeyListener(this);
```

Next, go to the update() event and look for the line of code that draws the background and make the change noted in bold. Then, a few lines further down, add the new line of code shown in bold.

```
//draw the background
g2d.drawImage(background.getImage(),0,0,SCREENWIDTH-1,
SCREENHEIGHT-1,this);

//draw the game graphics
drawAsteroids();
drawShip();
drawBullets();
drawExplosions();
```

Now, while you're still in the update() method, scroll down a few lines to the part of the method that draws status information on the screen and add the following code to display the ship's current state.

```
if (ship.state()==STATE_NORMAL)
    g2d.drawString("State: NORMAL", 5, 70);
else if (ship.state()==STATE_COLLIDED)
    g2d.drawString("State: COLLIDED", 5, 70);
else if (ship.state()==STATE_EXPLODING)
    g2d.drawString("State: EXPLODING", 5, 70);
```

Now, scroll down past the three draw methods and add the following method after drawAsteroids(). This is just the first version of the explosion code, and it only draws a single animated explosion. Later, the game will need to support several explosions at a time.

```
public void drawExplosions() {
    //explosions don't need separate update method
    if (explosion.alive()) {
        explosion.updateAnimation();
        if (explosion.currentFrame() == explosion.totalFrames()-1) {
            explosion.setCurrentFrame(0);
            explosion.setAlive(false);
        }
```

```
        else {
            explosion.draw();
        }
    }
}
```

Next, scroll down a bit more to the gameUpdate() method. Modify it with the additional lines of code shown in bold.

```
private void gameUpdate() {
    checkInput();
    updateShip();
    updateBullets();
    updateAsteroids();
    if (collisionTesting) {
        checkCollisions();
        handleShipCollisions();
        handleBulletCollisions();
        handleAsteroidCollisions();
    }
}
```

Scroll down just past the checkCollisions() method and add the following new methods to the game. The two collision handler routines for asteroids and bullets are not implemented yet, as the goal is first to get a response for ship-asteroid collisions along with an animated explosion. The handleShipCollisions() method uses the ship sprite's state property extensively to monitor the current state of a collision, and it adds a three-second delay after a collision has occurred so the player can get out of the way before collisions start to occur again.

```
public void handleShipCollisions() {
    if (ship.state() == STATE_COLLIDED) {
        collisionTimer = System.currentTimeMillis();
        ship.setVelocity(new Point2D(0,0));
        ship.setState(STATE_EXPLODING);
        startExplosion(ship);
    }
    else if (ship.state() == STATE_EXPLODING) {
        if (collisionTimer + 3000 < System.currentTimeMillis()) {
            ship.setState(STATE_NORMAL);
        }
    }
}
```

```
public void startExplosion(Sprite sprite) {
    if (!explosion.alive()) {
        double x = sprite.position().X() -
            sprite.getBounds().width / 2;
        double y = sprite.position().Y() -
            sprite.getBounds().height / 2;
        explosion.setPosition(new Point2D(x, y));
        explosion.setCurrentFrame(0);
        explosion.setAlive(true);
    }
}

public void handleBulletCollisions() {
    for (int n = 0; n<BULLETS; n++) {
        if (bullet[n].state() == STATE_COLLIDED) {
            //nothing to do yet
        }
    }
}

public void handleAsteroidCollisions() {
    for (int n = 0; n<ASTEROIDS; n++) {
        if (ast[n].state() == STATE_COLLIDED) {
            //nothing to do yet
        }
    }
}
```

WHAT YOU HAVE LEARNED

This chapter tackled the difficult subject of sprite collision detection. Adding support for collision testing is not an easy undertaking, but this chapter provided you with the knowledge and explained the collision code in the core classes that make it possible. You can now draw two or more sprites on the screen and *very easily* determine when they have intersected or collided, and then respond to such events.

REVIEW QUESTIONS

The following questions will help you to determine how well you have learned the subjects discussed in this chapter. The answers are provided in Appendix A, "Chapter Quiz Answers."

1. What is the name of the method that makes collision detection possible?

2. How many collisions can the game detect within a single update of the game loop?

3. What would happen if the ship were to fire a projectile that "warps" around the screen and then hits the ship? Would a collision take place? Why or why not?

4. What should happen to the player's ship after it has been destroyed by a collision with an asteroid? Describe a better way to "respawn" the ship than what is currently being done.

5. What type of transform could you apply to the explosion sprite to change its size?

6. How does the ship's velocity affect the result of a collision when the ship is destroyed? Should the ship continue to exert momentum even while blowing up?

7. How can the collision routine be improved upon, so that collisions are more precise?

8. What is the name of the constant applied to the ship when a collision has taken place?

9. What is the name of the method that updates a sprite's animation sequence?

10. What is the name of the method that handles the game loop for Galactic War?

ON YOUR OWN

Since we are constantly improving the game with each new chapter, there is little you can do now that will not be addressed in the next chapter. However, some improvements can be made now that are not added in future chapters. Here is one such example: Add another explosion to Galactic War so that the asteroids blow up like the player's ship when they collide with the ship.

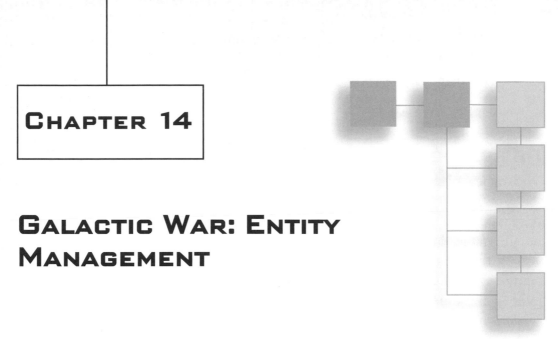

CHAPTER 14

GALACTIC WAR: ENTITY MANAGEMENT

You have learned the basics of web game programming in previous chapters, and you have been building the Galactic War game here in Part III. The source code for an applet-based game is becoming a bit tedious at this point. You've seen that there is a lot of code that does not change very much from one game to the next, now that you know how to write a typical game in Java. Aren't you getting tired of seeing the key and mouse handlers in every code listing? I sure am! I don't want to enforce too much structure for your own game projects, but I think it will be helpful to add some organization to the code.

There are a lot of events and methods that must be called and monitored regularly, and since this code doesn't change very often (if ever), it would clean up the source code considerably if we could move reusable code into a separate class. This chapter shows you how to create a base class for an applet-based framework—or rather, a *game engine*. You will be able to write a game very easily by inheriting from the new Game class, and your game won't need to implement the interfaces (such as Runnable) any longer. Instead, you will be able to focus on high-level game design and gameplay.

Here are the specific topics you will learn about:

- Event-driven game programming
- Creating a Java applet–based game engine

- Internalizing the sprite handler
- Adapting Galactic War to the new game engine

ADJUSTING TO EVENT-DRIVEN PROGRAMMING

The biggest obstacle to the adoption of a game framework, or a game engine, is that you must give up direct (active) control of the game and accept an indirect (passive) programming methodology. Adapting Galactic War from a direct to a passive game was very challenging, and I would like to share my experience with you so that you will not have to go through the pains of developing your own game engine the hard way. I could have completed the game two or three times over in the time I've spent building the Game class in this chapter, but the end result is a powerful engine for creating additional games for delivery on the web.

Exploring the Class Library

Let's take a look at the class library as it exists at this point, after the changes made in the previous chapter. Figure 14.1 shows a diagram of the four main

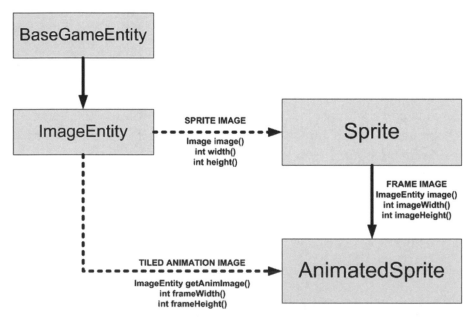

Figure 14.1
The four key Java classes for working with game graphics.

classes we've developed so far. The diagram doesn't show the VectorEntity class since it is no longer being used.

First, BaseGameEntity contains the basic movement and orientation variables that are passed on to the ImageEntity class. This class adds the capability to move, rotate, and draw bitmap images, and it is the core class. From this point, a new class called Sprite was developed. Now, Sprite does not *inherit* from ImageEntity, but rather, it *uses* this core class to store its internal image used for drawing sprites. That is why the link from ImageEntity to Sprite is a dotted line. Next we have AnimatedSprite, which is the core of the game engine due to its support for animation.

When you look at this diagram and resolve the connections in the reverse direction, you find that AnimatedSprite inherits from Sprite several key properties: an image, width, and height. AnimatedSprite also makes use of an ImageEntity to handle the large, tiled images containing frames of animation. The Sprite class likewise, looking backward, consumes an image and its width and height properties. You can use this diagram if you ever start to feel overwhelmed while perusing the Galactic War source code in these final chapters, because the game is becoming *tighter*. When an AnimatedSprite loads its source bitmap, that is passed up to the "super" or "parent" class (Sprite) that handles the image. This is inheritance at work, because the AnimatedSprite class doesn't actually need to handle its image at all.

I use the word "tight" to describe the situation in which the source code is not becoming *bloated,* as is often the case when a game becomes more advanced. Instead, Galactic War will evolve from a direct, actively coded model to an indirect, passively coded model using the game engine developed in this chapter. The source code listing for the game is about the same length as it was before, but the game has been *completely rewritten*. The Game class is quite complex, but the "front end" or "user" source code file, GalacticWar.java, is *much, much simpler*. That is the benefit of a game engine—it handles all of the messy details for you, allowing you to focus on building gameplay. From the engine's point of view, "You are too skilled to be bothered with such minutiae as sprite management. Let me take care of that for you, while you focus on making this game as fun as possible!"

Building the New Game Class

The purpose of the game engine is to encapsulate the *platform code* on which the game is developed. In this case, we're talking about a Java applet that runs in a web browser. So, the goal of this chapter is to build a game engine that simplifies building web games with Java. The first step is to create a new class. I opened the Galactic War project from the last chapter and began modifying it. First, I created a new class called Game. The Game class extends (or inherits from) the Applet class, as our programs have for the last 13 chapters. This new class will also need to implement the keyboard and mouse listener interfaces. It will also need to handle the game loop thread on its own, so the derived game will not need to be bothered with such details (or rather, *logistics*, since we're trying to manage the logistics of an applet).

Encapsulating a Standard Java Applet

Here are the main events that you're accustomed to seeing in a Java applet–based program up to this point. I'm including the mouse events because they are going to be part of the engine, even if we haven't used them very much in Galactic War. You are welcome to add mouse support if you wish; I'm just not sure how you would control the ship with a mouse.

```
public void init()
public void update(Graphics g)
public void paint(Graphics g)
public void start()
public void run()
public void stop()
public void keyTyped(KeyEvent k)
public void keyPressed(KeyEvent k)
public void keyReleased(KeyEvent k)
public void mousePressed(MouseEvent e)
public void mouseReleased(MouseEvent e)
public void mouseMoved(MouseEvent e)
public void mouseDragged(MouseEvent e)
public void mouseEntered(MouseEvent e)
public void mouseExited(MouseEvent e)
public void mouseClicked(MouseEvent e)
```

Even if you ignore the mouse listener events, there are a lot of raw events in this listing that every applet-based game must implement at a minimum. As for things such as key events, we want to completely replace the stock events with a keyboard handler that supports multiple key presses and releases. I experimented with quite a few different ways to do this, and I came up with a solution that is versatile but not totally internal to the Game class. The key events are passed on to the game, which can then use a few global boolean variables to keep track of keys needed by the game. The mouse events are parsed, and several mouse properties are made available to provide your game with mouse button and movement information.

Custom Game Events

In place of the standard applet events, I want this class to send events to the game that are directly related to gameplay issues, such as sprite collision and screen refresh. The most crucial methods in the Game class use the Animated-Sprite class. The Game class has the following features:

- Performs automatic double buffering
- Maintains a consistent frame rate
- Handles the input listeners
- Manages the game loop thread
- Maintains an internal linked list for sprites
- Performs an automatic frame rate calculation
- Automatically moves and draws all active sprites
- Performs collision testing on all active sprites
- Passes important events on to the game

That's an impressive list of goals for any sprite-based game engine. This engine allows you to build far more complex games than would be possible with the simple arrays we've been using in the previous chapters. The key to the sprite handler is the java.util.LinkedList class. By using a linked list containing AnimatedSprite objects, you can dynamically add and remove sprites without adversely affecting performance. I've managed to get 300 sprites on the screen at once, with full collision testing, and the game still runs at the desired frame rate. Keep in mind, the target platform here is a web browser! Anytime you add some overhead to a system, you will inherently introduce some inefficiency.

There's a tradeoff between simple speed and your desire to have an engaging, complex game with a lot of graphics on the screen. I like having the ability to add an explosion to the game at any point without having to worry about that explosion after it has finished animating itself. AnimatedSprite has a lot of properties and methods that make this possible (such as the lifetime and lifeage variables that the Game class uses to terminate a sprite when its lifespan is completed). I want to tell the game engine, "Hey, the player's ship has exploded *right here* [provide X,Y position]. Please display an explosion here." The game engine should not only animate the explosion at that location, it should also handle timing and then remove the explosion from the linked list *automatically*.

Tip

The linked list that handles sprites in the game engine is a global class variable called sprites(). You can access this object anywhere in your program when it inherits from Game.

Here are the new events introduced in the sprite engine. These events are declared as abstract because the inheriting class must implement them. They do not contain any source code in the Game class, although Game does call them. This is what gives the sprite engine the ability to pass events on to the game while still handling all the real work behind the scenes.

```
void gameStartup()
void gameTimedUpdate()
void gameRefreshScreen()
void gameShutdown()
void gameKeyDown(int keyCode)
void gameKeyUp(int keyCode)
void gameMouseDown()
void gameMouseUp()
void gameMouseMove()
void spriteUpdate(AnimatedSprite sprite)
void spriteDraw(AnimatedSprite sprite)
void spriteDying(AnimatedSprite sprite)
void spriteCollision(AnimatedSprite spr1, AnimatedSprite spr2)
```

Know what's really great about these events? They describe *exactly* what you need to know in your game. What does spriteDying mean? This is called just before a sprite is removed from the linked list! What about spriteUpdate and spriteDraw? These two work hand in hand to give *your code* an opportunity to monitor a sprite as it is updated and drawn (both of them are handled for you). For instance, you use spriteDraw to draw the bounding box around a sprite if you turn on the bounding box display option (B key). The sprites are already drawn by the time spriteDraw is called. This just gives you notice that the sprite has been drawn, and you can do whatever you want with it. Likewise, when spriteUpdate is called, the sprite will have already moved (based on velocity). It's up to you to keep the sprite from going out of the screen bounds, or performing any other behavior you want.

The Game Class Source Code

Here is the complete source code listing for the Game class, which I have been describing to you thus far. Much of this code should be familiar to you because we've used it extensively in previous chapters. I will highlight in bold the *crucial code* that is not directly related to the applet. While perusing the source code for the Game class, pay close attention to all bold lines of code, and then take note of the rest of the code. This should help you to grasp exactly what this class does.

```
/****************************************************
* Applet Game Framework class
****************************************************/
import java.applet.*;
import java.awt.*;
import java.awt.event.*;
import java.awt.image.*;
import java.lang.System;
import java.util.*;

abstract class Game extends Applet implements Runnable, KeyListener,
    MouseListener, MouseMotionListener {

    //the main game loop thread
    private Thread gameloop;

    //internal list of sprites
    private LinkedList _sprites;
    public LinkedList sprites() { return _sprites; }

    //screen and double buffer related variables
    private BufferedImage backbuffer;
```

```java
private Graphics2D g2d;
private int screenWidth, screenHeight;

//keep track of mouse position and buttons
private Point2D mousePos = new Point2D(0,0);
private boolean mouseButtons[] = new boolean[4];

//frame rate counters and other timing variables
private int _frameCount = 0;
private int _frameRate = 0;
private int desiredRate;
private long startTime = System.currentTimeMillis();

//local applet object
public Applet applet() { return this; }

//game pause state
private boolean _gamePaused = false;
public boolean gamePaused() { return _gamePaused; }
public void pauseGame() { _gamePaused - true; }
public void resumeGame() { _gamePaused = false; }

//declare the game event methods that sub-class must implement
abstract void gameStartup();
abstract void gameTimedUpdate();
abstract void gameRefreshScreen();
abstract void gameShutdown();
abstract void gameKeyDown(int keyCode);
abstract void gameKeyUp(int keyCode);
abstract void gameMouseDown();
abstract void gameMouseUp();
abstract void gameMouseMove();
abstract void spriteUpdate(AnimatedSprite sprite);
abstract void spriteDraw(AnimatedSprite sprite);
abstract void spriteDying(AnimatedSprite sprite);
abstract void spriteCollision(AnimatedSprite spr1,AnimatedSprite spr2);

/*****************************************************
 * constructor
 *****************************************************/
```

```java
public Game(int frameRate, int width, int height) {
    desiredRate = frameRate;
    screenWidth = width;
    screenHeight = height;
}

//return g2d object so sub-class can draw things
public Graphics2D graphics() { return g2d; }

//current frame rate
public int frameRate() { return _frameRate; }

//mouse buttons and movement
public boolean mouseButton(int btn) { return mouseButtons[btn]; }
public Point2D mousePosition() { return mousePos; }

/*******************************************************
 * applet init event method
 *******************************************************/
public void init() {
    //create the back buffer and drawing surface
    backbuffer = new BufferedImage(screenWidth, screenHeight,
        BufferedImage.TYPE_INT_RGB);
    g2d = backbuffer.createGraphics();

    //create the internal sprite list
    _sprites = new LinkedList<AnimatedSprite>();

    //start the input listeners
    addKeyListener(this);
    addMouseListener(this);
    addMouseMotionListener(this);

    //this method implemented by sub-class
    gameStartup();
}

/*******************************************************
 * applet update event method
 *******************************************************/
```

```java
public void update(Graphics g) {
    //calculate frame rate
    _frameCount++;
    if (System.currentTimeMillis() > startTime + 1000) {
        startTime = System.currentTimeMillis();
        _frameRate = _frameCount;
        _frameCount = 0;

        //once every second all dead sprites are deleted
        purgeSprites();
    }
    //this method implemented by sub-class
    gameRefreshScreen();

    //draw the internal list of sprites
    if (!gamePaused()) {
        drawSprites();
    }

    //redraw the screen
    paint(g);
}

/*****************************************************
  * applet window paint event method
  *****************************************************/
public void paint(Graphics g) {
    g.drawImage(backbuffer, 0, 0, this);
}

/*****************************************************
  * thread start event - start the game loop running
  *****************************************************/
public void start() {
    gameloop = new Thread(this);
    gameloop.start();
}
/*****************************************************
  * thread run event (game loop)
  *****************************************************/
```

```java
public void run() {
    //acquire the current thread
    Thread t = Thread.currentThread();

    //process the main game loop thread
    while (t == gameloop) {
        try {
            //set a consistent frame rate
            Thread.sleep(1000 / desiredRate);
        }
        catch(InterruptedException e) {
            e.printStackTrace();
        }

        //update the internal list of sprites
        if (!gamePaused()) {
            updateSprites();
            testCollisions();
        }

        //allow main game to update if needed
        gameTimedUpdate();

        //refresh the screen
        repaint();
    }
}

/*****************************************************
 * thread stop event
 *****************************************************/
public void stop() {
    //kill the game loop
    gameloop = null;

    //this method implemented by sub-class
    gameShutdown();
}

/*****************************************************
 * key listener events
 *****************************************************/
```

```java
public void keyTyped(KeyEvent k) { }
public void keyPressed(KeyEvent k) {
    gameKeyDown(k.getKeyCode());
}
public void keyReleased(KeyEvent k) {
    gameKeyUp(k.getKeyCode());
}


/*****************************************************
 * checkButtons stores the state of the mouse buttons
 *****************************************************/
private void checkButtons(MouseEvent e) {
        switch(e.getButton()) {
        case MouseEvent.BUTTON1:
            mouseButtons[1] = true;
            mouseButtons[2] = false;
            mouseButtons[3] = false;
            break;
        case MouseEvent.BUTTON2:
            mouseButtons[1] = false;
            mouseButtons[2] = true;
            mouseButtons[3] = false;
            break;
        case MouseEvent.BUTTON3:
            mouseButtons[1] = false;
            mouseButtons[2] = false;
            mouseButtons[3] = true;
            break;
        }
}


/*****************************************************
 * mouse listener events
 *****************************************************/
public void mousePressed(MouseEvent e) {
    checkButtons(e);
    mousePos.setX(e.getX());
    mousePos.setY(e.getY());
    gameMouseDown();
}
```

```java
public void mouseReleased(MouseEvent e) {
    checkButtons(e);
    mousePos.setX(e.getX());
    mousePos.setY(e.getY());
    gameMouseUp();
}
public void mouseMoved(MouseEvent e) {
    checkButtons(e);
    mousePos.setX(e.getX());
    mousePos.setY(e.getY());
    gameMouseMove();
}
public void mouseDragged(MouseEvent e) {
    checkButtons(e);
    mousePos.setX(e.getX());
    mousePos.setY(e.getY());
    gameMouseDown();
    gameMouseMove();
}
public void mouseEntered(MouseEvent e) {
    mousePos.setX(e.getX());
    mousePos.setY(e.getY());
    gameMouseMove();
}
public void mouseExited(MouseEvent e) {
    mousePos.setX(e.getX());
    mousePos.setY(e.getY());
    gameMouseMove();
}
//this event is not needed
public void mouseClicked(MouseEvent e) { }

/******************************************************
 * X and Y velocity calculation functions
 ******************************************************/
protected double calcAngleMoveX(double angle) {
    return (double)(Math.cos(angle * Math.PI / 180));
}
protected double calcAngleMoveY(double angle) {
    return (double) (Math.sin(angle * Math.PI / 180));
}
```

```
/********************************************************
 * update the sprite list from the game loop thread
 ********************************************************/
protected void updateSprites() {
    for (int n=0; n < _sprites.size(); n++) {
        AnimatedSprite spr = (AnimatedSprite) _sprites.get(n);
        if (spr.alive()) {
            spr.updatePosition();
            spr.updateRotation();
            spr.updateAnimation();
            spriteUpdate(spr);
            spr.updateLifetime();
            if (!spr.alive()) {
                spriteDying(spr);
            }
        }
    }
}


/********************************************************
 * perform collision testing of all active sprites
 ********************************************************/
protected void testCollisions() {
  //iterate through the sprite list, test each sprite against
  //every other sprite in the list
  for (int first=0; first < _sprites.size(); first++) {

    //get the first sprite to test for collision
    AnimatedSprite spr1 = (AnimatedSprite) _sprites.get(first);
    if (spr1.alive()) {
        //look through all sprites again for collisions
        for (int second = 0; second < _sprites.size(); second++) {
          //make sure this isn't the same sprite
          if (first != second) {
              //get the second sprite to test for collision
              AnimatedSprite spr2 = (AnimatedSprite)
                  _sprites.get(second);
              if (spr2.alive()) {
                  if (spr2.collidesWith(spr1)) {
                      spriteCollision(spr1, spr2);
```

```
                                        break;
                                }
                                else
                                    spr1.setCollided(false);
                        }
                    }
                }
            }
        }
    }


    /******************************************************
     * draw all active sprites in the sprite list
     * sprites lower in the list are drawn on top
     ******************************************************/
    protected void drawSprites() {
        //draw sprites in reverse order (reverse priority)
        for (int n=0; n<_sprites.size(); n++) {
            AnimatedSprite spr = (AnimatedSprite) _sprites.get(n);
            if (spr.alive()) {
                spr.updateFrame();
                spr.transform();
                spr.draw();
                spriteDraw(spr); //notify player
            }
        }
    }


    /******************************************************
     * once every second during the frame update, this method
     * is called to remove all dead sprites from the linked list
     ******************************************************/
    private void purgeSprites() {
        for (int n=0; n < _sprites.size(); n++) {
            AnimatedSprite spr = (AnimatedSprite) _sprites.get(n);
            if (!spr.alive()) {
                _sprites.remove(n);
            }
        }
    }
}
```

ENHANCING GALACTIC WAR

You will be surprised to learn that the source code for Galactic War has remained about the same in length, even though the game is dramatically more complex with significant new gameplay features. It is truly only a few steps away from completion, and my goal in the next chapter will be to add more gameplay features (such as power-ups). Just play the game for a few seconds, and you'll immediately see a need for power-ups! This game is *hard*! If you can manage to keep from destroying some of the larger asteroids while working on the smaller ones, you might have a chance, but once you start letting bullets fly and asteroids begin to break into smaller pieces, you will have to be quick on the maneuvering to keep from becoming space dust (which I have just become—see Figure 14.2).

Exploring the New Galactic War Source Code

Rather than go over the source code solely from a functional point of view, I'm going to take you on a tour of the code along with screenshots of key aspects of

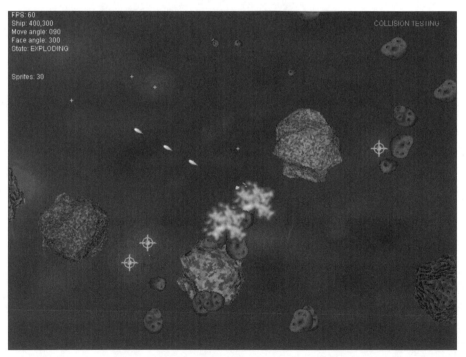

Figure 14.2
My ship has just been demolished by three medium-sized asteroids.

the game that are impacted by specific sections of the source code. For a game this complex, 630 or so lines of code is surprising (not counting the support classes). I have highlighted all key lines of code in bold text so they will stand out. If you pay close attention to the bold lines of code, the code listings should make more sense to you.

Let's get started with the opening credits for the game, where all the initial variables and objects are defined. The most significant thing about this code is the short class definition! The GalacticWar class just extends Game—and that's it! Beyond that, the initialization of the game's graphics is all done here. The images defined and loaded at the beginning are used whenever a new sprite needs to be added to the internal sprite list.

```java
/*****************************************************
 * GALACTIC WAR, Chapter 14
 *****************************************************/
import java.awt.*;
import java.util.*;
import java.lang.System;
import java.awt.event.*;

public class GalacticWar extends Game {
    //these must be static because they are passed to a constructor
    static int FRAMERATE = 60;
    static int SCREENWIDTH = 800;
    static int SCREENHEIGHT = 600;

    //misc global constants
    final int ASTEROIDS = 10;
    final int BULLET_SPEED = 4;
    final double ACCELERATION = 0.05;
    final double SHIPROTATION = 5.0;

    //sprite state values
    final int STATE_NORMAL = 0;
    final int STATE_COLLIDED = 1;
    final int STATE_EXPLODING = 2;

    //sprite types
    final int SPRITE_SHIP = 1;
```

```
final int SPRITE_ASTEROID_BIG = 10;
final int SPRITE_ASTEROID_MEDIUM = 11;
final int SPRITE_ASTEROID_SMALL = 12;
final int SPRITE_ASTEROID_TINY = 13;
final int SPRITE_BULLET = 100;
final int SPRITE_EXPLOSION = 200;

//various toggles
boolean showBounds = false;
boolean collisionTesting = true;

//define the images used in the game
ImageEntity background;
ImageEntity bulletImage;
ImageEntity[] bigAsteroids = new ImageEntity[5];
ImageEntity[] medAsteroids = new ImageEntity[2];
ImageEntity[] smlAsteroids = new ImageEntity[3];
ImageEntity[] tnyAsteroids = new ImageEntity[4];
ImageEntity[] explosions = new ImageEntity[2];
ImageEntity[] shipImage = new ImageEntity[2];

//create a random number generator
Random rand = new Random();

//used to make ship temporarily invulnerable
long collisionTimer = 0;

//some key input tracking variables
boolean keyLeft, keyRight, keyUp, keyFire, keyB, keyC;

/******************************************************
 * constructor
 ******************************************************/
public GalacticWar() {
    //call base Game class' constructor
    super(FRAMERATE, SCREENWIDTH, SCREENHEIGHT);
}

/******************************************************
  * gameStartup event passed by game engine
  ******************************************************/
```

```java
void gameStartup() {
    //load the background image
    background = new ImageEntity(this);
    background.load("bluespace.png");

    //create the ship sprite--first in the sprite list
    shipImage[0] = new ImageEntity(this);
    shipImage[0].load("spaceship.png");
    shipImage[1] = new ImageEntity(this);
    shipImage[1].load("ship_thrust.png");

    AnimatedSprite ship = new AnimatedSprite(this, graphics());
    ship.setSpriteType(SPRITE_SHIP);
    ship.setImage(shipImage[0].getImage());
    ship.setFrameWidth(ship.imageWidth());
    ship.setFrameHeight(ship.imageHeight());
    ship.setPosition(new Point2D(SCREENWIDTH/2, SCREENHEIGHT/2));
    ship.setAlive(true);
    ship.setState(STATE_NORMAL);
    sprites().add(ship);

    //load the bullet sprite image
    bulletImage = new ImageEntity(this);
    bulletImage.load("plasmashot.png");

    //load the explosion sprite image
    explosions[0] = new ImageEntity(this);
    explosions[0].load("explosion.png");
    explosions[1] = new ImageEntity(this);
    explosions[1].load("explosion2.png");

    //load the big asteroid images (5 total)
    for (int n = 0; n<5; n++) {
        bigAsteroids[n] = new ImageEntity(this);
        String fn = "asteroid" + (n+1) + ".png";
        bigAsteroids[n].load(fn);
    }
    //load the medium asteroid images (2 total)
    for (int n = 0; n<2; n++) {
        medAsteroids[n] = new ImageEntity(this);
        String fn = "medium" + (n+1) + ".png";
```

```
                medAsteroids[n].load(fn);
            }
            //load the small asteroid images (3 total)
            for (int n = 0; n<3; n++) {
                smlAsteroids[n] = new ImageEntity(this);
                String fn = "small" + (n+1) + ".png";
                smlAsteroids[n].load(fn);
            }
            //load the tiny asteroid images (4 total)
            for (int n = 0; n<4; n++) {
                tnyAsteroids[n] = new ImageEntity(this);
                String fn = "tiny" + (n+1) + ".png";
                tnyAsteroids[n].load(fn);
            }

            //create the random asteroid sprites
            for (int n = 0; n<ASTEROIDS; n++) {
                createAsteroid();
            }
        }
```

Game Loop Update and Screen Refresh

Now let's take a look at some key events passed here from the Game class. Remember, these methods were defined as *abstract* in Game so that they would be implemented here in the derived source code file. The gameTimedUpdate() method is called from within the timed game loop thread. The gameRefreshScreen() method is called from the applet update() event. I'm not currently using gameShutdown(), but it is available if you need to clean house before the program ends.

Now let's take a look at Figure 14.3, which shows the game fairly early on in the run. The same toggles are still available in the game, including collision testing and bounding box display. There are four stages to destroying an asteroid:

■ Large, detailed asteroids

■ Medium asteroid chunks

■ Small asteroid pieces

■ Tiny asteroids

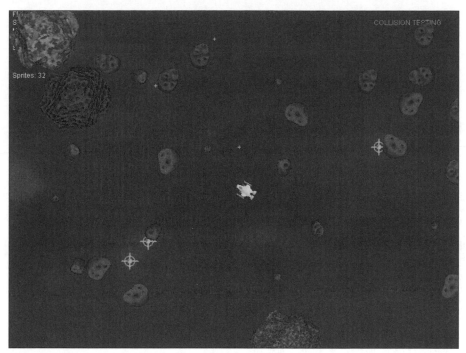

Figure 14.3
The large asteroids break up into smaller ones, either when they hit your ship or when you fire a plasma bolt.

Don't let the tiny asteroids fool you—they will still damage your ship, and they can be destroyed by your guns. Speaking of damage, the game would be more fun if the ship's health were displayed somewhere on the screen—a good feature to add in the next chapter.

```
/******************************************************
 * gameTimedUpdate event passed by game engine
 ******************************************************/
void gameTimedUpdate() {
    checkInput();
}


/******************************************************
 * gameRefreshScreen event passed by game engine
 ******************************************************/
```

```java
void gameRefreshScreen() {
    Graphics2D g2d = graphics();

    //the ship is always the first sprite in the linked list
    AnimatedSprite ship = (AnimatedSprite)sprites().get(0);

    //draw the background
    g2d.drawImage(background.getImage(),0,0,SCREENWIDTH-1,
        SCREENHEIGHT-1,this);

    //print status information on the screen
    g2d.setColor(Color.WHITE);
    g2d.drawString("FPS: " + frameRate(), 5, 10);
    long x = Math.round(ship.position().X());
    long y = Math.round(ship.position().Y());
    g2d.drawString("Ship: " + x + "," + y , 5, 25);
    g2d.drawString("Move angle: " +
        Math.round(ship.moveAngle())+90, 5, 40);
    g2d.drawString("Face angle: " +
        Math.round(ship.faceAngle()), 5, 55);
    if (ship.state()==STATE_NORMAL)
        g2d.drawString("State: NORMAL", 5, 70);
    else if (ship.state()==STATE_COLLIDED)
        g2d.drawString("State: COLLIDED", 5, 70);
    else if (ship.state()==STATE_EXPLODING)
        g2d.drawString("State: EXPLODING", 5, 70);

    //display the number of sprites currently in use
    g2d.drawString("Sprites: " + sprites().size(), 5, 120);

    if (showBounds) {
        g2d.setColor(Color.GREEN);
        g2d.drawString("BOUNDING BOXES", SCREENWIDTH-150, 10);
    }
    if (collisionTesting) {
        g2d.setColor(Color.GREEN);
        g2d.drawString("COLLISION TESTING", SCREENWIDTH-150, 25);
    }
}
```

```
/*****************************************************
 * gameShutdown event passed by game engine
 *****************************************************/
void gameShutdown() {
    //oh well, let the garbage collector have at it..
}
```

Updating and Drawing Sprites

Next, let's take a look at the `spriteUpdate()` and `spriteDraw()` events, which are passed on by the Game class. The `spriteDying()` event is also available here, but it's not currently being used in the game. You would use this event to keep a sprite alive if you wanted to keep it around by setting `alive` back to true.

The game engine processes all of the sprites in the linked list automatically (by the game loop thread). After each sprite is updated, control is sent to `spriteUpdate()` to give you a chance to fool around with the sprite if you need to. (It is passed as a parameter.) You can make any changes you want to the sprite, and those changes will be stored back in the linked list because you are working with an object reference—the actual object in the linked list, not just a copy.

This is truly where the sprite engine shows its power. You can fire as many weapons as you want, and they will strike an unknown number of sprites, which will each blow up in an animated explosion—and the linked list keeps track of all these details for you. All we really have to do is put together a new scratch sprite, give it an image from one of our global images, and then pop it off to the sprite list. This sprite will then automatically move around on the screen, rotate (if rotation is set), and animate (if frames exist). This new sprite will also be included in collision testing. The engine allows you to determine whether a collision "sticks" by giving you control at the key point where a collision has occurred, passing both sprites to your implementation of the `spriteCollision()` event.

When I was first developing the engine, I thought it would be too limiting to move all of the sprites into the list. I kept the ship outside the list for a while, and then realized that to truly make the internal sprite handler work the way it is supposed to, you really need to give it all of the sprites it needs to update, draw, and test for collision. When you get tired of a sprite, just set its `alive` property to false, and then the game engine will remove it from the list a few seconds later! Furthermore, as you learned in the previous chapter, you can make use of the

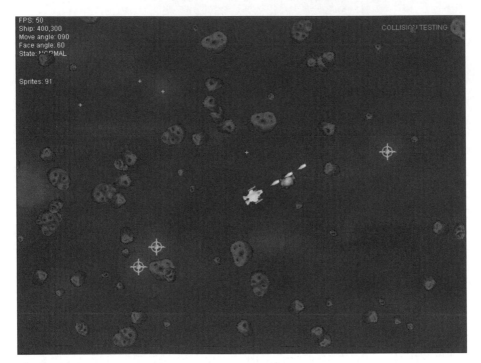

Figure 14.4
The ship is overwhelmed by asteroids and in need of some weapon upgrades!

features in AnimatedSprite for limiting the lifetime of a sprite. By setting the lifespan of a sprite, you can have it automatically terminate after a certain number of passes through the game loop. For instance, the "flaming plasma" projectiles fired from the ship are given a lifetime of 200 loops. The engine detects when the age is beyond the lifespan threshold, and then kills the sprite automatically!

Figure 14.4 shows the game after all of the large asteroids have been broken down into smaller ones. The game is truly crazy at this point, with close to a hundred small asteroids floating around your ship on various random trajectories! It's hard enough just to spin and shoot frantically, let alone move around. I even had to cheat to keep from getting blown up repeatedly! (I'll share the cheat with you at our next stop in this trip through the source code.)

```
/*****************************************************
 * spriteUpdate event passed by game engine
 *****************************************************/
```

```
public void spriteUpdate(AnimatedSprite sprite) {
    switch(sprite.spriteType()) {
    case SPRITE_SHIP:
        warp(sprite);
        break;

    case SPRITE_BULLET:
        warp(sprite);
        break;

    case SPRITE_EXPLOSION:
        if (sprite.currentFrame() == sprite.totalFrames()-1) {
            sprite.setAlive(false);
        }
        break;

    case SPRITE_ASTEROID_BIG:
    case SPRITE_ASTEROID_MEDIUM:
    case SPRITE_ASTEROID_SMALL:
    case SPRITE_ASTEROID_TINY:
        warp(sprite);
        break;
    }
}

/*******************************************************
 * spriteDraw event passed by game engine
 * called by the game class after each sprite is drawn
 * to give you a chance to manipulate the sprite
 *******************************************************/
public void spriteDraw(AnimatedSprite sprite) {
    if (showBounds) {
        if (sprite.collided())
            sprite.drawBounds(Color.RED);
        else
            sprite.drawBounds(Color.BLUE);
    }
}

/*******************************************************
 * spriteDying event passed by game engine
 * called after a sprite's age reaches its lifespan
```

```
 * at which point it will be killed off, and then removed from
 * the linked list. you can cancel the purging process here.
 ****************************************************/
public void spriteDying(AnimatedSprite sprite) {
    //currently no need to revive any sprites
}
```

Handling Sprite Collisions

The most important event in the game is probably the spriteCollision() event, which is passed from the engine to your source code automatically. The engine goes through the list of active sprites (where the alive property is true) and tests each one for collision with all the other sprites in the list (except for the same one—we don't want to have objects blow themselves up for no reason!).

Take a look at Figure 14.5, which shows the ship firing several volleys of flaming plasma bolts toward asteroids. There are several bolts traveling away from the

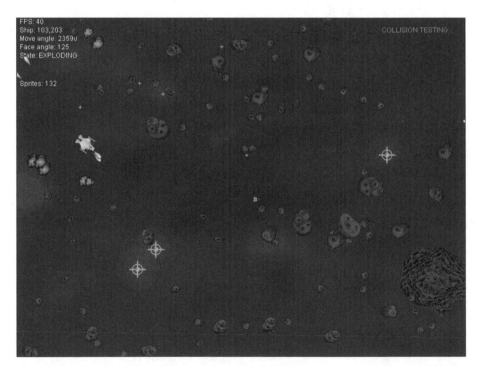

Figure 14.5
Projectiles fired from the ship eventually get passed through the spriteCollision() event when they collide with asteroids.

ship at various angles and several explosions that are animating on the screen. Figure 14.5 shows sprite collision testing in progress. The engine, as implemented in the Game class and inherited by GalacticWar, goes through the sprites and tests them all for collision—but that's all it does. Look at the sprite counter in this figure—132 sprites! This number includes the ship, bullets, asteroids, and explosions, and the number rises and falls dynamically with the gameplay. (The engine clears out unused sprites that have "died" once every second when the frame rate is calculated.)

There is no more logic going on behind the scenes than the test for collision itself. The engine simply passes both sprites that have interacted to the sprite Collision() method. At this point, it's entirely up to you to decide what to do with the conflicting sprites. You can destroy them, have them bounce away from each other, or anything else. So all you have to do is figure out what kinds of sprites have been passed to you through the spriteCollision() event. You can do this with your own predefined constants (defined as a static int in Java). For example, I have defined SPRITE_EXPLOSION for all explosions. Yes, explosion sprites are tested for collision like everything else—but we simply ignore them, let them play out, and then disappear. The value of each constant is not important, as long as each one is different. Since I defined each of the four types of asteroids with a separate constant, I had to write a helper method called isAsteroid() to handle them all in the same way when they are passed through the event handlers.

Now, how about that cheat I promised? When I get into a tough spot in the game, I hold down the left or right arrow key to spin while hitting *both* fire buttons (the Ctrl keys). This launches twice as many volleys of plasma bolts, as Figure 14.6 shows.

```
/****************************************************
 * spriteCollision event passed by game engine
 ****************************************************/
public void spriteCollision(AnimatedSprite spr1,AnimatedSprite spr2) {
    //jump out quickly if collisions are off
    if (!collisionTesting) return;

    //figure out what type of sprite has collided
    switch(spr1.spriteType()) {
```

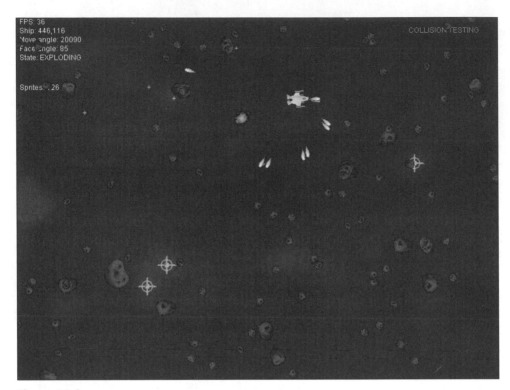

Figure 14.6
You can launch twice as many bolts using *both* Ctrl keys!

```
case SPRITE_BULLET:
    //did bullet hit an asteroid?
    if (isAsteroid(spr2.spriteType())) {
        spr1.setAlive(false);
        spr2.setAlive(false);
        breakAsteroid(spr2);
    }
    break;
case SPRITE_SHIP:
    //did asteroid crash into the ship?
    if (isAsteroid(spr2.spriteType())) {
        if (spr1.state() == STATE_NORMAL) {
            collisionTimer = System.currentTimeMillis();
            spr1.setVelocity(new Point2D(0, 0));
            double x = spr1.position().X() - 10;
            double y = spr1.position().Y() - 10;
```

```
                    startBigExplosion(new Point2D(x, y));
                    spr1.setState(STATE_EXPLODING);
                    spr2.setAlive(false);
                    breakAsteroid(spr2);
                }
                //make ship temporarily invulnerable
                else if (spr1.state() == STATE_EXPLODING) {
                    if (collisionTimer + 3000 <
                        System.currentTimeMillis()) {
                        spr1.setState(STATE_NORMAL);
                    }
                }
            }
            break;
        }
    }
```

Keyboard and Mouse Events

The keyboard and mouse handlers are not always used, but you must still implement them in your program. You might wonder, then, how is this any better than just using the listeners directly in the game's source code file? That's a good question! Basically, we want to homogenize the events as much as possible. Note that the keyboard events pass nothing but the key scan code, and the mouse events pass nothing at all—you must access the mouse information through the mousePos and mouseButtons variables (with their associated accessor methods). Simply knowing about a keyboard or mouse event is enough; we don't need all of the extra information that Java sends the program.

```
/*****************************************************
 * gameKeyDown event passed by game engine
 *****************************************************/
public void gameKeyDown(int keyCode) {
    switch(keyCode) {
    case KeyEvent.VK_LEFT:
        keyLeft = true;
        break;
    case KeyEvent.VK_RIGHT:
        keyRight = true;
        break;
```

```java
        case KeyEvent.VK_UP:
            keyUp = true;
            break;
        case KeyEvent.VK_CONTROL:
            keyFire = true;
            break;
        case KeyEvent.VK_B:
            //toggle bounding rectangles
            showBounds = !showBounds;
            break;
        case KeyEvent.VK_C:
            //toggle collision testing
            collisionTesting = !collisionTesting;
            break;
        }
    }

    /*******************************************************
     * gameKeyUp event passed by game engine
     *******************************************************/
    public void gameKeyUp(int keyCode) {
        switch(keyCode) {
        case KeyEvent.VK_LEFT:
            keyLeft = false;
            break;
        case KeyEvent.VK_RIGHT:
            keyRight = false;
            break;
        case KeyEvent.VK_UP:
            keyUp = false;
            break;
        case KeyEvent.VK_CONTROL:
            keyFire = false;
            fireBullet();
            break;
        }
    }

    /*******************************************************
     * mouse events passed by game engine
```

```
 * the game is not currently using mouse input
 *****************************************************/
public void gameMouseDown() { }
public void gameMouseUp() { }
public void gameMouseMove() { }
```

Asteroid Manipulation Methods

The asteroids are the most complicated part of Galactic War. First of all, there are *four types* of asteroids in the game, each with several different images available (which are chosen randomly when a new asteroid is created). I have written several methods for working with asteroids, mainly called from the collision events that occur. The larger asteroids are destroyed and replaced by smaller asteroids, while an explosion is animated over the old asteroid.

Figure 14.7 shows the game with bounding boxes turned on so you can see the dimensions of each sprite in the game. Note how even the explosions have a

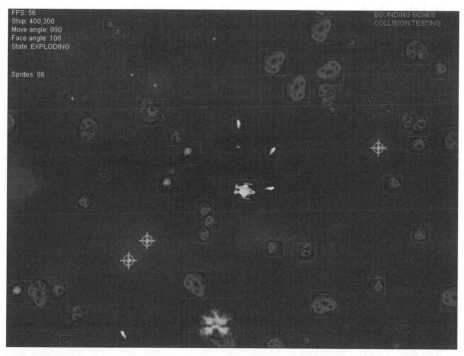

Figure 14.7
The bounding boxes and collision testing can still be toggled on or off in the game.

bounding box—they are included in collision testing as well, even though the game ignores them. All of the original asteroids have been destroyed and replaced with increasingly smaller ones. If you want to grab some power-ups (something that will be added in the next chapter), you will have to be careful not to destroy all of the larger asteroids—the smaller ones are next to impossible to get around, and your ship will get hosed by them in short order if you let the guns go carelessly. As a result of this gameplay factor, this game involves some strategy.

This section of code marks the end of the game engine events. From this point forward, all of the methods are custom programmed and provide the real gameplay in Galactic War.

```
/****************************************************
 * break up an asteroid into smaller pieces
 ****************************************************/
private void breakAsteroid(AnimatedSprite sprite) {
    switch(sprite.spriteType()) {
    case SPRITE_ASTEROID_BIG:
        //spawn medium asteroids over the old one
        spawnAsteroid(sprite);
        spawnAsteroid(sprite);
        spawnAsteroid(sprite);
        //draw big explosion
        startBigExplosion(sprite.position());
        break;
    case SPRITE_ASTEROID_MEDIUM:
        //spawn small asteroids over the old one
        spawnAsteroid(sprite);
        spawnAsteroid(sprite);
        spawnAsteroid(sprite);
        //draw small explosion
        startSmallExplosion(sprite.position());
        break;
    case SPRITE_ASTEROID_SMALL:
        //spawn tiny asteroids over the old one
        spawnAsteroid(sprite);
        spawnAsteroid(sprite);
        spawnAsteroid(sprite);
        //draw small explosion
```

```
            startSmallExplosion(sprite.position());
            break;
        case SPRITE_ASTEROID_TINY:
            //spawn a random powerup
            spawnPowerup(sprite);
            //draw small explosion
            startSmallExplosion(sprite.position());
            break;
    }
}


/******************************************************
 * spawn a smaller asteroid based on passed sprite
 ******************************************************/
private void spawnAsteroid(AnimatedSprite sprite) {
    //create a new asteroid sprite
    AnimatedSprite ast = new AnimatedSprite(this, graphics());
    ast.setAlive(true);

    //set pseudo-random position around source sprite
    int w = sprite.getBounds().width;
    int h = sprite.getBounds().height;
    double x = sprite.position().X() + w/2 + rand.nextInt(20)-40;
    double y = sprite.position().Y() + h/2 + rand.nextInt(20)-40;
    ast.setPosition(new Point2D(x,y));

    //set rotation and direction angles
    ast.setFaceAngle(rand.nextInt(360));
    ast.setMoveAngle(rand.nextInt(360));
    ast.setRotationRate(rand.nextDouble());

    //set velocity based on movement direction
    double ang = ast.moveAngle() - 90;
    double velx = calcAngleMoveX(ang);
    double vely = calcAngleMoveY(ang);
    ast.setVelocity(new Point2D(velx, vely));

    //set some size-specific properties
    switch(sprite.spriteType()) {
    case SPRITE_ASTEROID_BIG:
```

```
            ast.setSpriteType(SPRITE_ASTEROID_MEDIUM);

            //pick one of the random asteroid images
            int i = rand.nextInt(2);
            ast.setImage(medAsteroids[i].getImage());
            ast.setFrameWidth(medAsteroids[i].width());
            ast.setFrameHeight(medAsteroids[i].height());

            break;
        case SPRITE_ASTEROID_MEDIUM:
            ast.setSpriteType(SPRITE_ASTEROID_SMALL);

            //pick one of the random asteroid images
            i = rand.nextInt(3);
            ast.setImage(smlAsteroids[i].getImage());
            ast.setFrameWidth(smlAsteroids[i].width());
            ast.setFrameHeight(smlAsteroids[i].height());
            break;

        case SPRITE_ASTEROID_SMALL:
            ast.setSpriteType(SPRITE_ASTEROID_TINY);

            //pick one of the random asteroid images
            i = rand.nextInt(4);
            ast.setImage(tnyAsteroids[i].getImage());
            ast.setFrameWidth(tnyAsteroids[i].width());
            ast.setFrameHeight(tnyAsteroids[i].height());
            break;
    }

    //add the new asteroid to the sprite list
    sprites().add(ast);
}


/*****************************************************
 * create a random powerup at the supplied sprite location
 * (this will be implemented in the next chapter)
 *****************************************************/
private void spawnPowerup(AnimatedSprite sprite) {
}
```

```
/******************************************************
 * create a random "big" asteroid
 ******************************************************/
public void createAsteroid() {
    //create a new asteroid sprite
    AnimatedSprite ast = new AnimatedSprite(this, graphics());
    ast.setAlive(true);
    ast.setSpriteType(SPRITE_ASTEROID_BIG);

    //pick one of the random asteroid images
    int i = rand.nextInt(5);
    ast.setImage(bigAsteroids[i].getImage());
    ast.setFrameWidth(bigAsteroids[i].width());
    ast.setFrameHeight(bigAsteroids[i].height());

    //set to a random position on the screen
    int x = rand.nextInt(SCREENWIDTH-128);
    int y = rand.nextInt(SCREENHEIGHT-128);
    ast.setPosition(new Point2D(x, y));

    //set rotation and direction angles
    ast.setFaceAngle(rand.nextInt(360));
    ast.setMoveAngle(rand.nextInt(360));
    ast.setRotationRate(rand.nextDouble());

    //set velocity based on movement direction
    double ang = ast.moveAngle() - 90;
    double velx = calcAngleMoveX(ang);
    double vely = calcAngleMoveY(ang);
    ast.setVelocity(new Point2D(velx, vely));

    //add the new asteroid to the sprite list
    sprites().add(ast);
}


/******************************************************
 * returns true if passed sprite type is an asteroid type
 ******************************************************/
private boolean isAsteroid(int spriteType) {
    switch(spriteType) {
```

```
        case SPRITE_ASTEROID_BIG:
        case SPRITE_ASTEROID_MEDIUM:
        case SPRITE_ASTEROID_SMALL:
        case SPRITE_ASTEROID_TINY:
            return true;
        default:
            return false;
        }
    }
```

Handling Multiple Key Presses

I spent a lot of time trying to incorporate a multiple key-press system into the
game engine itself, but this proved to be too troublesome. As a result, the main
game keeps track of key presses and releases using global boolean variables.
Since only a handful of keys are ever used in an arcade-style game like this, a
more complex form of key handler is not necessary. As it is implemented here,
the engine calls a few events and passes the key code when a key is pressed or
released so that you don't have to bother decoding the KeyEvent, MouseEvent, or
MouseMotionEvent class.

```
/***************************************************
 * process keys that have been pressed
 ***************************************************/
public void checkInput() {
    //the ship is always the first sprite in the linked list
    AnimatedSprite ship = (AnimatedSprite)sprites().get(0);
    if (keyLeft) {
        //left arrow rotates ship left 5 degrees
        ship.setFaceAngle(ship.faceAngle() - SHIPROTATION);
        if (ship.faceAngle() < 0)
            ship.setFaceAngle(360 - SHIPROTATION);
    }
    else if (keyRight) {
        //right arrow rotates ship right 5 degrees
        ship.setFaceAngle(ship.faceAngle() + SHIPROTATION);
        if (ship.faceAngle() > 360)
            ship.setFaceAngle(SHIPROTATION);
    }
```

```
if (keyUp) {
    //up arrow applies thrust to ship
    ship.setImage(shipImage[1].getImage());
    applyThrust();
}
else
    //set ship image to normal non-thrust image
    ship.setImage(shipImage[0].getImage());
}
```

Moving the Spaceship

The spaceship in Galactic War is rotated using the left and right arrow keys, and thrust is applied by pressing the up arrow key. The applyThrust() method handles the acceleration of the ship while keeping the ship within a reasonable velocity threshold.

```
/*****************************************************
 * increase the thrust of the ship based on facing angle
 *****************************************************/
public void applyThrust() {
    //the ship is always the first sprite in the linked list
    AnimatedSprite ship = (AnimatedSprite)sprites().get(0);

    //up arrow adds thrust to ship (1/10 normal speed)
    ship.setMoveAngle(ship.faceAngle() - 90);

    //calculate the X and Y velocity based on angle
    double velx = ship.velocity().X();
    velx += calcAngleMoveX(ship.moveAngle()) * ACCELERATION;
    if (velx < -10) velx = -10;
    else if (velx > 10) velx = 10;
    double vely = ship.velocity().Y();
    vely += calcAngleMoveY(ship.moveAngle()) * ACCELERATION;
    if (vely < -10) vely = -10;
    else if (vely > 10) vely = 10;
    ship.setVelocity(new Point2D(velx, vely));
}
```

Firing Weapons

The most significant area of improvement for the game is in the weaponry department, so some time will be spent in the next chapter adding power-ups to the game. You will be able to grab power-up icons that are dropped by exploding asteroids, which will then enhance the ship in various ways. The current version of the game here has not changed from the previous chapter, except that it now functions with the game engine. The Ctrl key is used to fire weapons, but you can change this to another key if you want by examining the key handlers.

```java
/*****************************************************
 * fire a bullet from the ship's position and orientation
 *****************************************************/
public void fireBullet() {
    //the ship is always the first sprite in the linked list
    AnimatedSprite ship = (AnimatedSprite)sprites().get(0);

    //create the new bullet sprite
    AnimatedSprite bullet = new AnimatedSprite(this,graphics());
    bullet.setImage(bulletImage.getImage());
    bullet.setFrameWidth(bulletImage.width());
    bullet.setFrameHeight(bulletImage.height());
    bullet.setSpriteType(SPRITE_BULLET);
    bullet.setAlive(true);
    bullet.setLifespan(200);
    bullet.setFaceAngle(ship.faceAngle());
    bullet.setMoveAngle(ship.faceAngle() - 90);

    //set the bullet's starting position
    double x = ship.center().X() - bullet.imageWidth()/2;
    double y = ship.center().Y() - bullet.imageHeight()/2;
    bullet.setPosition(new Point2D(x,y));

    //set the bullet's velocity
    double angle = bullet.moveAngle();
    double svx = calcAngleMoveX(angle) * BULLET_SPEED;
    double svy = calcAngleMoveY(angle) * BULLET_SPEED;
    bullet.setVelocity(new Point2D(svx, svy));

    //add bullet to the sprite list
    sprites().add(bullet);
}
```

Give Me Something to Blow Up!

There are two main methods for starting explosions. I could have come up with a craftier way to do this, but I decided to just write two similar methods: one for initiating large explosions and another for smaller explosions. They use images stored in the explosions array (of ImageEntity objects). There are currently only two explosion animations. The large explosion is used when you hit a large asteroid. The small explosion is drawn when you hit smaller asteroids. I think the result looks pretty good.

Because there are *a lot* of small asteroids and bullets flying every which way, you don't want too complex of an explosion sucking up the game's resources when there could be a couple dozen such explosions animating at a time. Check out Figure 14.8. The large explosion's frames are 96 × 96 pixels in size and there are 16 frames; the small explosion has 8 frames, and each one is only 40 × 40 pixels in size. The big explosion is used for the ship and large asteroids. This should be used sparingly because it is such a large image.

```
/*****************************************************
 * launch a big explosion at the passed location
 *****************************************************/
public void startBigExplosion(Point2D point) {
    //create a new explosion at the passed location
    AnimatedSprite expl = new AnimatedSprite(this,graphics());
    expl.setSpriteType(SPRITE_EXPLOSION);
    expl.setAlive(true);
    expl.setAnimImage(explosions[0].getImage());
```

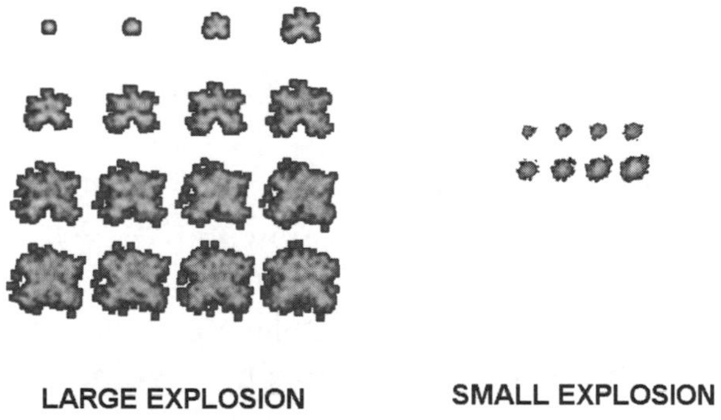

LARGE EXPLOSION   **SMALL EXPLOSION**

Figure 14.8
The two explosion animations compared side by side.

```
        expl.setTotalFrames(16);
        expl.setColumns(4);
        expl.setFrameWidth(96);
        expl.setFrameHeight(96);
        expl.setFrameDelay(2);
        expl.setPosition(point);

        //add the new explosion to the sprite list
        sprites().add(expl);
    }


    /*****************************************************
     * launch a small explosion at the passed location
     *****************************************************/
    public void startSmallExplosion(Point2D point) {
        //create a new explosion at the passed location
        AnimatedSprite expl = new AnimatedSprite(this,graphics());
        expl.setSpriteType(SPRITE_EXPLOSION);
        expl.setAlive(true);
        expl.setAnimImage(explosions[1].getImage());
        expl.setTotalFrames(8);
        expl.setColumns(4);
        expl.setFrameWidth(40);
        expl.setFrameHeight(40);
        expl.setFrameDelay(2);
        expl.setPosition(point);

        //add the new explosion to the sprite list
        sprites().add(expl);
    }
```

Additional Game Logic

The last method in the game is called warp(), and it has the duty of making sprites wrap around the edges of the screen (right, left, top, and bottom). This is kind of a strange occurrence if you think about it, but a lot of games use this technique. The idea is that this makes an otherwise small playing field appear larger because objects can just travel through *ether-space* behind the monitor and magically reappear on the other side, otherwise unscathed. It helps to contain the gameplay when a scrolling game world is not a goal for the game.

```
/*****************************************************
 * cause sprite to warp around the edges of the screen
 *****************************************************/
public void warp(AnimatedSprite spr) {
    //create some shortcut variables
    int w = spr.frameWidth()-1;
    int h = spr.frameHeight()-1;

    //wrap the sprite around the screen edges
    if (spr.position().X() < 0-w)
        spr.position().setX(SCREENWIDTH);
    else if (spr.position().X() > SCREENWIDTH)
        spr.position().setX(0-w);
    if (spr.position().Y() < 0-h)
        spr.position().setY(SCREENHEIGHT);
    else if (spr.position().Y() > SCREENHEIGHT)
        spr.position().setY(0-h);
}
}
```

WHAT YOU HAVE LEARNED

This was a code-heavy chapter that involved significant changes to the coding model we've been following in each chapter up to this point. Now that Galactic War is event-driven and makes use of a sprite engine, the game has many more upgrade possibilities than it might have had before (where each new sprite had to be implemented from scratch). Here are the key topics you learned:

■ How to create an event-driven game engine

■ How to use the new Game class

■ How to handle all sprites uniformly, regardless of type

■ How to adapt Galactic War to an event-driven game

REVIEW QUESTIONS

The following questions will help you to determine how well you have learned the subjects discussed in this chapter. The answers are provided in Appendix A, "Chapter Quiz Answers."

1. What is the name of the new game engine class developed in this chapter?

2. How many sprites can the new engine handle on the screen simultaneously?

3. Which of the four key classes in the game engine handles image loading?

4. How many different asteroid sizes does the game use?

5. True or False: Collisions are handled inside the game engine.

6. What type of object is `animImage`, a private variable in `AnimatedSprite`?

7. Which class is responsible for rendering a single frame of an animation in `AnimatedSprite`?

8. What is the maximum velocity value for the player's spaceship?

9. Which class does the game/sprite engine pass in some of its events?

10. What is the name of the support method in `AnimatedSprite` that returns a properly formed URL for a file to be loaded?

On Your Own

The following exercise will help you to see how well you have integrated the new material in this chapter with your existing knowledge of Java game programming.

There are currently two methods used to start an explosion—a custom method for large explosions and another one for small explosions. These methods do the same thing, but they use a few different properties. How could you revise one of them to handle both cases for a large or small explosion with a single method?

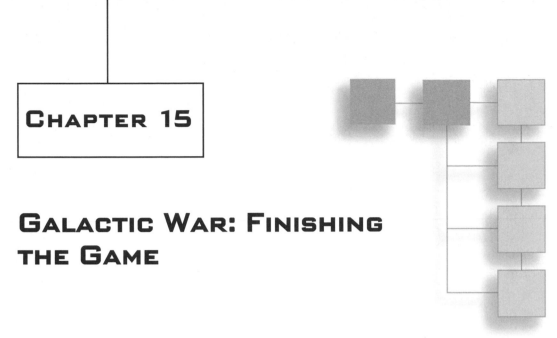

CHAPTER 15

GALACTIC WAR: FINISHING THE GAME

The things you have learned in this book all culminate in this last chapter involving Galactic War. The game will be enhanced, polished, and ready for a production environment at the end of this chapter. All that will remain to do is to package up the entire game, resources and all, into a JAR file for distribution on the web (which is covered in the next and final chapter of the book).

Here are the key topics of interest in this chapter:

- Adding power-ups to the game
- Implementing a global game state with a start and end screen
- Polishing the game and preparing it for production

LET'S TALK ABOUT POWER-UPS

Let's face it; Galactic War is a difficult game. It's nearly impossible to clear the asteroids with the weapon we've been using up to this point—a single peashooter, for the most part. I want to totally enhance the game in this chapter and make it ready for primetime—for distribution on the web. To meet that lofty goal, there are quite a few things to cover in this chapter. I'll itemize what I'd like to accomplish:

- Add power-ups to upgrade the ship's weapons system

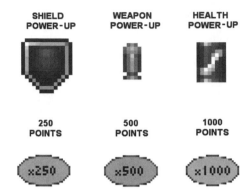

Figure 15.1
Galactic War has six different power-ups that enhance the ship and increase your score.

- Add power-ups to restore health and shields
- Add power-ups to gain extra score points

Figure 15.1 shows the six power-ups that will be added to the game in this chapter.

Tip

The finished version of the game can be played online at www.jharbour.com/BeginningJava. You need to have the Java Runtime Environment for SE 6 Update 22 installed (the same as required for all of the book's examples).

Ship and Bonus-Point Power-Ups

There are three different power-ups that simply increase your score for 250, 500, and 1,000 points. These power-ups are released randomly when you destroy a tiny asteroid—the last stage of the asteroid's deterioration after the large, medium, and small stages.

The shield power-up will increase your shield strength by 1/4 (not the full refill that you were expecting?). Likewise, the cola can increases your ship's health by 1/4, up to the maximum value displayed in the health bar at the top of the screen. Figure 15.2 shows the three states the ship can take on during gameplay.

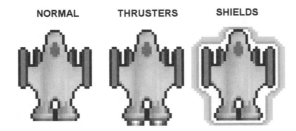

Figure 15.2
There are now three modes for the ship: normal, thrusters, and shields.

Wait, the ship doesn't have any shields! Oh, right; that's a feature we'll add to the game in this chapter as well.

Weapon Upgrades

The weapon upgrade power-up is by far the most interesting new feature of the game, and it is very welcome given how difficult it is to stay alive in this game! You can earn up to five levels of weapon upgrades in this game. I had my son, Jeremiah, help me design the weapon patterns for each upgrade, and the result is shown in Figure 15.3.

The upgrades were implemented a little differently than our design here, but the result is unmistakable. The biggest difference is upgrade level five: Rather than firing side to side, the two additional shots go upward at a slight angle. I made this adjustment while playing the game when it seemed to be more effective than

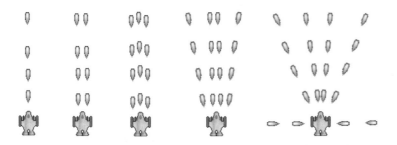

Figure 15.3
The five levels of weapon upgrades for your ship.

firing them at 90-degree angles. Let's take a tour of the five weapon upgrades as they were implemented in the game.

Standard Weapon

The standard weapon is shown being fired in Figure 15.4. Note the single bullet icon in the upper-right corner of the screen, showing the current weapon upgrade level.

Weapon Level Two

The first weapon upgrade allows the ship to fire two shots at the same time, as shown in Figure 15.5. There are now two bullet icons at the upper-right. After play testing the game for a while, I decided to make this the starting weapon level. You can still lose this by getting hit and then drop down to the standard weapon if you aren't careful.

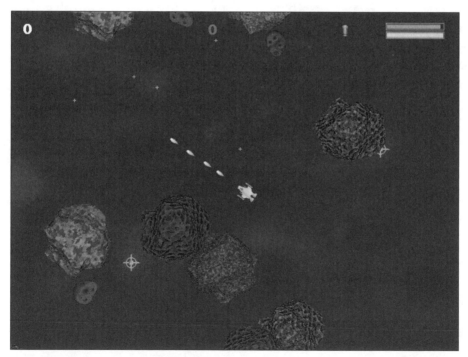

Figure 15.4
The standard weapon is a single bullet.

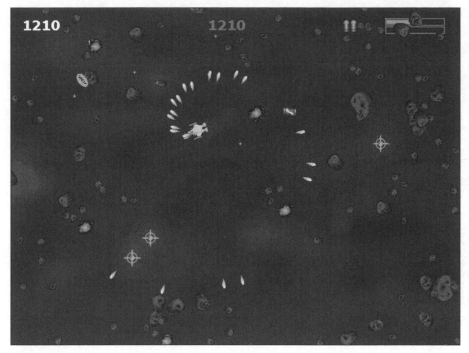

Figure 15.5
Two bullets definitely do a lot more damage!

Weapon Level Three

Weapon upgrade level three allows the ship to fire three shots at the same time, as shown in Figure 15.6. There are now three bullet icons at the upper-right.

Weapon Level Four

The fourth weapon upgrade gives you four shots at a time, spreading out at slightly wider angles than the previous level, capable of meting out massive damage to the horde of asteroids, as shown in Figure 15.7.

Weapon Level Five

Heavy gunner! Weapon level five is truly staggering, delivering massive amounts of firepower to the ship. Take care, though—if you get hit, your ship is taken down a notch to level four again. The angles of spread at level five are slightly wider than level four, and two additional shots fire out roughly sideways from the ship (see Figure 15.8).

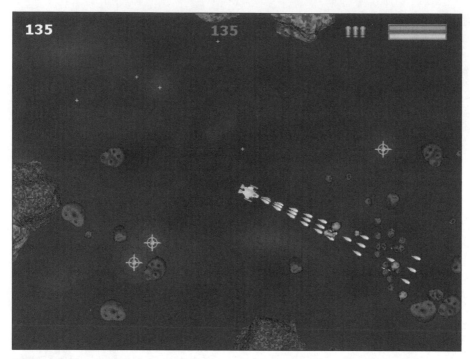

Figure 15.6
The third weapon upgrade will keep you alive much longer.

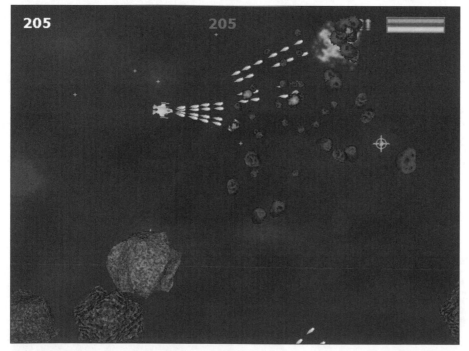

Figure 15.7
Four shots at a time is good for your self-confidence.

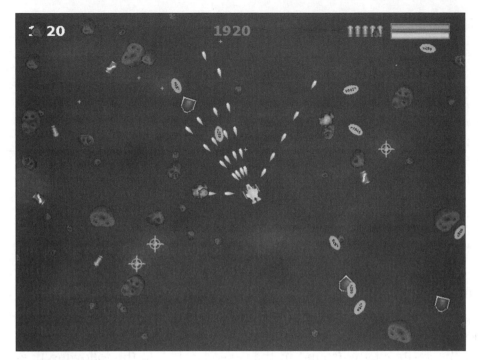

Figure 15.8
Weapon upgrade level five gives your ship *six* projectiles!

ENHANCING GALACTIC WAR

I'm going to start at the top of the GalacticWar.java file and note the changes made as we move down through the source code. We'll take a look at a few screenshots along the way to explain what's happening in the code. As you can clearly see in the pages to follow, the new game engine (via the Game class) makes enhancements incredibly easy to add to the game.

Tip

If you run into any problems updating the source code with the new improvements, I recommend you open up the complete Galactic War project, located in the chapter resources.

New Sprite Types

The first change to the program involves adding some new sprite type definitions in GalacticWar.java. Near the top of the program listing is a set of sprite types. Add the new items shown in bold text.

```
//sprite types
final int SPRITE_SHIP = 1;
final int SPRITE_ASTEROID_BIG = 10;
final int SPRITE_ASTEROID_MEDIUM = 11;
final int SPRITE_ASTEROID_SMALL = 12;
final int SPRITE_ASTEROID_TINY = 13;
final int SPRITE_BULLET = 100;
final int SPRITE_EXPLOSION = 200;
final int SPRITE_POWERUP_SHIELD = 300;
final int SPRITE_POWERUP_HEALTH = 301;
final int SPRITE_POWERUP_250 = 302;
final int SPRITE_POWERUP_500 = 303;
final int SPRITE_POWERUP_1000 = 304;
final int SPRITE_POWERUP_GUN = 305;
```

New Game States

To give the game the ability to start, play, and end (with the option to restart), we need to add some conditional gameplay states and make use of the pause property in the sprite engine (found in the Game class). Add the following lines just below the new sprite definitions, above the toggle variables. The new code is shown in bold.

```
//game states
final int GAME_MENU = 0;
final int GAME_RUNNING = 1;
final int GAME_OVER = 2;

//various toggles
boolean showBounds = false;
boolean collisionTesting = true;
```

When the game first starts up, you see the title screen, which is shown in Figure 15.9. This screen shows the keys you press to control the ship.

New Sprite Images

Now let's add some new sprite image definitions using the ImageEntity class. The ship has a new shield feature, and we have a whole bunch of new images for power-ups and the updated user interface (such as the health and shield meters).

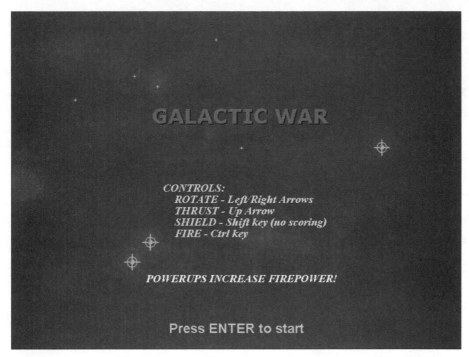

Figure 15.9
The title screen of Galactic War displays the key controls.

Scroll down a bit more to the block of code showing definitions for all of the `ImageEntity` objects used in the game. Add the new code shown in bold. (Note also the minor change to the `shipImage` array, which now has three elements.)

```
//define the images used in the game
ImageEntity background;
ImageEntity bulletImage;
ImageEntity[] bigAsteroids = new ImageEntity[5];
ImageEntity[] medAsteroids = new ImageEntity[2];
ImageEntity[] smlAsteroids = new ImageEntity[3];
ImageEntity[] tnyAsteroids = new ImageEntity[4];
ImageEntity[] explosions = new ImageEntity[2];
ImageEntity[] shipImage = new ImageEntity[3];
ImageEntity[] barImage = new ImageEntity[2];
ImageEntity barFrame;
ImageEntity powerupShield;
ImageEntity powerupHealth;
ImageEntity powerup250;
```

```
ImageEntity powerup500;
ImageEntity powerup1000;
ImageEntity powerupGun;
```

Health/Shield Meters, Score, Firepower, and Game State Variables

Now let's add some global variables to keep track of such things as the ship's health, shield power, game state, as well as more obvious things such as current score, high score, and weapon upgrade level. Add the following code after the image definitions, before the Random line. New code is shown in bold.

```
//health/shield meters and score
int health = 20;
int shield = 20;
int score = 0;
int highscore = 0;
int firepower = 1;
int gameState = GAME_MENU;

//create a random number generator
Random rand = new Random();
```

New Input Keys

We need to add support for the new shield ability. I've defined the Shift key to activate the ship's shield, but you may change this key if you prefer a different one. Locate the key input tracking variables a few lines below the last change you just made, and note the new variable added in bold.

The collision toggle and bounding box toggle are both still active in the game. Although they were used for testing, they are now known as undocumented *hidden cheats* in the game!

```
//some key input tracking variables
boolean keyLeft, keyRight, keyUp, keyFire, keyB, keyC, keyShield;
```

Sound and Music Objects

Immediately below the key tracking variable definitions, add the following code for the sound and music objects (or make sure the code looks like this, if it differs in your source code listing). Note the changes in bold.

```
//some key input tracking variables
boolean keyLeft, keyRight, keyUp, keyFire, keyB, keyC, keyShield;

//sound effects and music
MidiSequence music = new MidiSequence();
SoundClip shoot = new SoundClip();
SoundClip explosion = new SoundClip();
```

Loading Media Files

Unfortunately, all of these new features come with a price—load times. The game loads up very fast on your local PC, but can take 10 to 20 seconds to load from a website, depending on your connection speed. All the images and sounds used in this game are fairly small because they are stored in the compressed PNG format. The biggest file is the background, which is about 300 KB. All remaining image and sound files are well under 100 KB, and most of them are in the 1 to 10 KB range, which is extremely small indeed. I suspect that without the background image and the large explosion, the game would load up almost instantly. When packaged into a JAR (which is covered in the next chapter), the entire game is 600 KB.

Let's add all of the new code to gameStartup() to load all of the new images, sounds, and music in the game. There are also some gameplay-related changes in this method that you should look out for. All new code and changes are highlighted in bold.

```
void gameStartup() {
    //load sounds and music
    music.load("music.mid");
    shoot.load("shoot.au");
    explosion.load("explode.au");

    //load the health/shield bars
    barFrame = new ImageEntity(this);
    barFrame.load("barframe.png");
    barImage[0] = new ImageEntity(this);
    barImage[0].load("bar_health.png");
    barImage[1] = new ImageEntity(this);
    barImage[1].load("bar_shield.png");
```

```
//load powerups
powerupShield = new ImageEntity(this);
powerupShield.load("powerup_shield2.png");
powerupHealth = new ImageEntity(this);
powerupHealth.load("powerup_cola.png");
powerup250 = new ImageEntity(this);
powerup250.load("powerup_250.png");
powerup500 = new ImageEntity(this);
powerup500.load("powerup_500.png");
powerup1000 = new ImageEntity(this);
powerup1000.load("powerup_1000.png");
powerupGun = new ImageEntity(this);
powerupGun.load("powerup_gun.png");

//load the background image
background = new ImageEntity(this);
background.load("bluespace.png");

//create the ship sprite--first in the sprite list
shipImage[0] = new ImageEntity(this);
shipImage[0].load("spaceship.png");
shipImage[1] = new ImageEntity(this);
shipImage[1].load("ship_thrust.png");
shipImage[2] = new ImageEntity(this);
shipImage[2].load("ship_shield.png");

AnimatedSprite ship = new AnimatedSprite(this, graphics());
ship.setSpriteType(SPRITE_SHIP);
ship.setImage(shipImage[0].getImage());
ship.setFrameWidth(ship.imageWidth());
ship.setFrameHeight(ship.imageHeight());
ship.setPosition(new Point2D(SCREENWIDTH/2, SCREENHEIGHT/2));
ship.setAlive(true);
//start ship off as invulnerable
ship.setState(STATE_EXPLODING);
collisionTimer = System.currentTimeMillis();
sprites().add(ship);

//load the bullet sprite image
bulletImage = new ImageEntity(this);
```

```
bulletImage.load("plasmashot.png");

//load the explosion sprite image
explosions[0] = new ImageEntity(this);
explosions[0].load("explosion.png");
explosions[1] = new ImageEntity(this);
explosions[1].load("explosion2.png");

//load the big asteroid images (5 total)
for (int n = 0; n<5; n++) {
    bigAsteroids[n] = new ImageEntity(this);
    String fn = "asteroid" + (n+1) + ".png";
    bigAsteroids[n].load(fn);
}
//load the medium asteroid images (2 total)
for (int n = 0; n<2; n++) {
    medAsteroids[n] = new ImageEntity(this);
    String fn = "medium" + (n+1) + ".png";
    medAsteroids[n].load(fn);
}
//load the small asteroid images (3 total)
for (int n = 0; n<3; n++) {
    smlAsteroids[n] = new ImageEntity(this);
    String fn = "small" + (n+1) + ".png";
    smlAsteroids[n].load(fn);
}
//load the tiny asteroid images (4 total)
for (int n = 0; n<4; n++) {
    tnyAsteroids[n] = new ImageEntity(this);
    String fn = "tiny" + (n+1) + ".png";
    tnyAsteroids[n].load(fn);
}

//start off in pause mode
pauseGame();
```

//delete this block of code, which has been moved to another method
```
/**** moved to resetGame
    //create the random asteroid sprites
    for (int n = 0; n<ASTEROIDS; n++) {
```

```
        createAsteroid();
    }
*/
}
```

Game State Issue—Resetting the Game

The game used to just start up with asteroids flying at your ship, without any chance to prepare yourself! To avoid this problem, I've added an overall state system to the game, which now starts off in GAME_MENU mode. During normal gameplay, the state is GAME_PLAYING. When your ship blows up, the state is GAME_OVER. To make it possible to restart the game after dying (in which case, the high score is retained), we need a way to reset the key variables and objects—but the game should *not* reload any files! Add the resetGame() method just below gameStartup().

```
private void resetGame() {
    //restart the music soundtrack
    music.setLooping(true);
    music.play();

    //save the ship for the restart
    AnimatedSprite ship = (AnimatedSprite) sprites().get(0);

    //wipe out the sprite list to start over!
    sprites().clear();

    //add the saved ship to the sprite list
    ship.setPosition(new Point2D(SCREENWIDTH/2, SCREENHEIGHT/2));
    ship.setAlive(true);
    ship.setState(STATE_EXPLODING);
    collisionTimer = System.currentTimeMillis();
    ship.setVelocity(new Point2D(0, 0));
    sprites().add(ship);

    //create the random asteroid sprites
    for (int n = 0; n<ASTEROIDS; n++) {
        createAsteroid();
    }

    //reset variables
```

```
        health = 20;
        shield = 20;
        score = 0;
        firepower = 2;
    }
```

Detecting the Game-Over State

The next method in the source code listing is gameTimedUpdate(), an event passed by the parent Game class. We need to add a bit of code here to handle the GAME_OVER state, which occurs when there is only one sprite left in the game—the ship. Figure 15.10 shows the game in this state after the health meter has dropped to zero.

```
void gameTimedUpdate() {
    checkInput();

    if (!gamePaused() && sprites().size() == 1) {
```

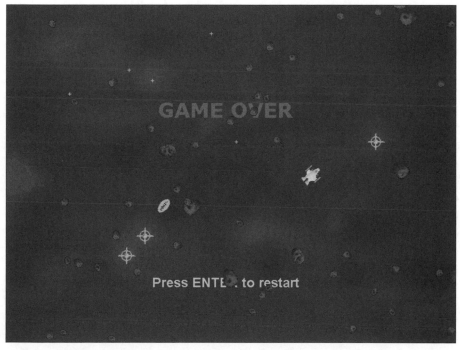

Figure 15.10
If your health drops to zero, the game is over—you lose!

```
            resetGame();
            gameState = GAME_OVER;
        }
    }
```

Screen Refresh Updates

I've made a whole bunch of changes to the game screen, which is refreshed regularly during the applet's update() and paint() events. I've removed the testing/debugging displays, which showed the ship's vitals and other things. We want the game screen to look nice now, without any clutter. Because there are so many changes involved, you may want to just delete any commented-out code and rewrite this method as indicated. I will show new or changed code in bold and deleted code in italics.

```
    void gameRefreshScreen() {
        Graphics2D g2d = graphics();

//*** REMOVE OR COMMENT OUT THIS BLOCK
        //the ship is always the first sprite in the linked list
        AnimatedSprite ship = (AnimatedSprite)sprites().get(0);
******/


        //draw the background
        g2d.drawImage(background.getImage(),0,0,SCREENWIDTH-1,SCREEN-
HEIGHT-1,this);

//*** REMOVE OR COMMENT OUT THIS BLOCK
/*      //print status information on the screen
        g2d.setColor(Color.WHITE);
        g2d.drawString("FPS: " + frameRate(), 5, 10);
        long x = Math.round(ship.position().X());
        long y = Math.round(ship.position().Y());
        g2d.drawString("Ship: " + x + "," + y , 5, 25);
        g2d.drawString("Move angle: " + Math.round(ship.moveAngle())+90, 5, 40);
        g2d.drawString("Face angle: " +  Math.round(ship.faceAngle()), 5, 55);
        if (ship.state()==STATE_NORMAL)
            g2d.drawString("State: NORMAL", 5, 70);
        else if (ship.state()==STATE_COLLIDED)
```

```
        g2d.drawString("State: COLLIDED", 5, 70);
    else if (ship.state()==STATE_EXPLODING)
        g2d.drawString("State: EXPLODING", 5, 70);
    g2d.drawString("Sprites: " + sprites().size(), 5, 120);

    if (showBounds) {
        g2d.setColor(Color.GREEN);
        g2d.drawString("BOUNDING BOXES", SCREENWIDTH-150, 10);
    }
    if (collisionTesting) {
        g2d.setColor(Color.GREEN);
        g2d.drawString("COLLISION TESTING", SCREENWIDTH-150, 25);
    }
******/

    //what is the game state?
    if (gameState == GAME_MENU) {
        g2d.setFont(new Font("Verdana", Font.BOLD, 36));
        g2d.setColor(Color.BLACK);
        g2d.drawString("GALACTIC WAR", 252, 202);
        g2d.setColor(new Color(200,30,30));
        g2d.drawString("GALACTIC WAR", 250, 200);

        int x = 270, y = 15;
        g2d.setFont(new Font("Times New Roman", Font.ITALIC | Font.BOLD,
20));
        g2d.setColor(Color.YELLOW);
        g2d.drawString("CONTROLS:", x, ++y*20);
        g2d.drawString("ROTATE - Left/Right Arrows", x+20, ++y*20);
        g2d.drawString("THRUST - Up Arrow", x+20, ++y*20);
        g2d.drawString("SHIELD - Shift key (no scoring)", x+20, ++y*20);
        g2d.drawString("FIRE - Ctrl key", x+20, ++y*20);

        g2d.setColor(Color.WHITE);
        g2d.drawString("POWERUPS INCREASE FIREPOWER!", 240, 480);

        g2d.setFont(new Font("Ariel", Font.BOLD, 24));
        g2d.setColor(Color.ORANGE);
        g2d.drawString("Press ENTER to start", 280, 570);
    }
```

```
        else if (gameState == GAME_RUNNING) {
            //draw health/shield bars and meters
            g2d.drawImage(barFrame.getImage(), SCREENWIDTH - 132, 18, this);
            for (int n = 0; n < health; n++) {
                int dx = SCREENWIDTH - 130 + n * 5;
                g2d.drawImage(barImage[0].getImage(), dx, 20, this);
            }
            g2d.drawImage(barFrame.getImage(), SCREENWIDTH - 132, 33, this);
            for (int n = 0; n < shield; n++) {
                int dx = SCREENWIDTH - 130 + n * 5;
                g2d.drawImage(barImage[1].getImage(), dx, 35, this);
            }

            //draw the bullet upgrades
            for (int n = 0; n < firepower; n++) {
                int dx = SCREENWIDTH - 220 + n * 13;
                g2d.drawImage(powerupGun.getImage(), dx, 17, this);
            }

            //display the score
            g2d.setFont(new Font("Verdana", Font.BOLD, 24));
            g2d.setColor(Color.WHITE);
            g2d.drawString("" + score, 20, 40);
            g2d.setColor(Color.RED);
            g2d.drawString("" + highscore, 350, 40);
        }
        else if (gameState == GAME_OVER) {
            g2d.setFont(new Font("Verdana", Font.BOLD, 36));
            g2d.setColor(new Color(200, 30, 30));
            g2d.drawString("GAME OVER", 270, 200);

            g2d.setFont(new Font("Arial", Font.CENTER_BASELINE, 24));
            g2d.setColor(Color.ORANGE);
            g2d.drawString("Press ENTER to restart", 260, 500);
        }
    }
```

Preparing to End

The gameShutdown() event comes next. As you'll recall, this method was left empty in the previous chapter, but now we need to use it properly. A well-behaved Java program will free up resources before the program ends. In the case of Galactic War, I prefer to rely on Java's built-in garbage collector to free up resources automatically. However, it is necessary to shut off the music and any sound effects currently playing before the applet ends because sometimes a MIDI sequence will keep playing after the game has ended.

```
void gameShutdown() {
    music.stop();
    shoot.stop();
    explosion.stop();
}
```

Updating New Sprites

Next up is the spriteUpdate() event method. There are a lot of new additions here but no changes, as we have all these new power-ups that need to be handled when they appear on the screen. The most important thing to do here is to warp the power-ups along with everything else in the game. Then, in addition, the power-ups need to *wobble*, or alternate the rotation back and forth, so they stand out from the other sprites.

Just as an example, take a look at Figure 15.11. This zoom-in of the ship firing shows how much the sprite engine is handling at one time. In this figure, I count 60 sprites in just this small portion of the screen (which, granted, is where most of the action is currently taking place). All of the asteroids are rotating by some random value. The flaming bullets are rotated and adjusted every time they move along their paths. The ship rotates with user input. Every time you destroy a tiny sprite, an eight-frame animation is played. That's a lot of action! It's a good thing we developed the sprite engine in the last chapter, or none of this would have been possible using the old method of handling sprites with arrays. (Oh, and in case you were wondering—the bullets have not passed through any of those tiny sprites; they have just been spawned by the destruction of a larger sprite and will soon be annihilated by the incoming fire.)

The new code in spriteUpdate(), marked in bold, adds additional cases to the switch statement for dealing with the power-ups.

```
public void spriteUpdate(AnimatedSprite sprite) {
    switch(sprite.spriteType()) {
    case SPRITE_SHIP:
```

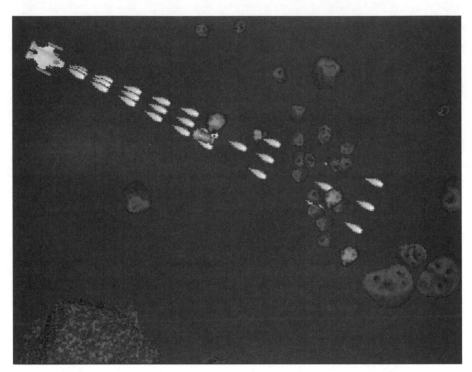

Figure 15.11
There are a lot of sprites in any normal game, but this is only 1/4 of the screen.

```
        warp(sprite);
        break;
    case SPRITE_BULLET:
        warp(sprite);
        break;
    case SPRITE_EXPLOSION:
        if (sprite.currentFrame() == sprite.totalFrames()-1) {
            sprite.setAlive(false);
        }
        break;
    case SPRITE_ASTEROID_BIG:
    case SPRITE_ASTEROID_MEDIUM:
    case SPRITE_ASTEROID_SMALL:
    case SPRITE_ASTEROID_TINY:
        warp(sprite);
        break;
```

```
        case SPRITE_POWERUP_SHIELD:
        case SPRITE_POWERUP_HEALTH:
        case SPRITE_POWERUP_250:
        case SPRITE_POWERUP_500:
        case SPRITE_POWERUP_1000:
        case SPRITE_POWERUP_GUN:
            warp(sprite);
            //make powerup animation wobble
            double rot = sprite.rotationRate();
            if (sprite.faceAngle() > 350) {
                sprite.setRotationRate(rot * -1);
                sprite.setFaceAngle(350);
            }
            else if (sprite.faceAngle() < 10) {
                sprite.setRotationRate(rot * -1);
                sprite.setFaceAngle(10);
            }
            break;
    }
}
```

Grabbing Power-Ups

Next in the source code listing is the spriteCollision() event. All we need to do
here is handle all the new power-ups that are in the game; this means that only
the ship should collide with the power-ups. I've moved the test for the collision
testing toggle to the top of this method, out of the keyboard handling code,
because it belongs here instead. Some new lines have been added to increase the
score whenever a bullet hits an asteroid and to deal with collisions when the
shield is up. Note the changes in bold, as usual.

```
public void spriteCollision(AnimatedSprite spr1, AnimatedSprite spr2) {
    //jump out quickly if collisions are off
    if (!collisionTesting) return;

    //figure out what type of sprite has collided
    switch(spr1.spriteType()) {
    case SPRITE_BULLET:
        //did bullet hit an asteroid?
        if (isAsteroid(spr2.spriteType())) {
            bumpScore(5);
```

```java
                spr1.setAlive(false);
                spr2.setAlive(false);
                breakAsteroid(spr2);
            }
            break;
        case SPRITE_SHIP:
            //did asteroid crash into the ship?
            if (isAsteroid(spr2.spriteType())) {
                if (spr1.state() == STATE_NORMAL) {
                    if (keyShield) {
                        shield -= 1;
                    }
                    else {
                        collisionTimer = System.currentTimeMillis();
                        spr1.setVelocity(new Point2D(0, 0));
                        double x = spr1.position().X() - 10;
                        double y = spr1.position().Y() - 10;
                        startBigExplosion(new Point2D(x, y));
                        spr1.setState(STATE_EXPLODING);
                        //reduce ship health after a hit
                        health -= 1;
                        if (health < 0) {
                            gameState = GAME_OVER;
                        }
                        //lose firepower when you get hit
                        firepower--;
                        if (firepower < 1) firepower = 1;
                    }
                    spr2.setAlive(false);
                    breakAsteroid(spr2);
                }
                //make ship temporarily invulnerable
                else if (spr1.state() == STATE_EXPLODING) {
                    if (collisionTimer + 3000 <
                        System.currentTimeMillis()) {
                        spr1.setState(STATE_NORMAL);
                    }
                }
            }
            break;
```

```
case SPRITE_POWERUP_SHIELD:
    if (spr2.spriteType()==SPRITE_SHIP) {
        shield += 5;
        if (shield > 20) shield = 20;
        spr1.setAlive(false);
    }
    break;

case SPRITE_POWERUP_HEALTH:
    if (spr2.spriteType()==SPRITE_SHIP) {
        health += 5;
        if (health > 20) health = 20;
        spr1.setAlive(false);
    }
    break;

case SPRITE_POWERUP_250:
    if (spr2.spriteType()==SPRITE_SHIP) {
        bumpScore(250);
        spr1.setAlive(false);
    }
    break;

case SPRITE_POWERUP_500:
    if (spr2.spriteType()==SPRITE_SHIP) {
        bumpScore(500);
        spr1.setAlive(false);
    }
    break;

case SPRITE_POWERUP_1000:
    if (spr2.spriteType()==SPRITE_SHIP) {
        bumpScore(1000);
        spr1.setAlive(false);
    }
    break;

case SPRITE_POWERUP_GUN:
    if (spr2.spriteType()==SPRITE_SHIP) {
        firepower++;
```

```
            if (firepower > 5) firepower = 5;
            spr1.setAlive(false);
        }
        break;
    }
}
```

New Input Keys

The game now uses the Shift key to engage the ship's shields and the Enter key to continue when the game is in the GAME_MENU or GAME_OVER state. There's also a way to exit out of the game now: When the game is running, you can hit Escape to end the game (see Figure 15.12).

Here are the new key handlers in bold.

```
public void gameKeyDown(int keyCode) {
    switch(keyCode) {
    case KeyEvent.VK_LEFT:
```

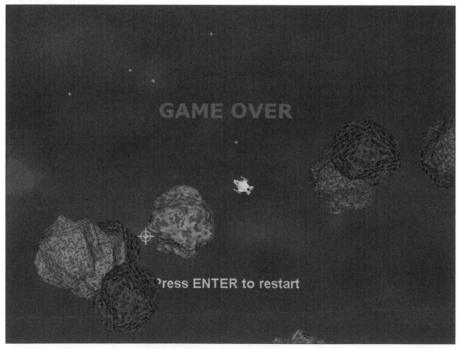

Figure 15.12
The Escape key will end the game immediately and allow you to start over.

```
        keyLeft = true;
        break;
case KeyEvent.VK_RIGHT:
        keyRight = true;
        break;
case KeyEvent.VK_UP:
        keyUp = true;
        break;
case KeyEvent.VK_CONTROL:
        keyFire = true;
        break;
case KeyEvent.VK_B:
        //toggle bounding rectangles
        showBounds = !showBounds;
        break;
case KeyEvent.VK_C:
        //toggle collision testing
        collisionTesting = !collisionTesting;
        break;
case KeyEvent.VK_SHIFT:
        if ((!keyUp) && (shield > 0))
            keyShield = true;
        else
            keyShield = false;
        break;
case KeyEvent.VK_ENTER:
        if (gameState == GAME_MENU) {
            resetGame();
            resumeGame();
            gameState = GAME_RUNNING;
        }
        else if (gameState == GAME_OVER) {
            resetGame();
            resumeGame();
            gameState = GAME_RUNNING;
        }
        break;
case KeyEvent.VK_ESCAPE:
        if (gameState == GAME_RUNNING) {
            pauseGame();
```

```
                gameState = GAME_OVER;
            }
            break;
        }
    }
```

Now let's add a single new case to the gameKeyUp() event as well.

```
public void gameKeyUp(int keyCode) {
    switch(keyCode) {
    case KeyEvent.VK_LEFT:
        keyLeft = false;
        break;
    case KeyEvent.VK_RIGHT:
        keyRight = false;
        break;
    case KeyEvent.VK_UP:
        keyUp = false;
        break;
    case KeyEvent.VK_CONTROL:
        keyFire = false;
        fireBullet();
        break;
    case KeyEvent.VK_SHIFT:
        keyShield = false;
        break;
    }
}
```

Spawning Power-Ups

In the previous chapter we added a new method to the game called spawnPowerup(), which was left empty at the time. Due to that foresight, we do not have to make any changes to the breakAsteroid() method that makes this call. Instead, here is the fully functional spawnPowerup(). At the top of the code, a random percentage determines whether the power-up is actually created. I have it currently set to 12 percent, which provides some fair gameplay. If you want to make the game more difficult, reduce this value. To make it easier, increase it.

Even though 12 percent doesn't sound like very many power-ups, keep in mind that every large asteroid produces three "mediums," each of which produces three "smalls," each of which produces three "tinys" (see Figure 15.13). That's a

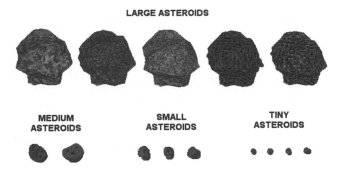

LARGE ASTEROIDS

**MEDIUM
ASTEROIDS**

**SMALL
ASTEROIDS**

**TINY
ASTEROIDS**

Figure 15.13
Here are all of the asteroids you'll run into in the game (pun intended).

whopping 27 tiny asteroids for every large one, and since the game starts out with 10 large ones—well, you can do that kind of math. In a single game session, 12 percent will generate about 30 power-ups! I think this value should be reduced to about 20 to make the game a bit more challenging, but each power-up has a limited lifetime, so it's possible in the heat of battle that the player will only manage to grab a few of them.

The spawnPowerup() method creates a single power-up sprite with some standard properties that all power-ups share, and then it sets the specific properties using a random number. Since there are six power-ups, this random number determines the type of power-up.

```
private void spawnPowerup(AnimatedSprite sprite) {
    //only a few tiny sprites spit out a powerup
    int n = rand.nextInt(100);
    if (n > 12) return;

    //use this powerup sprite
    AnimatedSprite spr = new AnimatedSprite(this, graphics());
    spr.setRotationRate(8);
    spr.setPosition(sprite.position());
    double velx = rand.nextDouble();
    double vely = rand.nextDouble();
    spr.setVelocity(new Point2D(velx, vely));
    spr.setLifespan(1500);
    spr.setAlive(true);
```

```
//customize the sprite based on powerup type
switch(rand.nextInt(6)) {
case 0:
    //create a new shield powerup sprite
    spr.setImage(powerupShield.getImage());
    spr.setSpriteType(SPRITE_POWERUP_SHIELD);
    sprites().add(spr);
    break;
case 1:
    //create a new health powerup sprite
    spr.setImage(powerupHealth.getImage());
    spr.setSpriteType(SPRITE_POWERUP_HEALTH);
    sprites().add(spr);
    break;
case 2:
    //create a new 250-point powerup sprite
    spr.setImage(powerup250.getImage());
    spr.setSpriteType(SPRITE_POWERUP_250);
    sprites().add(spr);
    break;
case 3:
    //create a new 500-point powerup sprite
    spr.setImage(powerup500.getImage());
    spr.setSpriteType(SPRITE_POWERUP_500);
    sprites().add(spr);
    break;
case 4:
    //create a new 1000-point powerup sprite
    spr.setImage(powerup1000.getImage());
    spr.setSpriteType(SPRITE_POWERUP_1000);
    sprites().add(spr);
    break;
case 5:
    //create a new gun powerup sprite
    spr.setImage(powerupGun.getImage());
    spr.setSpriteType(SPRITE_POWERUP_GUN);
    sprites().add(spr);
    break;
}
}
```

Making the Shield Work

Although the key events turn the ship's shield on or off, the real work is done in the `checkInput()` method shown here. Let's take a close-up look at the shield in action. Figure 15.14 shows the ship bombarded with asteroids, but the shield is taking all of the impact and protecting the ship (at least until the shield runs out!).

We also need to make a change to the new global game state so it will ignore input events unless the game is running—in other words, it should ignore gameplay input changes when in the GAME_MENU or GAME_OVER state. The new code is shown in bold.

```
public void checkInput() {
    if (gameState != GAME_RUNNING) return;

    //the ship is always the first sprite in the linked list
    AnimatedSprite ship = (AnimatedSprite)sprites().get(0);
    if (keyLeft) {
        //left arrow rotates ship left 5 degrees
```

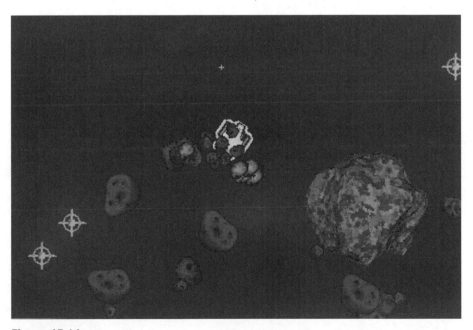

Figure 15.14
This close-up view shows multiple asteroids impacting the ship's shields (and breaking apart into small asteroids or just blowing up).

```
            ship.setFaceAngle(ship.faceAngle() - SHIPROTATION);
            if (ship.faceAngle() < 0)
                ship.setFaceAngle(360 - SHIPROTATION);

        } else if (keyRight) {
            //right arrow rotates ship right 5 degrees
            ship.setFaceAngle(ship.faceAngle() + SHIPROTATION);
            if (ship.faceAngle() > 360)
                ship.setFaceAngle(SHIPROTATION);
        }
        if (keyUp) {
            //up arrow applies thrust to ship
            ship.setImage(shipImage[1].getImage());
            applyThrust();
        }
        else if (keyShield) {
            ship.setImage(shipImage[2].getImage());
        }
        else
            //set ship image to normal non-thrust image
            ship.setImage(shipImage[0].getImage());
    }
```

Making Use of Weapon Upgrade Power-Ups

The new weapon upgrades are awesome, as you saw earlier in the chapter—wouldn't you agree? This is the most interesting new gameplay feature, without a doubt. Each time you get a weapon upgrade, it adds another gun to your ship. However, if your ship gets hit, you lose an upgrade, so it's pretty tough to keep those upgrades. The good news is, when you get level-four or level-five guns, your ship is so powerful that it's fairly easy to clear out the asteroids in short order.

To support weapon upgrades, the code in fireBullet() has been completely rewritten, and two new support methods were needed: adjustDirection() and stockBullet(). The new "bullets" emerge from the center of the ship, and then spread out in various patterns, based on the upgrade level (which is in a variable called firepower). I'll show you the new code for fireBullet() first.

```
public void fireBullet() {
    //create the new bullet sprite
    AnimatedSprite[] bullets = new AnimatedSprite[6];
```

```
switch(firepower) {
case 1: //single shot
    bullets[0] = stockBullet();
    sprites().add(bullets[0]);
    break;
case 2: //double shot
    bullets[0] = stockBullet();
    adjustDirection(bullets[0], -4);
    sprites().add(bullets[0]);
    bullets[1] = stockBullet();
    adjustDirection(bullets[1], 4);
    sprites().add(bullets[1]);
    break;
case 3: //triple shot
    bullets[0] = stockBullet();
    adjustDirection(bullets[0], -4);
    sprites().add(bullets[0]);
    bullets[1] = stockBullet();
    sprites().add(bullets[1]);
    bullets[2] = stockBullet();
    adjustDirection(bullets[2], 4);
    sprites().add(bullets[2]);
    break;
case 4: //4-shot
    bullets[0] = stockBullet();
    adjustDirection(bullets[0], -5);
    sprites().add(bullets[0]);
    bullets[1] = stockBullet();
    adjustDirection(bullets[1], 5);
    sprites().add(bullets[1]);
    bullets[2] = stockBullet();
    adjustDirection(bullets[2], -10);
    sprites().add(bullets[2]);
    bullets[3] = stockBullet();
    adjustDirection(bullets[3], 10);
    sprites().add(bullets[3]);
    break;
case 5: //5-shot
    bullets[0] = stockBullet();
    adjustDirection(bullets[0], -6);
```

```
                    sprites().add(bullets[0]);
                    bullets[1] = stockBullet();
                    adjustDirection(bullets[1], 6);
                    sprites().add(bullets[1]);
                    bullets[2] = stockBullet();
                    adjustDirection(bullets[2], -15);
                    sprites().add(bullets[2]);
                    bullets[3] = stockBullet();
                    adjustDirection(bullets[3], 15);
                    sprites().add(bullets[3]);
                    bullets[4] = stockBullet();
                    adjustDirection(bullets[4], -60);
                    sprites().add(bullets[4]);
                    bullets[5] = stockBullet();
                    adjustDirection(bullets[5], 60);
                    sprites().add(bullets[5]);
                    break;
            }
            shoot.play();
    }
```

Here's the new adjustDirection() support method, which basically just cuts
down on the amount of code in fireBullet() because this code is repeated for
every single bullet launched. This method is new, so you should add it below the
fireBullet() method in your code listing for GalacticWar.java.

```
    private void adjustDirection(AnimatedSprite sprite, double angle) {
        angle = sprite.faceAngle() + angle;
        if (angle < 0) angle += 360;
        else if (angle > 360) angle -= 360;
        sprite.setFaceAngle(angle);
        sprite.setMoveAngle(sprite.faceAngle()-90);
        angle = sprite.moveAngle();
        double svx = calcAngleMoveX(angle) * BULLET_SPEED;
        double svy = calcAngleMoveY(angle) * BULLET_SPEED;
        sprite.setVelocity(new Point2D(svx, svy));
    }
```

The next support method that helps out fireBullet() is called stockBullet().
This method creates a stock bullet sprite with all of the standard values needed
to fire a single bullet from the center of the ship. The custom upgraded bullets

are modified from this stock bullet to create the various firepower patterns you see in the game. This method returns a new `AnimatedSprite` object.

```
private AnimatedSprite stockBullet() {
    //the ship is always the first sprite in the linked list
    AnimatedSprite ship = (AnimatedSprite)sprites().get(0);

    AnimatedSprite bul = new AnimatedSprite(this, graphics());
    bul.setAlive(true);
    bul.setImage(bulletImage.getImage());
    bul.setFrameWidth(bulletImage.width());
    bul.setFrameHeight(bulletImage.height());
    bul.setSpriteType(SPRITE_BULLET);
    bul.setLifespan(90);
    bul.setFaceAngle(ship.faceAngle());
    bul.setMoveAngle(ship.faceAngle() - 90);

    //set the bullet's velocity
    double angle = bul.moveAngle();
    double svx = calcAngleMoveX(angle) * BULLET_SPEED;
    double svy = calcAngleMoveY(angle) * BULLET_SPEED;
    bul.setVelocity(new Point2D(svx, svy));

    //set the bullet's starting position
    double x = ship.center().X() - bul.imageWidth()/2;
    double y = ship.center().Y() - bul.imageHeight()/2;
    bul.setPosition(new Point2D(x,y));

    return bul;
}
```

Tallying the Score

The final change to the Galactic War source code is the addition of a new method called `bumpScore()`. This is called in the collision routine to increase the player's score for every asteroid hit by a weapon. (Collisions with the ship don't count.)

```
public void bumpScore(int howmuch) {
    score += howmuch;
```

```
        if (score > highscore)
            highscore = score;
    }
```

What You Have Learned

This has certainly been an eye-opening chapter! It's amazing what is possible now that we have a sprite engine with such dynamic sprite-handling capabilities. It's now possible, as you have seen, to add new power-ups and entirely new gameplay elements by simply adding new cases to the switch statements in the key event methods, as well as adding the few lines of code to load new images. The end result is now a fully polished, retail-quality game that's ready to take on any game in the web-based casual game market.

Here's what you have learned:

- How to add power-ups to the game
- How to enhance gameplay with new features
- How to fire a spread of bullets at various angles
- How to add a game state to give the game a start and an ending

Review Questions

The following questions will help you to determine how well you have learned the subjects discussed in this chapter. The answers are provided in Appendix A, "Chapter Quiz Answers."

1. What method in GalacticWar.java makes it possible to add power-ups to the game when a tiny asteroid is destroyed?

2. What construct does the sprite engine (in Game.java) use to manage the sprites?

3. How many weapon upgrades are available now in Galactic War?

4. How many different point-value power-ups are there in the game?

5. What method in GalacticWar.java returns a stock bullet sprite object, which is then tweaked to produce the upgraded bullet spreads?

6. How many different asteroid images are there in Galactic War?

7. If you wanted to add another weapon upgrade to the game, which method would you need to modify?

8. How many sprites is the sprite engine capable of handling at a time?

9. How many bullets are fired at a time with the fifth-level weapon upgrade?

10. What is the name of the static int that represents the game state when the game is running normally?

ON YOUR OWN

There are so many possibilities with this game that I hardly know where to start. Since I consider the game finished in the sense that it is sufficiently stocked with features and gameplay elements to meet the goals I laid out for this book, I will just make some suggestions for the game.

I would like to add a black hole that randomly crosses the screen from time to time, sucking in everything it touches. Wouldn't that be cool?

Another great feature would be to have an alien spacecraft come onto the screen from time to time and shoot at the player. To keep the alien ship from getting hit by asteroids, the ship would engage a shield whenever it collides with an asteroid; otherwise, it would have to navigate through the asteroid field, and that's some code I would not care to write!

Here is yet another idea to improve gameplay, since the game is *really* hard. The game could start off with a single big asteroid for Level 1, and then add an additional big asteroid to each level the player completes. Although the game can handle an unlimited number of sprites, I would end the game at level 10 to keep it reasonable. Since the game currently just throws 10 asteroids at the player from the start, switching to a level-based system would greatly improve the fun factor!

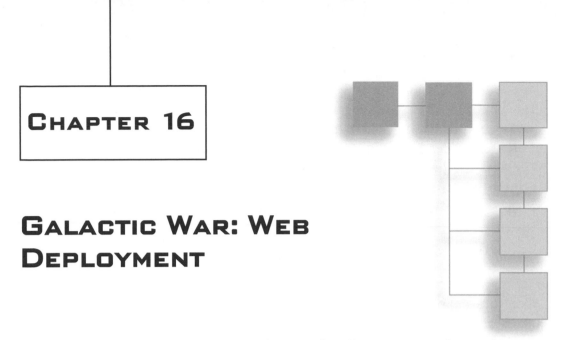

CHAPTER 16

GALACTIC WAR: WEB DEPLOYMENT

This chapter finishes the book by explaining the all-important subject of how to deploy your Java applet–based games to the web. I assume you already have some knowledge about how to use FTP to copy your game to a web server. I will show you how to prepare the applet so that it will run from your own web page! (Even if you use a free hosting service, if you can upload the files to your website, then very likely the game will run from your site.) You will also learn how to use the Java Archive tool to bundle your entire game (with class files and all media files together) in a Java Archive file.

Here are the key topics in this chapter:

- Packaging an applet in a Java Archive (JAR)
- Using the JAR command-line program
- Packaging Galactic War into a JAR file
- Creating a host HTML file for the applet

PACKAGING AN APPLET IN A JAVA ARCHIVE (JAR)

The Java Development Kit (JDK) comes with a command-line tool called jar.exe that is used to create Java Archive files. JARs, as they are known, use the ZIP compression method when storing files. JARs can greatly reduce the size of a Java applet—which is crucial for web deployment.

To use the JAR tool, you will need to open a command-prompt window (also known as a *shell* in some operating systems), and then set the path to the JDK if it is not already set. By default, on a Windows system, the JDK is installed at C:\Program Files\Java, and under this folder there will be a folder containing the JDK and the Java Runtime Environment (JRE). You need to set the path to include the \bin folder located in the JDK. This will differ depending on the version of JDK you have installed. Currently on my system, the jar.exe tool is located here:

C:\Program Files\Java\jdk1.6.0_22\bin

You can open the command prompt by going to Start, Program Files, Accessories. You can also run cmd.exe manually using Start, Run. On Linux and Mac systems, the JDK is usually already added to the path when it is installed.

Tip

If you added Java to your system path as described back in Chapter 1, then you should be able to run jar.exe from anywhere.

Using the jar.exe Program

The JAR tool is a bit finicky. If you don't use the parameters exactly right and in the correct order, JAR will complain and fail to create the JAR file you wanted it to create. The order of the parameters should not be significant, but it is in this case. The general syntax of the JAR command can be viewed by typing JAR at the command line. The output looks something like Figure 16.1.

Creating a New JAR File

The parameters in this Help listing are deceptive. Not only should you *not* use the dash (−), but these parameters must be specified in a specific order. For instance, we use the "c" parameter to tell JAR to create a new JAR file. But this parameter *must* be used along with "f" to specify the filename. I can't imagine a situation where you would want to use the JAR tool without using a JAR file, but I guess that's just me. After the "cf" parameters, you specify the JAR file name, and then the files you want to add. Here is an example:

```
jar cf test.jar *.class
```

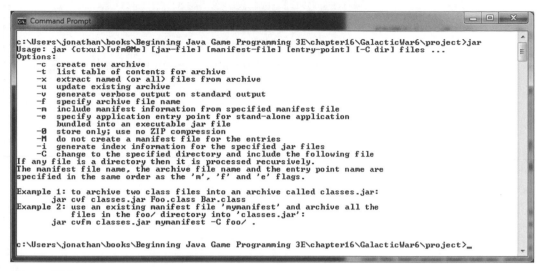

Figure 16.1
Verifying that the JAR program is available at the command prompt.

This command will create a new JAR file called test.jar and add all .class files found in the current folder to the JAR file. After doing so, if the JAR tool successfully created the new JAR file, it will simply exit and not print anything out. (So remember, no display equals no problems.)

Listing the Contents of a JAR File

To display the contents of a JAR file, use the "tf" parameter, like so:

```
jar tf test.jar
```

You can also include the "v" option to display the contents of the JAR file with details. This option also works when creating a new JAR file, but you must be careful to include the "v" option after the "c" or "t" parameter. Here's an example of both cases:

```
jar cvf test.jar *.class
jar tvf test.jar
```

Extracting Files from a JAR File

You can extract a single file or all files from a JAR file using the "x" option, like this:

```
jar xvf test.jar *.*
```

Updating a JAR File

You can update a JAR file using the "u" parameter. Any files you specify will replace existing files in the archive, and any new files will be added.

```
jar uvf test.jar HelloWorld.class
```

Manifest Files

Java archives can include a manifest file that tells the JRE the name of the .class file it should run (automatically) when it opens the JAR file. Since this is a fairly common occurrence, and manifest files are a cinch, it makes sense to include one in a JAR file that will run on the web. The general format of the manifest file looks like this:

```
Main-Class: Filename
```

You should not include the .class extension. There are more options for manifest files, but this is the only one you need to be concerned with when the goal is to run an applet stored in a JAR file on the web.

Caution

Be sure to add a blank line after this single line in the manifest file, or the JAR tool will complain.

To use a manifest file when creating a new archive, you can use the "m" parameter option. Just be sure that this is the *last* letter in the options you include.

```
jar cvfm test.jar manifest.txt *.class *.png
```

Note

Given the Java community's obsession with clichés, I'm surprised the JAR program was not called MUG instead, since one does not usually drink a hot beverage from a JAR.

Packaging Galactic War in a Java Archive

The JAR program is fairly easy to use once you get used to its specific requirements. Now let's use this tool to package Galactic War into a Java archive. This will save a little space and will keep the game together in a single file so you won't leave any media files behind when copying the game or uploading it to a website.

Caution

You must load files in a certain way in your code so that the JRE will know how to read them from a JAR file when you have deployed the applet to a website. I've shown you a couple of different ways to load images and other media files in this book.

The method you must use when a game is deployed in a JAR uses the `java.net.URL` class and the `getResource()` method to create a URL that you can pass to the appropriate image or sound loader. The `getResource()` method is available from `this.getClass()`. This method will correctly pull a media file from the local file system or from a JAR file when resources are stored within a JAR. Here is an example:

```
URL url = this.getClass().getResource(filename);
```

The first order of business is to copy your project folder to a new location so you don't accidentally mess up the original. Essentially, this new folder contains the runtime files for the game—the .class files and all assets. You do not need to add the .java files to the .jar file that will be distributed to the web server.

Reviewing the Project Files

Now let's create a Java archive to contain the files needed by this game. The manifest.txt file and index.html file (covered next) are found in the GalacticWar folder. I have copied all of the Galactic War media and class files into a folder called GalacticWar\project. Included are 30 image (PNG) files, two audio files, and one MIDI file. In addition, we have these nine Java class files:

- AnimatedSprite.class
- BaseGameEntity.class
- Game.class
- ImageEntity.class
- Point2D.class
- Sprite.class
- GalacticWar.class
- MidiSequence.class
- SoundClip.class

These files were compiled using Java SE 6. That's a lot of files for a single game! The last thing I want to do is deploy this game to a web server by copying all of the files along with index.html, although that is definitely a workable option. In fact, if you just edit the HTML file (which you'll learn to do here shortly), you can simply copy these files to a website and run the game over the web. But a Java archive works so much better, and it saves some space too. Instead of streaming all of those many dozens of bitmaps, classes, and audio clips to the applet, it just streams the single .jar file.

Building the Java Archive

Using the CD command in the command prompt, I've changed the current folder to chapter12\GalacticWar. (This may be slightly different on your system.) You can perform this step from any folder where your project files are located. I've copied all of the class and media files to a subfolder called "project" to keep things tidy. So, all I have in this main GalacticWar folder are index.html, manifest.txt, and the project subfolder (see Figure 16.2).

The manifest.txt file for Galactic War contains this line:

```
Main-Class: GalacticWar
```

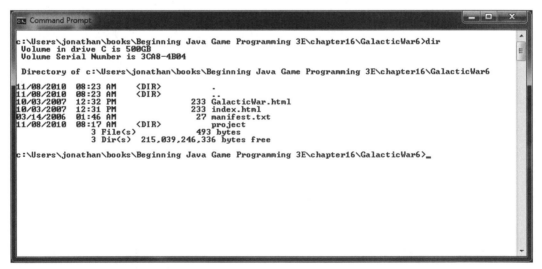

Figure 16.2
Listing the contents of the GalacticWar folder.

This tells the JRE which of the .class files to open up and start running after opening the JAR file. (Be sure to include a blank line after the Main-Class property line.)

You will need to use an optional parameter of the JAR program that lets you specify a subfolder where the actual files are located. You don't want to just tell it to include .\project*.* because that will add .\project to the internal structure of the JAR file. Instead, you want to grab all the files inside of .\project, but not include the folder name. The option is "C" (uppercase is important). Here's the command to create the GalacticWar.jar file:

```
jar cvfm GalacticWar.jar manifest.txt -C project *.*
```

This line tells JAR to create a new Java archive called GalacticWar.jar, to include the manifest information stored in manifest.txt, to use the project subfolder, and to add all files in that subfolder to the JAR file. Figure 16.3 shows the output of the command.

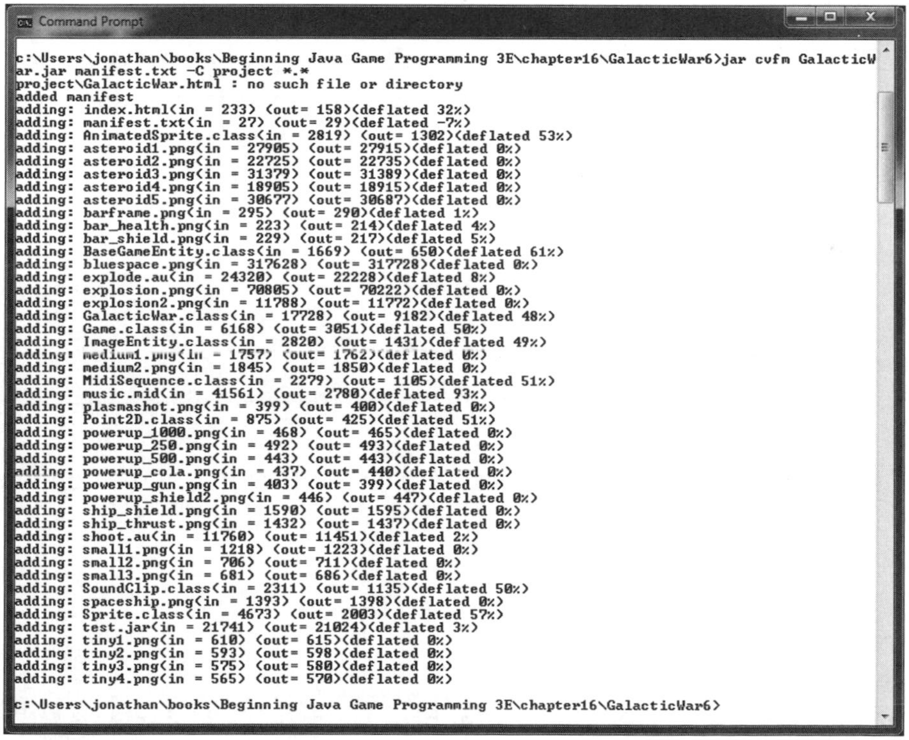

Figure 16.3
Creating the deployable JAR file.

If these additional steps get on your nerves, just lump everything together in a single folder and run the JAR program in the same folder as all your Java project's files, without using the C option, like so:

```
jar cvfm GalacticWar.jar manifest.txt *.*
```

CREATING AN HTML HOST FILE FOR YOUR APPLET

HTML is short for *Hypertext Markup Language*, and it is the water flowing through the world wide web. To run a Java applet on the web, you have to *embed* the applet inside a webpage. This involves creating an HTML file with an <applet> tag that specifies the details about how to run the applet and where it is contained. If you use an IDE such as NetBeans, then just launch the program as an applet and the IDE will generate the HTML container file for you. But, if you want to deploy your applet to a web server, then you do need to create your own HTML file.

A Simple HTML File

The most basic format for an HTML file that will host an applet looks like the following code. This code assumes that a file called game.class is available in the same web folder as the HTML file.

```
<html><head>
<title>This is my game</title>
</head>
<body>
<applet code = game.class
 width=800 height=600>
</applet>
</body></html>
```

The key to running an applet inside a Java archive is to add another option within the <applet> tag called archive.

```
<applet code=game.class
 archive=game.jar
 width=800 height=600>
</applet>
```

The webpage file is usually called index.html because that is the name of a file that web servers will send the web browser automatically if you don't specify the

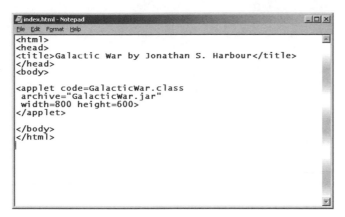

Figure 16.4
Creating a webpage file called GalacticWar.html.

HTML file directly. For instance, when you go to www.jharbour.com, the web server delivers index.html automatically. You can create this simple HTML file using a text editor such as Notepad (as shown in Figure 16.4). If you want your applet to be stored with your other web files, including your already-existing index file, then just use a different name, such as GalacticWar.html.

Testing the Deployed Applet Game

When you have the HTML host file and a JAR file ready to go, it's time to upload them to your web server. I've created a folder on my web server called /BeginningJava that I'll use to deploy the Galactic War files. The indcx.html and GalacticWar.jar files are both uploaded to www.jharbour.com/BeginningJava and are ready to run from this location. When you open this URL, the web browser fires up the JRE, which displays an attractive logo image and a progress bar while it downloads the JAR file (see Figure 16.5). (Note that this logo may look slightly different on your system.)

Tip

The great thing about an applet is that your web browser will store it in the web cache. That is why the applet seems to just open up immediately when you go to the same URL again. The applet does not need to be downloaded again when it is stored in the local web cache.

Figure 16.5
The Java runtime displays this progress bar while downloading the JAR file.

When the applet has completely downloaded to your local system, it will access the files in the JAR locally rather than hitting the web server for every file. Remember the list of 40+ media files in Galactic War? If the game were deployed to the web server with all of those individual files, the applet would have to download every single file individually over the Internet. That's a lot of file transfers! But when your applet is stored in a JAR, that single JAR file is downloaded to your PC, and the applet runs from there. All media files are drawn directly from the JAR file instead of from the web server. If all goes well during the downloading of the JAR file, the game should come up as shown in Figure 16.6.

What You Have Learned

Java applets can grow quite large when you are writing a game because most games use dozens of media files. By packaging a Java applet–based game into a

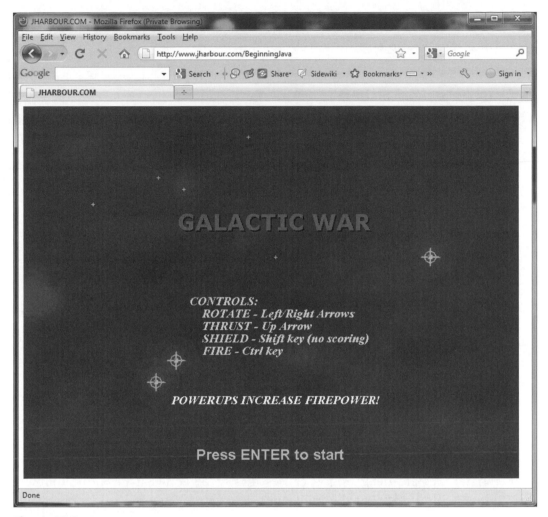

Figure 16.6
Galactic War is now running on a real web server from within an efficient JAR file.

Java Archive (JAR) file, you dramatically improve the time it takes to download and run the game from a web server. You also cut down on the number of transfers that must be made when individual files are stored directly on the server instead of inside an archive file.

Here are the key topics you learned:

- Packaging an applet inside a Java archive

- Creating an HTML host file for your applet
- Running the applet from a website

REVIEW QUESTIONS

The following questions will help you to determine how well you have learned the subjects discussed in this chapter. The answers are provided in Appendix A, "Chapter Quiz Answers."

1. What does the acronym JAR stand for?

2. What is the name of the program used to work with JAR files?

3. What types of files can be stored inside a JAR file?

4. What compression method does the JAR format use?

5. What method must you use in conjunction with the $java.net.URL$ class for loading media files when an applet has been deployed in a JAR file?

6. What command would you enter to create a new JAR file, called test.jar, that contains all files in the current folder?

7. What command would you enter to create the same archive but also include a manifest file called manifest.txt?

8. What command would you enter to list the contents of a file called MyGame.jar with verbose listing enabled?

9. What JAR parameter option causes files to be added from a different folder without adding the folder name to the files stored in the archive?

10. What type of web server do you need to host a Java applet–based game?

EPILOGUE

This concludes the final chapter of the book! I hope you have enjoyed this book and learned a lot from it. I'll admit that it was quite a challenge! For a while I didn't think this Galactic War game would ever see the light of day. There are so many advanced topics that we didn't have time to cover in this book, the likes of which a diehard Java programmer would have liked to see. However, I believe a completely functional game, created from scratch and actually finished within the pages of a book, is far more educational than any "advanced" material we might have spent more time studying instead. The game engine developed in the previous chapter, which was based on all the material in this book, is a viable game engine that can be used for many different types of games. My hope is that you have learned enough from this book to build your own blockbuster Java game for the online casual game market. Good luck!

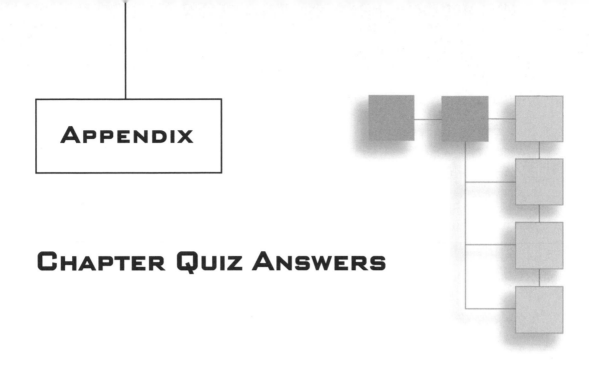

APPENDIX

CHAPTER QUIZ ANSWERS

Here are the answers to the quizzes at the end of each chapter.

CHAPTER 1

1. What does the acronym "JDK" stand for?
   Answer: Java Development Kit

2. What version of the JDK are we focusing on in this book?
   Answer: 6 or Java 6 or Java SE 6

3. What is the name of the company that created Java?
   Answer: Sun Microsystems

4. Where on the web will you find the text editor called TextPad?
   Answer: www.textpad.com

5. In what year was Java first released?
   Answer: 1995

6. Where on the web is the primary download site for Java?
   Answer: http://java.sun.com

7. What type of Java program do you run with the java.exe tool?
Answer: application

8. What type of Java program runs in a web browser?
Answer: applet

9. What is the name of the command-line tool used to run a web-based Java program?
Answer: appletviewer.exe

10. What is the name of the parameter passed to the `paint()` event method in an applet?
Answer: Graphics g

CHAPTER 2

1. What is the name of the JDK tool used to compile Java programs?
Answer: javac.exe

2. Which JDK command-line tool is used to run a Java application?
Answer: java.exe

3. Which JDK command-line tool is used to run a Java applet?
Answer: appletviewer.exe

4. What are two good, free Java IDEs recommended in this chapter?
Answer: Eclipse, NetBeans, or TextPad

5. Encapsulation, polymorphism, and inheritance are the keys to what programming methodology?
Answer: OOP: Object-Oriented Programming

6. What's the main difference between a Java application and an applet?
Answer: applets run in a Web browser

7. Which method of the `Graphics` class can you use to print a text message on the screen?
Answer: drawString()

8. How many bits make up a Java integer (the *int* data type)?
Answer: 32

9. How many bits are there in a Java long integer (the *long* data type)?
   Answer: 64

10. What programming language was Java based on?
    Answer: C++

CHAPTER 3

1. What is the name of the method that calculates the velocity for X?
   Answer: calcAngleMoveX()

2. What is the base class from which Ship, Asteroid, and Bullet are inherited?
   Answer: BaseVectorShape

3. Which classic Atari game inspired the game developed in this chapter?
   Answer: Asteroids

4. Which type of collision testing does this game use?
   Answer: Bounding Rectangle

5. Which method of the Shape class does this game use for collision testing?
   Answer: contains()

6. Which geometric shape class do the Ship and Asteroid classes use?
   Answer: Polygon

7. Which geometric shape class does the Bullet class use?
   Answer: Rectangle (pixel also acceptable)

8. Which applet event actually draws the screen?
   Answer: paint()

9. What is the name of the interface class used to add threading support to the game?
   Answer: Runnable

10. What math function does calcAngleMoveX use to calculate the X velocity?
    Answer: Math.cos()

CHAPTER 4

1. What is the primary class we've been using to manipulate vector graphics in this chapter?

   Answer: Graphics2D

2. What is the name of the Applet event that refreshes the screen?

   Answer: paint() or update()

3. What is the name of the Graphics2D method that draws a filled rectangle?

   Answer: fillRect()

4. Define the words comprising the acronym "AWT."

   Answer: Abstract Window Toolkit

5. What class makes it possible to perform translation, rotation, and scaling of shapes?

   Answer: AffineTransform

6. Which Graphics2D method draws a polygon?

   Answer: draw()

7. Which transform method moves a shape to a new location?

   Answer: translate()

8. What method initializes the keyboard listener interface?

   Answer: addKeyListener()

9. What method in the Random class returns a double-precision floating-point value?

   Answer: nextDouble()

10. Which KeyListener event detects key presses?

    Answer: keyPressed()

CHAPTER 5

1. What is the primary class we've been using to manipulate bitmapped graphics in this chapter?

   Answer: Graphics2D

2. What method initializes the keyboard listener interface?

   Answer: addKeyListener()

3. What Graphics2D method is used to draw an image?

   Answer: drawImage()

4. Which Java class contains the getImage() method?

   Answer: Applet

5. What class makes it possible to perform translation, rotation, and scaling of images?

   Answer: AffineTransform

6. Which Graphics2D method draws an image?

   Answer: drawImage()

7. Which transform method moves an image to a new location?

   Answer: translate()

8. What is the name of the "transparency" channel in a 32-bit PNG image?

   Answer: alpha channel

9. What is the Applet class method used to load a resource from a JAR?

   Answer: getResource()

10. Which KeyListener event detects key presses?

    Answer: keyPressed()

CHAPTER 6

1. What is the name of the support class created in this chapter to help the Sprite class manage position and velocity?

    Answer: `Point2D`

2. During which keyboard event should you disable a keypress variable, when detecting multiple key presses with global variables?

    Answer: `keyReleased()`

3. What are the three types of parameters can you pass to the `collidesWith()` method?

    Answer: `Rectangle`, `Sprite`, *and* `Point2D`

4. What Java class provides an alternate method for loading images that is not tied to the applet?

    Answer: `Toolkit`

5. Which Java package do you need to import to use the `Graphics2D` class?

    Answer: `java.awt.Graphics2D`

6. What numeric data type does the `Point2D` class (created in this chapter) use for internal storage of the X and Y values?

    Answer: double

7. What data types can the `Point2D` class work with at the constructor level?

    Answer: `int`, `float`, *and* `double`

8. Which sprite property determines the angle at which the sprite will move?

    Answer: `moveAngle`

9. Which sprite property determines at which angle an image is pointed, regardless of movement direction?

    Answer: `faceAngle`

10. Which `AffineTransform` methods allow you to translate, rotate, and scale a sprite?

    Answer: `translate()`, `rotate()`, *and* `scale()`

CHAPTER 7

1. What is the name of the animation class created in this chapter?
   Answer: `AnimatedSprite`

2. From which class does the new animation class inherit?
   Answer: `Sprite`

3. How many frames of animation were there in the animated ball sprite?
   Answer: 64

4. What do you call an animation that is stored inside many files?
   Answer: sequence

5. What do you call an animation that is all stored in a single file?
   Answer: tiled

6. What type of parameter does the `AnimatedSprite.setVelocity` method accept?
   Answer: `Point2D`

7. What arithmetic operation is used to calculate an animation frame's Y position?
   Answer: division

8. What arithmetic operation is used to calculate an animation frame's X position?
   Answer: modulus

9. What is a good class to use when you need to create a bitmap in memory?
   Answer: `BufferedImage`

10. Which `AnimatedSprite` method draws the current frame of animation?
    Answer: `draw()`

CHAPTER 8

1. What is the name of the method used to enable keyboard events in your program?

   Answer: `addKeyListener()`

2. What is the name of the keyboard event interface?

   Answer: `KeyListener`

3. What is the virtual key code for the Enter key?

   Answer: `VK_ENTER`

4. Which keyboard event will tell you the code of a pressed key?

   Answer: Technically, any of the three (`keyPressed()`, `keyReleased()`, *and* `keyTyped()` *)*

5. Which keyboard event will tell you when a key has been released?

   Answer: `keyPressed()` *or* `keyTyped()`

6. Which keyboard event will tell you the character of a pressed key?

   Answer: Technically, any of the three (`keyPressed()`, `keyReleased()`, *and* `keyTyped()` *)*

7. Which `KeyEvent` method returns a key code value?

   Answer: `getKeyCode()`

8. What is the name of the method used to enable mouse motion events?

   Answer: `addMouseMotionListener()`

9. What is the name of the class used as a parameter for all mouse event methods?

   Answer: `MouseEvent`

10. Which mouse event reports the actual movement of the mouse?

    Answer: `mouseDragged()` *or* `mouseMoved()`

CHAPTER 9

1. What is the name of Java's digital sound system class?

   Answer: `AudioSystem`

2. What is the name of Java's MIDI music system class?

   Answer: `MidiSystem` *(*`Sequencer` *also acceptable)*

3. Which Java class handles the loading of a sample file?

   Answer: `AudioInputStream` *(*`AudioSystem` *also acceptable)*

4. Which Java class handles the loading of a MIDI file?

   Answer: `Sequence` *(*`MidiSystem` *also acceptable)*

5. What type of exception error will Java generate when it cannot load a sound file?

   Answer: `UnsupportedAudioFileException` *(*`LineUnavailableException` *and* `IOException` *are also technically acceptable)*

6. Which method of the MIDI system returns the sequencer object?

   Answer: `MidiSystem.getSequencer()`

7. What is the main Java class hierarchy for the audio system class?

   Answer: javax.sound.sampled

8. What is the main Java class hierarchy for the MIDI system class?

   Answer: javax.sound.midi

9. What three digital sound file formats does Java support?

   Answer: AIFF, AU, and WAV

10. What rare exception error will occur when no MIDI sequencer is available?

    Answer: `MidiUnavailableException`

CHAPTER 10

1. What is the name of the interface class that provides thread support?
   Answer: Runnable

2. What is the name of the thread execution method that you can use to run code inside the separate thread?
   Answer: run()

3. What is the name of the class that handles vector-based graphics?
   Answer: Shape

4. What Thread method causes the thread to pause execution for a specified time?
   Answer: sleep()

5. What System method returns the current time in milliseconds?
   Answer: currentTimeMillis()

6. What is the name of the method that returns the directory containing the applet (or HTML container) file?
   Answer: getCodeBase()

7. What is the name of the method that returns the entire URL string including the applet (or HTML container) file?
   Answer: getDocumentBase()

8. What class do you use to store a bitmap image?
   Answer: Image or BufferedImage

9. Which Graphics2D method is used to draw a bitmap?
   Answer: drawImage()

10. Which class helps to improve gameplay by providing random numbers?
    Answer: Random

CHAPTER 11

1. What is the name of the class that handles bitmaps?

   Answer: Image or BufferedImage

2. Which class in Galactic War detects when bullets hit the asteroids?

   Answer: Rectangle or Bullet

3. What is the maximum number of sprites that can be supported by the game?

   Answer: virtually unlimited (based on available memory)

4. Which method in the Graphics2D class actually draws the image of a sprite?

   Answer: drawImage()

5. What is the name of the Applet method that redraws the window?

   Answer: paint()

6. How many key presses can the game detect at a single time?

   Answer: virtually unlimited (limited only by the operating system)

7. What method do you use to track the mouse's movement?

   Answer: mouseMoved() or mouseDragged()

8. What type of graphics entity does the game use for the asteroids?

   Answer: Shape

9. Regarding ship rotation, by how many angles can the ship be rotated?

   Answer: 360

10. What method provides the game with support for collision detection?

    Answer: Rectangle.contains()

CHAPTER 12

1. Which support class helps manage the position and velocity of sprites?

   Answer: `Point2D`

2. During which keyboard event should you disable a `keypress` variable, when detecting multiple key presses with global variables?

   Answer: `keyReleased`

3. What is the name of the sprite collision detection routine used in Galactic War?

   Answer: `Rectangle.contains()`

4. Which method in the `Applet` class provides a way to load images from a JAR file?

   Answer: `getResource()`

5. Which Java package do you need to import to use the `Graphics2D` class?

   Answer: `java.awt.Graphics2D`

6. What numeric data type does the `Point2D` class (created in this chapter) use for internal storage of the X and Y values?

   Answer: `double`

7. How does the use of a class such as `Point2D` improve a game's source code, versus using simple variables?

   Answer: A single parameter handles two variables (x and y)

8. Which property in the `Sprite` class determines the angle at which the sprite will move?

   Answer: `moveAngle`

9. Which property in the `Sprite` class determines the angle at which a sprite is pointed?

   Answer: `faceAngle`

10. How many milliseconds must the game use as a delay in order to achieve a frame rate of 60 frames per second?

    Answer: 1000/60 = 16.67 ms

CHAPTER 13

1. What is the name of the method that makes collision detection possible?

   Answer: `Rectangle.contains()`

2. How many collisions can the game detect within a single update of the game loop?

   Answer: the square of the number of sprites

3. What would happen if the ship were to fire a projectile that "warps" around the screen and then hits the ship? Would a collision take place? Why or why not?

   Answer: No collision is handled between the ship and bullets

4. What should happen to the player's ship after it has been destroyed by a collision with an asteroid? Describe a better way to "respawn" the ship than what is currently being done.

   Answer: It should be destroyed and respawned. A better way might be to give the player some "invulnerable" time after respawn to improve gameplay.

5. What type of transform could you apply to the explosion sprite to change its size?

   Answer: scaling

6. How does the ship's velocity affect the result of a collision when the ship is destroyed? Should the ship continue to exert momentum even while blowing up?

   Answer: The ship currently stops when it explodes. A more realistic explosion would continue to move a little ways along the ship's trajectory.

7. How can the collision routine be improved upon, so that collisions are more precise?

   Answer: Either smaller bounding boxes can be used or every pixel of two sprites can be compared (which is usually overkill)

8. What is the name of the constant applied to the ship when a collision has taken place?

Answer: `STATE_EXPLODING`

9. What is the name of the method that updates a sprite's animation sequence?

Answer: `updateAnimation()`

10. What is the name of the method that handles the game loop for Galactic War?

Answer: `gameUpdate()`

CHAPTER 14

1. What is the name of the new game engine class developed in this chapter?

Answer: `Game`

2. How many sprites can the new engine handle on the screen simultaneously?

Answer: unlimited (with available memory)

3. Which of the four key classes in the game engine handles image loading?

Answer: `ImageEntity`

4. How many different asteroid sizes does the game use?

Answer: 4

5. True or False: Collisions are handled inside the game engine.

Answer: False (collisions are only detected, not handled)

6. What type of object is `animImage`, a private variable in `AnimatedSprite`?

Answer: `ImageEntity`

7. Which class is responsible for rendering a single frame of an animation in `AnimatedSprite`?

Answer: `Sprite` *(which, in turn, uses* `ImageEntity`*)*

8. What is the maximum velocity value for the player's spaceship?
Answer: 10

9. What class does the game/sprite engine pass in some of its events?
Answer: `AnimatedSprite`

10. What is the name of the support method in `AnimatedSprite` that returns a properly formed URL for a file to be loaded?
Answer: `getURL`

CHAPTER 15

1. What method in GalacticWar.java makes it possible to add powerups to the game when a tiny asteroid is destroyed?
Answer: `spawnPowerup()`

2. What construct does the sprite engine (in Game.java) use to manage the sprites?
Answer: `LinkedList`

3. How many weapon upgrades are available now in Galactic War?
Answer: 5

4. How many different point-value power-ups are there in the game?
Answer: 3

5. What method in GalacticWar.java returns a stock bullet sprite object, which is then tweaked to produce the upgraded bullet spreads?
Answer: `stockBullet()`

6. How many different asteroid images are there in Galactic War?
Answer: 14

7. If you wanted to add another weapon upgrade to the game, which method would you need to modify?
Answer: `fireBullet()`

8. How many sprites is the sprite engine capable of handling at a time?

Answer: unlimited (with available memory)

9. How many bullets are fired at a time with the fifth-level weapon upgrade?

Answer: 6

10. What is the name of the static `int` that represents the game state when the game is running normally?

Answer: GAME_RUNNING

CHAPTER 16

1. What does the acronym JAR stand for?

Answer: Java Archive

2. What is the name of the program used to work with JAR files?

Answer: jar.exe

3. What types of files can be stored inside a JAR file?

Answer: Any type of file

4. What compression method does the JAR format use?

Answer: ZIP compression

5. What method must you use in conjunction with the `java.net.URL` class for loading media files when an applet has been deployed in a JAR file?

Answer: getResource()

6. What command would you enter to create a new JAR file, called test.jar, that contains all files in the current folder?

*Answer: jar cf test.jar *.**

7. What command would you enter to create the same archive but also include a manifest file called manifest.txt?

*Answer: jar cfm test.jar manifest.txt *.**

8. What command would you enter to list the contents of a file called MyGame.jar with verbose listing enabled?

Answer: `jar tvf MyGame.jar`

9. What JAR parameter option causes files to be added from a different folder without adding the folder name to the files stored in the archive?

Answer: C

10. What type of web server do you need to host a Java applet–based game?

Answer: Any server will do; applets are client-side programs.

INDEX